ENVIRONMENTAL POLITICS IN LATIN AMERICA AND THE CARIBBEAN

Liverpool Latin American Textbooks

Series Editor: Professor Catherine Davies
(University of Nottingham)

Written in an engaging and accessible style, the books in this series facilitate teaching and learning on topics broadly relating to Latin American history, culture and society. As well as including original research, they offer a critical synthesis of research and scholarship to date on relevant themes as well as critical perspectives to encourage further discussion and debate.

Environmental Politics in Latin America and the Caribbean

Volume 1: Introduction

Gavin O'Toole

LIVERPOOL UNIVERSITY PRESS

To the memory of my grandparents,
Eustace Eugene Edwards and Marjorie Edwards, née Greenhow
A ddwg angau, nid adfer

First published 2014 by
Liverpool University Press
4 Cambridge Street
Liverpool
L69 7ZU

British Library Cataloguing-in-Publication data
A British Library CIP record is available

ISBN 978-1-78138-021-5 (hb)
ISBN 978-1-78138-022-2 (pb)

Typeset by Carnegie Book Production, Lancaster
Printed and bound by Booksfactory.co.uk

Contents

Boxes

Figures

Tables

Abbreviations

ABS	access and benefit-sharing
AFI	Ancient Forest International
AIDA	Asociación Interamericana para la Defensa del Ambiente (Inter-American Association for Environmental Defense)
ALIDES	Alianza Centroamericana de Desarrollo Sostenible (Alliance for the Sustainable Development of Central America)
Anapqui	Asociación Nacional de Productores de Quínua (National Association of Quinoa Producers)
ARPA	Amazon Region Protected Area
CABEI	Central American Bank for Economic Integration
CABS	Center for Applied Biodiversity Science
CAN	Comunidad Andina de Naciones (Andean Community of Nations)
CBD	Convention on Biological Diversity
CCAD	Comisión Centroamericana de Ambiente y Desarollo (Central American Commission on Sustainable Development)
CDM	clean development mechanism
CEC	Commission for Environmental Co-operation
CEDLA	Centro de Estudios y Documentación Latinoamericanos/Centro de Estudos e Documentaçaõ Latino-Americanos (Centre for Latin American Research and Documentation)
CELAC	Comunidad de Estados Latinoamericanos y Caribeños (Community of Latin American and Caribbean States)

CEPAL	Comisión Económica para América Latina [y el Caribe] (Economic Commission for Latin America)
CLAES	Centro Latinoamericano de Ecología Social (Latin American Centre for Social Ecology)
CMEA	Council of Mutual Economic Assistance
CODEFF	Comité Nacional Pro Defensa de la Fauna y Flora
CONACAMI	Confederación de Comunidades del Perú Afectadas por la Minería (Confederation of Communities in Peru Affected by Mining)
COO	Chief Operating Officer
CORFO	Corporación de Fomento de la Producción de Chile (Corporation for the Development of Production in Chile)
CPA	Clean Production Agreement
CPL	Consejo Nacional de Producción Limpia de Chile (Committee for the Development of Clean Production)
CSD	Commission on Sustainable Development
DiBio	Dirección de Biodiversidad
EACC	Economics of Adaptation to Climate Change
ECLA	Economic Commission for Latin America
ECLAC	Economic Commission for Latin America and the Caribbean
ECSP	Environmental Change and Security Program
EIA	environmental impact assessment
ENGO	environmental non-governmental organization
ENGOV	Environmental Governance in Latin America and the Caribbean
ENSO	El Niño/La Niña-Southern Oscillation
EPA	Environmental Protection Agency
ESPAS	European Strategy and Policy Analysis System
ETS	emission trading scheme
EZLN	Ejército Zapatista de Liberación Nacional
FAO	Food and Agriculture Organization
FBOMS	Fórum Brasileiro de ONGs e Movimentos Sociais para o Meio Ambiente e o Desenvolvimento (Brazilian

	Forum of NGOs and Social Movements for the Environment and Development)
FDI	foreign direct investment
FIDA	Foro Interamericano de Derecho Ambiental (Inter-American Forum on Environmental Law)
FME	free market environmentalism
FOCADES	Fondo Centroamericano de Ambiente y Desarrollo (Central American Fund for Environment and Development)
FONAES	Fondo Ambiental de El Salvador (Environmental Fund of El Salvador)
FONDESHU	Fondo para el Desarrollo Humano (Human Development Fund)
FPVA	Federación de Partidos Verdes de las Américas (Federation of Green Parties of the Americas)
FTAA	Free Trade Area of the Americas
FUNAI	Fundação Nacional do Índio (National Indian Foundation)
GCF	Green Climate Fund
GDP	gross domestic product
GEF	Global Environment Facility
GFN	Global Footprint Network
GHG	greenhouse gas
GLADA	Global Assessment of Land Degradation and Improvement
GM	genetically modified
GMO	genetically modified organism
HDI	Human Development Index
HIPC	highly indebted poor countries
IAI	Inter-American Institute for Global Change Research
IARC	Impact Assessment Research Centre
ICBG	International Co-operative Biodiversity Groups
IDB	Inter-American Development Bank
IDPM	Institute for Development Policy and Management
IEA	International Energy Agency

IFAD	International Fund for Agricultural Development
IIRSA	Initiative for the Integration of the Regional Infrastructure of South America
IISD	International Institute for Sustainable Development
IKAP	Indigenous Knowledge and Peoples
ILO	International Labour Organization
IMAZON	Instituto do Homem e Meio Ambiente da Amazônia
IMF	International Monetary Fund
INE	Instituto Nacional de Ecología
INPE	Instituto Nacional de Pesquisas Espaciais (National Institute for Space Research, Brazil)
INPE	Instituto Nacional de Pesquisas Espaciais
IOM	International Organization for Migration
IPCC	Intergovernmental Panel on Climate Change
ISAAA	International Service for the Acquisition of Agri-Biotech Applications
ISEE	International Society for Ecological Economics
ISI	import substitution industrialization
ISRIC	International Soil Reference and Information Centre
IUCN	International Union for Conservation of Nature
IWGIA	International Work Group for Indigenous Affairs
LAC-CORE	Latin American and Caribbean Council on Renewable Energy
LACEEP	Latin American and Caribbean Environmental Economics Program
LETS	local economic transaction schemes
LFPCC	Ley Federal para Prevenir y Controlar la Contaminación Ambiental (Law for the Prevention and Control of Pollution)
LPI	Living Planet Index
MBI	market-based instrument
MDB	multilateral development bank
Mercosur/Mercosul	Mercado Común del Sur/Mercado Comum do Sul (Common Market of the South)
MMA	Ministerio de Medio Ambiente

MNC	multinational corporation
NAAEC	North American Agreement on Environmental Co-operation
NACLA	North American Congress on Latin America
NAFTA	North American Free Trade Agreement
NEF	New Economics Foundation
NGLS	Non-Governmental Liaison Service
NGO	non-governmental organization
OAS	Organization of American States
OCMAL	Observatorio de Conflictos Mineros de América Latina (Observatory of Mining Conflicts in Latin America)
ODA	overseas development aid
OECD	Organization for Economic Cooperation and Development
OPEC	Organization of the Petroleum Exporting Countries
OPIP	Organization of Indigenous Peoples of Pastaza
PAHO	Pan American Health Organization
PES	Payments for Ecosystem Services
PLAC	Programa Latinoamericano del Carbono (Latin America Carbon Programme)
PRI	Principles for Responsible Investment
PT	Partido dos Trabalhadores (Workers' Party)
PV	Partido Verde (Green Party)
PVE	Partido Verde Ecologista (Green Ecological Party)
REFF-LAC	Renewable Energy Finance Forum–Latin America and Caribbean
RRI	Rights and Resources Initiative
SAEMC	South American Emissions Megacities and Climate
SDG	sustainable development goal
SEEA	System of Environmental and Economic Accounting
SEI	Stockholm Environment Institute
SEMARNAT	Secretaría de Medio Ambiente y Recursos Naturales
SERNA	Secretaria de Recursos Naturales y Ambiente
SHCP	Secretarías de Hacienda y Crédito Público

TEEB	The Economics of Ecosystems and Biodiversity
Unasur	Unión de Naciones Suramericanas (Union of South American Nations)
UNCCD	United Nations Convention to Combat Desertification
UNCED	United Nations Conference on Environment and Development
UNDP	United Nations Development Programme
UNEP FI	United Nations Environment Programme Finance Initiative
UNEP	United Nations Environment Programme
UNESCO	United Nations Educational, Scientific and Cultural Organization
UNFPA	United Nations Population Fund
WCMC	World Conservation Monitoring Centre
WDPA	World Database on Protected Areas
WMO	World Maritime Organization
WRI	World Resources Institute
WSP	Water and Sanitation Programme
WWF	World Wildlife Fund

Acknowledgements

We are grateful to the following for permission to reproduce their material:
Table 1.1: data in "Agricultural development indicators in Latin America and the Caribbean 2008–12, selected countries", from World Bank, Agriculture & Rural Development data (http://data.worldbank.org/topic/agriculture-and-rural-development), to Vivian Klein, Rights & Permissions, World Bank Publications, Washington, DC; Figure 2.1: "Desarrollo de la economía vs. cuidado medioambiental América Latina 1995–2011, Total por país 2011", from Latinobarómetro, *Informe 2011*, to Fabiana L Barbeira, Corporación Latinobarómetro, Santiago; Table 4.1: "Deforestation in the Legal Amazon, 2000–11", from Instituto Nacional de Pesquisas Espaciais (INPE) (National Institute for Space Research), Brazil, 2008 (www.obt.inpe.br/prodes/prodes_1988_2011.htm), to Márcia Alvarenga and Dr Julio Dalge, Director of Earth Observation at the Brazilian National Institute for Space Research; Figure 4.1: "Extent of accumulated deforestation in the Brazilian Amazon up to 2011", from IMAZON, Desmatamento na Amazônia Legal até 2011 (www.imazon.org.br/mapas/desmatamento-acumulado-2007-2010/desmatamento-acumulado-na-amazonia-legal-ate-2011/view), to Bruno Oliveira, Communications, Instituto do Homem e Meio Ambiente da Amazônia (IMAZON), Belém; Table 4.2: "Number of known species in Latin America and the Caribbean as a percentage of the total number of known species in the world", from UNEP 2010, *Latin America and the Caribbean: Environment Outlook GEO LAC 3*. Panama City: United Nations Environment Programme (www.unep.org/publications/contents/pub_details_search.asp?ID=4149), to Monika G MacDevette, Division of Early Warning & Assessment, United Nations Environment Programme; Table 4.4: "Latin America's contribution to greenhouse gas emissions compared to the developed world", from *Key World Energy Statistics 2012* © OECD/IEA 2012,

pp. 48–49, to Eleonor Grammatikas, Office of the Chief Legal Counsel, International Energy Agency, Paris; Table 6.1: "Willingness to pay 10 per cent more for gasoline to reduce air pollution", from The Environmental Monitor 2002, Environics International, p. 190, to Corinne Fontaine, COO, GlobeScan, Toronto; Table 6.2: "Total annual costs of adaptation for all sectors, by region, 2010–50", from World Bank, 2009, "The Cost to Developing Countries of Adapting to Climate Change: New Methods and Estimates", Consultation Draft 64087, Washington, DC: World Bank, p. 6 (http://climatechange.worldbank.org/climatechange/research), to Vivian Klein, Rights & Permissions, World Bank Publications, Washington, DC.

In some instances, permission to reproduce material has been requested and a response from the organization contacted is yet to be received. In each case we have credited the relevant material and are grateful in advance for: Table 4.3: "Latin America and the Caribbean: total motor-vehicle fleet, 2002–08, selected countries", from *ECLAC, Anuario estadístico de América Latina y el Caribe 2011*, Microsoft Excel file "3.8 Transpotre/Transport; 3.8.1.2 Parque automotora/Motor-Vehicle Fleet a/" (www.eclac.cl/publicaciones/xml/7/45607/LCG2513b.pdf); Figure 4.2: "Latin America and the Caribbean: summary of climate change patterns projected for 2100"; Table 4.6: "Latin America (selected countries): projections of degraded territory, 2050 and 2100", from *ECLAC 2010, Economics of Climate Change in Latin America and the Caribbean, Summary 2010.* Santiago: Economic Commission for Latin America and the Caribbean on the basis of information from National Institute of Space Research (www.eclac.cl/dmaah/publicaciones/xml/9/41909/2010-914-Climate_change-COMPLETO_WEB.pdf), to the Economic Commission for Latin America and the Caribbean, Santiago; Table 4.7: "Projected impacts on urban areas everywhere of changes in extreme weather and climate events", from UN-HABITAT 2011, *Global Report on Human Settlements 2011, Cities and Climate Change: Policy Directions*, to UN Human Settlements Programme (UN-HABITAT), Nairobi.

Introduction

In October 2010, Marina Silva, a former Brazilian environment minister running as the Partido Verde (PV, Green Party) candidate, polled almost 20 per cent of the vote in the first round of the country's presidential elections. The unprecedented performance for a green candidate in Latin America and the Caribbean – and the momentum it has given the PV as it gears up for presidential elections in 2014 – demonstrated the prominence that environmental politics has gained in the region in recent years. It also revealed how behind the glamour and grind of machine politics Latin America and the Caribbean has become the battleground for a new *kind* of political competition that combines traditional class, institutional and ideological struggles that often look backwards with new battles over identities, rights and future generations shaped by innovative alliances and concepts that look forwards. The growth of green parties and the prominence that disputes over the natural environment are gaining throughout the region – from the quality of life of its citizens and how they share power and resources to how they understand their very history and identity – are transforming Latin America and the Caribbean into a laboratory of environmental politics that extends its study far beyond the institutionalized and formalized structures of the developed world.

Yet, surprisingly, introductory textbooks that focus solely on the growing role played by the environment in the politics of this region are few and far between, and the literature is spread thinly across disciplines. Nor are there university courses that attempt to bring together and provide a single, clear sense of direction to environmental topics scattered throughout a diverse academic ecosystem in which political scientists hunt alongside geographers, anthropologists prey upon historians, and economists feed off sociologists. Only a few initiatives, such as the Environmental Governance in Latin America and the Caribbean (ENGOV) collaborative research project in the Netherlands funded by the European Commission, exist to understand how environmental governance is shaped in Latin America, and, according to Baud, de Castro and Hogenboom (2011), in the region itself there have been no systematic efforts to analyse the problems of environmental governance and new environmental challenges from a purely local perspective. In short, the environmental politics of Latin America and the Caribbean – much like the early way in which governments tried to get to grips with environmental issues themselves as they grew in public importance – has been approached in a fragmented and often piecemeal way across many disciplines that has left students none the wiser about this crucial theme. This collection of two volumes aims to address that by providing a comprehensive introductory framework for teaching environmental politics that seeks to appeal to undergraduates taking a broad range of courses from area, environmental and development studies to geography, anthropology and environmental economics.

Together, the two volumes of *Environmental Politics in Latin America and the Caribbean* aim to provide a comprehensive introduction to the historical, political, economic and cultural themes that have a bearing on the natural environment. This first volume should be of value wherever the environment is being studied and introduces students to the essential context in which green politics in the region are developing. It offers students from a broad range of disciplines who may not be familiar with comparative politics, or indeed with the study of Latin America and the Caribbean, a way of coming to this theme for the first time. It provides a broad overview of the region's environmental history, the political legacies and challenges that confront green parties and movements, the current state of its natural environment, and the key issues of political economy that explain how patterns of development in Latin America and the Caribbean have shaped its natural environment and their implications for sustainable development. The second volume is more specifically aimed at students of politics per se, taking and developing themes that are touched on in the first volume in greater detail and with more theoretical insight, such as institutions, public policies, international relations, political actors and environmental ideologies. For the scholar who wants a comprehensive overview of green politics in Latin America and the Caribbean, it is aimed to complement the first volume and to be read in conjunction with it.

There are good reasons to focus on Latin America and the Caribbean if we wish to enhance our understanding of environmental politics. First, the environment as a political issue has been giving Latin America and the Caribbean a global profile since the Earth Summit in Rio de Janeiro, Brazil, in 1992, which represented a turning point in global environmental consciousness and mobilization, spawning Agenda 21 – the official, mainstream platform on sustainable development adopted at the United Nations Conference on Environment and Development. Latin America and the Caribbean has also played an important international role in the development of environmental governance and its countries have occupied a key role in global debates on the causes of and solutions to environmental problems and climate change.

Second, Latin America and the Caribbean is at the very sharp end of global environmental change as one of the most ecologically diverse regions of the planet. It hosts about half of the world's tropical forests, a quarter of its potential arable land, a third of its fresh water reserves, has 227 globally significant "Ramsar" wetlands, and has vast mineral reserves. Although it constitutes only about 14 per cent of the Earth's surface, it is home to 20 per cent of the terrestrial, marine and fresh water ecoregions identified by the World Wildlife Fund (WWF) as priority areas for global conservation. It has more than 30,000 species of vascular plants, more than 3,000 species of birds, and the Amazon and its tributaries themselves are home to more than 2,000 kinds of fish. Yet Latin America and the Caribbean is also home to five of the 20 countries with the greatest number of endangered species of fauna, and seven with the greatest number of endangered plant species. The region accounts for one-third of the world's carbon emissions from land use changes and every country in it is affected in some way by soil degradation. The loss of forest cover has been identified as one of the most significant environmental issues facing the region and intensive farming has resulted in extensive pollution to agricultural land and water systems. Mining has caused large-scale deforestation, changed sedimentation patterns in watercourses and disturbed soils. The Amazon discharges nearly 20 per cent of the fresh water that the Earth's rivers empty into the sea – yet, despite abundant water resources, Latin American and Caribbean people still faces shortages. Pressure on coastal ecosystems from development, growing coastal populations and tourism is destroying biodiversity and degrading coral reefs, with the coverage of coral in the Caribbean Basin declining by as much as 10 per cent in the last three decades. Poverty, rapid growth, weak institutions and poor policymaking have meant that cities face serious environmental problems of poor air quality, dangerous waste-disposal practices and inadequate sanitation. Moreover, all these existing environmental problems are likely to be made worse by climate change, which is already having a significant effect on ecosystem goods and services and has risen up the agenda of public policymaking. Climate change will exacerbate the effects of extreme weather events generated by the El Niño phenomenon and will result in both droughts and floods by changing rainfall patterns, river flows, lake levels and systems that recharge groundwater. Higher temperatures, rising sea levels and elevated CO_2 will all affect agricultural production and prompt further land-use change. Climate change will have a significant impact on forests, and the Amazon is likely to be affected by significant species loss, increased insect infestation and the spread of infectious diseases. Mesoamerica and the Caribbean are considered biodiversity "hotspots" where climate change will take a heavy toll. The warming of coastal waters, the death of coral and the impact on fish stocks caused by climate change will heighten existing pressures on marine systems from industrial and artisanal fishing, fleet transport and tourism. Urban areas and industry face unique challenges of maintaining their water and energy supplies, and their physical infrastructure could be disproportionately affected by extreme weather.

The combined effects of climate change will have significant implications for politics, increasing pressures for state spending, exacerbating an urban bias in politics, reinforcing existing inequalities and poverty and fuelling migration. A study compiled for the Rio+20 summit in 2012 jointly produced by the Inter-American Development Bank, the Economic Commission for Latin America and the Caribbean and the World Wildlife Fund warned that the region faces annual damages to the tune of $100 bn by 2050 from diminishing agricultural yields, disappearing glaciers, flooding, droughts and other events triggered by a warming planet (IDB 2012). The region is not considered to be a main contributor of the greenhouse gas (GHG) emissions that are causing climate change, so far having contributed only about 4 per cent of global emissions, yet it is likely to be disproportionately affected by it. This makes Latin America and the Caribbean an important case study for discussions about the principle recognized by the UN Framework Convention on Climate Change agreed in 1992 in Rio acknowledging that countries have common but differentiated responsibilities when it comes to addressing climate change. Moreover, despite mounting global concern about climate change, evidence of it and of changes in biological systems in Latin America and the Caribbean remains woefully under-documented.

Third, as a region that has long struggled with high levels of poverty and inequality – yet today enjoys robust growth and is the target of unprecedented flows of foreign investment – Latin America and the Caribbean exemplifies a dilemma at the heart of all environmental politics: the difficulty of reconciling development with environmental protection. This issue is thrown into sharp relief both by the ambitious agenda of regional integration that is being pursued across the Americas, and by the aspirations of the left-of-centre governments that have come to power there in recent years. The ambitions of politicians such as Bolivia's president Evo Morales embody what this dilemma can mean in practice, as he struggles to reconcile the accelerating extraction of his country's valuable mineral resources under national control in an effort to tackle persistent poverty with the language of his indigenous constituency that warns of the threat posed by mining to "Pachamama" – "Mother Earth". Much of Latin American and Caribbean economic and social history can be understood as a long and traumatic engagement with an insatiable world market, and historically it has almost always been the varying priorities of export-led development that have determined the forms taken by political development in the region.

These volumes concentrate on Hispanic and Lusophone Latin America and the Caribbean – taking a geopolitical as opposed to an ecological focus – while also making some references to Anglophone Caribbean and South American states and to those that often fall outside the formal ambit of area studies by virtue of their peculiarities, such as Francophone Haiti and Spanish-speaking Puerto Rico, a protectorate whose people in 2012 voted in support of US statehood. As a discernible region, Latin American and Caribbean politics have distinctive features deriving from history and culture that make it both viable and necessary to take such a regional view. Nonetheless, this parameter of study is not intended to be a rigid constraint to understanding, and the region is characterized as much by its cultural diversity as by the essentially linguistic terms of reference by which it is defined: indeed, many millions of people in Latin America do not speak languages derived from Latin as a mother tongue and today about 800 indigenous languages are still in use. This diversity is driving political and institutional development in the region.

Diversity also characterizes the region's physical environment. It comprises geographically of parts of North America, the Central American Isthmus and Caribbean Islands and the South American sub-continent, and a key characteristic is its geographic and ecological variation. The region extends from sub-tropics in the northern hemisphere to sub-polar extremes in South America, and its largest portion is within the neotropics – the bioregion of tropical and sub-tropical America from Mexico and the Caribbean down into the southern cone of South America. Mexico and the isthmus of Central America host long mountain chains, hot plateaus and valleys, deserts, semi-arid, elevated sub-regions and coastal plains, and southern Mexico's Lacandón Jungle is the largest montane rainforest in North America. Volcanoes descend to fertile coastal plains on Central America's Pacific littoral and in the east montane cloud forests roll down towards the Caribbean. The Isthmus of Panama has been a crucial ecological bridge in the hemisphere's evolutionary history and connects Central America to the Pacific lowlands in north-western South America. The Caribbean is dotted by a 3,200 km-long crescent-shaped group of about 7,000 islands, islets, reefs and cays separating the Gulf of Mexico and Caribbean Sea from the Atlantic Ocean, which include flat, non-volcanic islands and those with craggy mountain ranges. In South America, the 9,000 km Andes mountain chain forms the spine of the sub-continent and contains glaciers and volcanoes that play a key role in regulating its climate. Eastern slopes descend to the huge broadleaf forest that covers the Amazon Basin, the world's most important rainforest, which spreads into nine countries. To the east are also Los Llanos, the vast tropical grassland plains in Colombia and Venezuela, and the elevated lands of the Guyanas. The high plateau along the central Andes, the "altiplano", also descends to the Amazon Basin, to the south of which is Brazil's vast tropical savanna, the *cerrado*. To the west of this are the astonishing Pantanal tropical wetlands that flood during rainy seasons and the semi-arid lowland Gran Chaco. To the south-east are the huge fertile lowland Pampas of Argentina and Uruguay. On the southern tip of South America is the Patagonian plateau, where many lakes punctuate vast plains.

Together, these two volumes aim to provide the skeleton of a 10- to 11-unit course on the environmental politics of Latin America and the Caribbean that will appeal to both newcomers to the region and to the study of politics itself as well as to those more familiar with these subjects. They seek to achieve a balance between the detailed and the general in scope, and a key dilemma facing works of this kind is what to omit and not what to include. Nonetheless, this area of scholarship remains significantly understudied, and there are major gaps in the literature on environmental politics in Latin America and the Caribbean that greatly hamper any aspiration to be fully comprehensive or to push this subject forward. The books are not works of original research and rely heavily on the labours of other scholars who, to their great credit, have devoted considerable time and attention to specific areas of study and to whom this author owes a debt of gratitude. References for further reading have been provided liberally in the hope that students will go and explore the literature – and to encourage them to do so page numbers have been omitted.

Volume 1 begins by examining the environmental history of Latin America and the Caribbean and its impact on political development. It explores the idea of nature in history – a key variable in how human societies interact with the natural environment – as well as attitudes towards production and consumption. It then provides an overview of key themes in the study of environmental politics: institutions, public policy, parties and social movements and political ideas. The volume brings the reader up to date by identifying the principal environmental challenges the region now faces, from land, air and water pollution to biodiversity loss to climate change. Those challenges are intimately related to the legacies of different patterns of development in Latin America and the Caribbean, and the final chapters of this first volume look at the political economy of the environment, tracing how changing models of development have transformed the natural landscape in response to the demands of the world market. It concludes by exploring how Latin American and Caribbean policy-makers are responding to the challenges of sustainable development and climate change.

Volume 2 examines the institutional and policymaking dimensions of the environment, and how environmental issues influence international relations in Latin America and the Caribbean. It looks at how states have created modern infrastructures for environmental governance, key variables in the processes by which environmental policy is formulated and the international and multilateral influences that are shaping the green agenda. This volume then introduces the student to the key political actors in struggles over the environment in Latin America and the Caribbean such as green parties, social movements and NGOs. It explores how both the indigenous movement and businesses are playing an increasingly prominent role in this arena, and sketches out the main ideas that inform green ideology such as environmental justice, eco-socialism and environmental scepticism.

CHAPTER ONE

From early civilization to industrialization

HISTORY IS AN IMPORTANT BUILDING BLOCK in the study of politics that enables us to explore the wider economic, social and cultural factors that shape how resources are distributed and used. Resource use is at the very heart of the exercise of power, which in turn is the principal focus of political science. A point of departure in the study of all history is to understand the underlying narrative – who wrote it and why – and environmental history is no different. This has as its main focus the natural world and our interactions with it, but like all variants of history it can take many forms, emphasize different factors and have contrasting objectives. In the case of Latin America and the Caribbean, environmental history remains a relatively new field. This chapter begins by putting this emerging discipline in context and considering the main issues of interest to environmental historians. As this is a book about politics, it takes as its framework how human society interacts with a natural environment that provides the resources which influence the way power is exercised. It explores this interaction in Latin America and the Caribbean according to broadly discernible periods commonly found in the study of the region's history: the pre-Columbian era; the Iberian conquest and colonial era; the period following Independence in the nineteenth century; the neocolonial relationships that developed amid the emerging global economy of the late nineteenth and early twentieth centuries; the creation of modern states favouring industrialization, eventually leading to a period of authoritarianism in the 1960s and 1970s; and then the debt crisis, market reforms and democratization since the 1980s. An inescapable characteristic of development in the region since the colonial era has been "globalization" of one form or another, which lies at the heart of environmental change. Lastly, the chapter identifies key themes that recur in any examination of how the environment and natural resources have influenced political development in Latin America and the Caribbean: imperialism, neocolonialism and dependence: state building and institutional change; social relations and conflict; and democracy.

Environmental history

Like all disciplines, environmental history is distinguished by debates and disagreements, and a discernible schism relates to the role played by human agency. Scholars often consider nature in relation to human history and how, in turn, we have influenced the dynamics of nature. Indeed, environmental history can trace its development as a discipline to the concerns that began to arise in the 1970s generated by growing awareness of the impact of humankind on the biosphere. Writing in 1990, Worster declared that this "new" discipline of environmental history – which he referred to as an "agroecological" perspective in the study of history – "rejects the common assumption that human experience has been exempt from natural constraints, that people are a separate and uniquely special species, that the ecological consequences of our past deeds can be ignored" (Worster 1990: 1088). The goal of environmental history, said Worster, is to deepen our understanding of how humans have been affected by their natural environment through time, and conversely how they have affected that environment and with what results. Human interaction with the environment is studied in many ways – but often concentrates on how societies exercise control over nature by shaping landscapes or stimulating exchanges of plants, animals and pathogens. This focus alludes to a question asked by environmental historians themselves about the ultimate aims of their work: should it inform debates about present-day environmental concerns in an effort to influence public policies concerning how we control nature? Since the 1980s, environmental history has been informed by an urgency about climate change and our responsibility for it.

A key debate in the field has been between technocentrism, an optimistic belief in society's ability to solve environmental problems deriving from a faith in science and technology, versus ecocentrism, a more radical position sceptical about technology that suggests natural systems provide models for human society on the basis that we are part of, and not separate to, nature (see Brannstrom and Gallini 2004). Differences in approaches to the environmental history of Latin America and the Caribbean have often reflected this distinction. For example, a history of Brazil's Atlantic forest by Dean (1995) emphasizes how human activity destroyed the forest, while a later history by Miller (2000) argued that damage to the forest was the result of barriers to its productive use.

At the same time, environmental history has tended to focus on the economic, social and political system that has emerged on a global scale over the last 500 years (see Castro Herrera 2008). This is of particular relevance to the Americas, the conquest and settlement of which inaugurated what we now understand as "modernity". However, as a discipline, the environmental history of Latin America and the Caribbean remains in its infancy, and so far there have been a limited number of comprehensive works in this field and most of these have been written by scholars from outside the region. This is a key observation: Castro Herrera (2001) provides a valuable historiography of this subject in Latin America and the Caribbean itself from the 1970s to the present, and stresses the importance of the cultural tradition from which environmental history is written. While North American and European histories of the Latin American environment have come to dominate the field, it would be wrong to suggest that they pioneered this theme. Castro Herrera highlights several early works by Latin American scholars themselves that represented a "promising start" to this discipline but that during the crisis-ridden 1980s faded into relative obscurity (see Sunkel and Gligo 1980; Vitale 1983; Ortiz Monasterio et al. 1987). Such limitations offer clues as to why the environment in Latin America and the Caribbean has rarely been considered as anything more than a passive backdrop to political and economic histories. The search is now on for a discernibly Latin American approach to environmental history based on the region's unique heritage and priorities.

Three issues have emerged as of particular interest to environmental historians: territories, commodities and knowledge (see Brannstrom

2004). These generate questions about how a society's *understanding* of the environment influenced the practices and technologies that determined how it fared within it (see Chapter 2). One example of this is the notion of "wilderness" found in US historiography compared with attitudes towards nature found within Latin American cultural history, in which romantic inclinations about empty landscapes have largely been absent (see Miller 2007).

If the work of environmental historians is to inform contemporary debates, then political boundaries and processes also become an unavoidable factor in understanding how human society has exercised control over nature. Castro Herrera (2001) argues that Latin American and Caribbean regional specificities are likely to be of decisive importance in the design of environmental policies. This is particularly so in the twenty-first century, he argues, as Latin Americans strive to create integrated societies against the backdrop of a dominant vision of nature that proclaims as "natural", not historical, the ways in which it has been reduced to being seen as a resource to be "managed" according to market demands.

Pre-Columbian society and Conquest

Human society was transforming the environment of the Americas long before the great civilizations encountered by the conquering Spanish and Portuguese, and the landscape of 1492 had already been shaped by 15,000 years of activity. In the pre-Columbian era complex societies flourished in fragile ecosystems such as in the dry areas of Mesoamerica, the high altitudes of the Andes or the lowlands of the Amazonian floodplain (Baud, de Castro and Hogenboom 2011). Farming techniques developed by civilizations that preceded the Aztecs, Incas and Brazil's Tupi kneaded the landscape through established landholding patterns and massive irrigation and terracing systems. The rich resources offered by rivers, tidal areas and mangroves nurtured large communities and archaeological evidence from the Amazon basin indicates that the fertile lowlands may once have supported millions of people in huge settlements (see Roberts and Thanos 2003). Chiefdoms emerged in Peru in about 2500 BC through abundance that yielded a surplus – and hence created wealth. In Mesoamerica, by 500–250 BC corn cultivation had led to the growth of major cities such as Teotihuacán, sustaining 150,000 people.

The Taino, who occupied the Caribbean islands, had a successful agriculture cultivating cassava, sweet potatoes and maize. Early Spanish visitors to Hispaniola noted extensive cultivation of manioc and sweet potato. Alongside corn and beans, the Aztecs consumed diverse sources of protein from animals, game, fish and insects to grain and algae growing on Lake Texcoco. By the time of Conquest, all the Mesoamerican cultures had developed highly productive agricultural methods that included the use of canals, terracing, raised and ridged fields, fertilizer from waste and seasonal swamps, agroforestry, hydrological management through dykes, dams, irrigation, reservoirs, shifting cultivation and slash-and-burn agriculture. In the Andes, pre-Inca groups and their successors made extensive use of raised-field agriculture in what is now Colombia and around Lake Titicaca bordering Peru and Bolivia. Highland Andean society recycled waste to create compost, using llama manure, and the Incas also mined guano bird droppings on islands off Peru's coast for fertilizer (see below). In the north-east of what is today Chile, the herding of camelids – llamas and alpacas – had been practised for thousands of years. Agriculture had also developed in large areas within the Amazon Basin well before the European conquest and nutrient-rich dark soils known as *terra preta* were created from concentrated wastes such as rotting vegetation, animal remains and manure. Lower Amazon communities practised agroforestry, and a significant proportion of the Amazon Basin today consists of forests that were partly man-made (see Hecht and Posey 1989; Roosevelt 1999). Amazonians also manipulated rivers and streams to modify the landscape (see Raffles and Winkler Prins 2003). Such was the extent to which they changed their surroundings that an emergent body of research on the Amazon sub-region now conceives of a "natural-cultural" or "biocultural" landscape (see, for example, Balée 1989, 1999; Denevan 1992, 2001; Hecht and Posey 1989; Raffles 1999, 2002; Roosevelt 1981, 1991; Demerritt 1994; Haraway 1997; Latour 1993). Some scholars believe that virtually all of the Amazon reflects a "managed succession" of use (see Hecht and Posey 1989; Posey 1985, 1992; Irvine 1989). Pre-Columbian peoples also devised innovations in production such as the *chinampa* in Mexico (see Box 1.1). Terracing was such an important feature of Inca agriculture that it bequeathed the name "Andes". The Tiwanaku culture on the perimeter of Lake Titicaca (1500 BC–AD 1200) built ridged fields called *camellones* where potato yields were very high. The

Moxos culture (1000 BC–AD 1400) in Beni, Bolivia, developed a huge hydraulic system based on embankments, lakes and ridges.

The European invaders encountered large societies and organized patterns of settlement with dense populations. Sophisticated empires existed in the highlands of Mexico and Peru that had themselves succeeded previous civilizations. The Spaniards came upon large cities whose peoples had built roads and earthworks, cleared fields and modified forests, created grasslands, disrupted wildlife, and in some places caused soil erosion.

Box 1.1 The *chinampa*

The lakes of central Mexico were a source of bounty and a means of transportation that became the foundation of pre-Columbian civilization. Before the Aztecs settled in the Valley of Mexico in about AD 1300, communities along the shores of Lake Texcoco were employing raised field wetland agriculture comprising floating plots made of layered mud and rotting vegetation on reed structures called *chinampas*. Eventually, using extensive chinampas around their capital of Tenochtitlán, the Aztecs would go on to produce abundant quantities of maize without fallowing as well as fresh fruit, vegetables and flowers. The *chinampa* was a significant technological development: it reduced labour, was irrigated from below, could be sustained by the composting and recycling of wastes (including that from public latrines), and it improved soil fertility over time while maintaining the lake ecosystems. These factors meant *chinampas* were highly productive, allowing several harvests per year, and could support a large population, helping to explain why at that time central Mexico had one of the world's densest populations. Similar forms of raised-field agriculture were also used by the Maya further south. As the Aztecs consolidated their empire, Lake Texcoco became criss-crossed with causeways to manage the *chinampas* and control the water around the fields, which warmed the air and helped to combat frost. Sophisticated water management enabled the Aztecs to combat salination, drought and the threat posed by flooding.

A key issue in environmental history has been the extent to which ecological factors were responsible for the disappearance of pre-Columbian civilizations and hence the extent to which these peoples used resources sustainably. This issue has attracted attention since the late 1980s because it coincides with the growing prominence of indigenous peoples in many environmental struggles (see Chapter 2). It raises important questions about how in many narratives indigenous peoples are portrayed as responsible stewards of nature.

There is debated evidence that as early as 12,000 years ago humans had already decimated some large species that once roamed the Americas (see Roberts and Thanos 2003). Archaeological debate has focused on the decline of the Classic Maya cities between the eighth and ninth centuries, when advanced centres of the southern lowlands were abandoned. Environmental factors from climate change to deforestation have formed the basis for theories about why this happened, with the most influential being the idea of drought exacerbated by thin tropical soils.

In some areas, the size of native populations and prolonged intensive agriculture may have caused land degradation. In some cases, indigenous societies clearly consumed timber, fuel, water and soil nutrients faster than they could be replaced, although it may have been the resulting socio-political impact of shortages that explain breakdown. Over-intensive resource use has been cited among explanations for the decline of the classical Maya cultures, and some archaeologists have pointed to evidence of a decline in agricultural yields, over-cultivation and soil depletion. The over-exploitation of resources probably contributed to the crisis of the Aztec empire, and evidence from lake-core sediments in Michoacán reveals significant levels of soil erosion. Elaborate customs surrounding war and human sacrifice that developed may have been one response to overuse.

Conquest and colonization by the Spanish and Portuguese had an irreversible impact on the landscape, transforming the ecology of large areas through the propagation of disease and non-native fauna and flora. Conquest initiated the demographic collapse of indigenous society, changed how resources were used and managed, and Europe-anized the flora and fauna of the New World by homogenizing cultural and productive systems and by changing the objectives of agriculture (see Miller 2007; Baud, de Castro and Hogenboom 2011). A loose consensus among scholars is that the indigenous population declined by 90 per cent, mostly within the first decade of the Europeans' arrival as a result of disease – from between 50 million and 100 million people in 1492 to between 5 million and 12 million at its lowest point in the seventeenth century. Demographic collapse had a significant impact on the natural environment: the Iberian conquerors were able to occupy fertile farmland and pasture now abandoned in order to pursue agriculture or ranching. Land-use patterns were overturned through a new system of tribute to the Spaniards, forced migration and relocation patterns, the Iberian monopolization of women and the forcible recruitment of males for mining. Population centres were reorganized to reflect the development of an economy now serving a worldwide trade network (see Castro Herrera 2008). By the middle of the sixteenth century, many Andean villages were deserted and the ancient irrigation networks and terraced fields that had held topsoil in place were abandoned.

The Spanish and Portuguese brought plants, animals and pests that had few natural predators and reproduced easily (see Brothwell 1994). European crops and those from their other territories in Africa and Asia spread, pushing native plants on to marginal lands. Spanish land-use reproduced the mono-crop economy based on the plantation, whereby land was cleared to introduce a foreign species and other plants were eradicated. Wheat was raised from the Río de la Plata to the Central American highlands, and within a generation of conquest, rice, sugar and bananas were being grown in Peru's wet lowlands (see Crosby 1991). Grapevines thrived in Peru, Chile, Tucumán and the Río de la Plata (see Lacoste 2007). The introduction of sugar cane in the fields of the Tupi in 1516 had a dramatic impact on the landscape, and between 1550 and 1600 Brazil became the world's most important producer of sugar through extensive plantation monoculture. Vast areas of the lowland coastal Atlantic Forest were felled to create canefields. Furnaces to boil cane juice consumed vast tracts of woodland and mangroves. Eventually, the coastal plains of the Caribbean islands and Brazil were deforested and irrigated to produce sugar, and the forests of Colombia, Venezuela, Central America, the Caribbean islands and the São Paulo plateau were cut down to grow coffee.

Spanish farming practices also spread local crops over larger areas, and the animals they brought with them transported seeds and weeds in their manure. New grasses and weeds colonized the South American pampas and Colombian and Venezuelan llanos, and turned grasslands in northern Mexico into scrub and thorn. Horses, dogs, pigs, cattle, chickens, sheep and goats were left to feed freely, and reproduced rapidly (see Crosby 1991). Swine thrived, competing for pasture with indigenous species. Horses made possible the great colonial cattle industry that had a significant environmental impact in the New World. Melville (1997) suggests that the introduction of sheep into Mexico's Valle del Mezquital initiated the rapid destruction of flora and desertification. The ox enabled new lands to be ploughed, and cultivation with a plough is more likely to cause soil erosion than with a hoe or digging stick. By the 1570s, the impact of rapidly increasing livestock herds was already noted in Hispaniola by observers, and by the 1580s overgrazing in Mexico was apparent.

The colonial era

Rapid depopulation and the limited scale of immigration during the early colonial era enabled, on the one hand, the renewal of depleted soils, waters, forests and wildlife; and, on the other, new extractive practices that could benefit from the disappearance of indigenous cultures.

Within 150 years after being emptied of indigenous people, the once occupied settlements, fields and savannas of Central America and Colombia had reverted to forest. The demographic collapse of the indigenous peoples of coastal areas and the Amazon Basin such as the Tupi and Omagua led to the regeneration of forestry as abandoned fields regrew, riverbanks were colonized by trees and river life revived. By the late eighteenth century, many ecosystems once exploited by large indigenous societies had recovered (Castro Herrera 2008). A limited population in the new Iberian territories meant that by the mid- to late sixteenth century food was abundant, allowing the slow recovery of indigenous populations themselves to begin.

The Spanish imperial system restricted immigration in the colonies, and Iberian land tenure further limited immigration because land grants were often huge, creating forms of monopoly (*latifundia*) to secure labour and limit competition in the production of crops or for limited resources such as firewood and water. Property that was not cultivated remained untouched as landholders had neither the capital nor labour to work it, and was not taxed, reducing the degree to which forests and soils were depleted. The most important strategic objective of the Spanish and Portuguese crowns was the search for precious metals, and mining was a driving force of colonial expansion (see Box 1.2).

Box 1.2 Mining in the colonial era

The Spanish conquistadors' obsession with precious metals is well documented. The enslavement by the Spanish of declining populations of Tainos, Caribs and Arawaks to pan rivers for alluvial gold accelerated their decline. Gold was the most sought-after commodity but by the 1550s, the exploitation of large silver deposits in Mexico and Peru turned this precious metal into the principal commodity exported from the Indies. From the mid-sixteenth century until the early nineteenth century, 85 per cent of the world's silver and 70 per cent of its gold came from Latin America. Silver mining became the engine of both economic growth in Mexico and of the early globalization of trade (see Ponzio 2005). From 1492 to 1900, the environmental impact of mining was concentrated in highland Mexico, Peru, Bolivia and Chile and later in the interior of Brazil. Mining was a major cause of ecological destruction, as forests were cut to provide timber for shafts and pasture for draft animals. The need to produce meat for the Spanish colonists and mules for the mines stimulated extensive deforestation for ranching. In the Caribbean, large areas were deforested to build the galleons that carried the silver to Europe. In 1554, at Pachuca, the "patio" method of extracting precious metals from ore by using mercury was developed, inaugurating a rapid expansion of silver production that would finance colonial administration, the construction of cities and, eventually, European industrialization. The pollution caused by this metal in Huancavelica in Peru and Potosí in Bolivia had a devastating effect on indigenous communities, and mercury entered rivers and poisoned the food chain and soil (see Robins 2011). Gold later discovered in Brazil's mountainous interior meant miners largely worked above ground, scarring the landscape, diverting rivers and digging canals to get at river beds. Deforestation combined with panning caused extensive soil erosion and pollution (see Dore 1991). Farmers and ranchers often followed gold rushes to slash and burn large areas. Across Latin America, the need for labour in the mines meant entire indigenous communities were enslaved to work them, abandoning ancient irrigation networks and terraced fields and further exacerbating soil erosion.

The Spanish imperial state began to tighten its grip over economic practices through protectionism and monopolies. An extractive economy in which the Crown played a significant role would shape

Latin American and Caribbean society forever. The new American lands gave the Spanish and Portuguese monarchs vast potential new sources of patronage, and they monopolized entire sectors – timber, tobacco, diamonds, mercury – in order to control prices and maximize revenues to the exchequer. Restrictions on production of commodities such as tobacco limited the impact they would have on the natural environment. In some cases, such as brazilwood, diamonds and whales, these forms of protectionism limited the environmental impact of the colonial export economy for centuries. It was not until the era of Bourbon reform in the late eighteenth century that Spanish monarchs opened more American ports for trade, and between 1778 and 1796 colonial trade grew rapidly.

The extractive economy greatly expanded the institutions of state, with the creation of a separate colonial infrastructure to administer the New World territories. Taxation was well organized, and trade between Spain and its overseas territories obeyed a monopoly under state supervision that persisted for much of the colonial era. The Iberian imperial states were the first to establish "enclave" economies, dominated by single interests serving overseas markets. The Amazon Basin had become an enclave dedicated to foreign extraction under the Portuguese through colonization and settlement by the 1750s, and retained this character into the early twentieth century (see Anderson 1999). Economic exploitation of forest and river goods – and competition between foreign states – have been at the heart of all subsequent penetration of the region (see Da Cunha 2006; Pádua 2012).

By the late sixteenth century, African slavery had become the dominant form of work organization in Central, South American and Caribbean plantations. Slavery cemented Latin America's links with the world economy as an exporter of raw materials, allowed elites to maintain outdated farming techniques and ignore the need to conserve the soil, and encouraged them to expand into the vast frontier in Brazil, coastal Central America and the Caribbean, burning forests and depleting soils.

Many of the ecological changes in the Americas resulted from colonial policies aimed at satisfying European demand (see Mintz 1991). It was an era distinguished by the development of tradable commodities, such as sugar. Most of the Caribbean islands were heavily wooded in 1492 but by 1700 nearly all the small sugar islands had been deforested to make way for planting and for the wood fuel needed to process cane, exposing soil to rain and heat that leached nutrients and caused erosion. Initially, Spain's economy was a significant beneficiary of the wealth produced by the colonies. By the mid-seventeenth century, however, weakening Spanish control over its American territories and the rise of a new Spanish American ruling class meant that great landed estates (*haciendas*) developed alongside mining as one of the region's most characteristic productive units. The nature of agriculture, subject to unpredictable climatic conditions, encouraged *hacendados* to minimize competition by achieving monopoly positions and to aspire to self-sufficiency by growing staples alongside cash crops and using land for pasture or allowing it to lie fallow. Although by the late sixteenth century significant exports in some agricultural commodities had evolved, it was not until the eighteenth century that other products such as coffee and cacao were exported in large volumes.

Colonization of the Americas also had significant implications for the natural environment in Europe. It made available to European farmers new species – maize, potatoes, tobacco – and agroecosystems now contained more varieties than ever before on both sides of the Atlantic (see Worster 1990). The conquest of the New World also inaugurated the age of imperialism that for the next 400 years would have a comprehensive impact on the global environment.

Independence and export capitalism

Independence at the start of the nineteenth century marked a new era in the history of ideas in Latin America with important consequences for resource use and attitudes towards nature (see Chapter 2). The liberalization of trade in the American colonies by the Spanish and Portuguese authorities in the late eighteenth century responded to the growing desire of creoles – American-born ethnic Spaniards – for free trade. Independence removed the Crown monopoly on commodities and gave rise to an export boom and, ultimately, the development of capitalism in the region. A new era based on Latin America's growing integration in the world economy through export-led growth began in the 1840s. The region's new national leaders were influenced by liberal economic ideas and fired by visions of national progress built on export revenues (see Chapter 5). At the same time, the demands of the Industrial Revolution in northern Europe and increasingly the US created hungry new markets (see Bulmer-Thomas 1994). The period between 1850 and 1914 was one of unprecedented growth that transformed the colonial pattern of exportation, based primarily on precious metals, and had the most profound impact on the environment to date. In much of Latin America and the Caribbean, the new products that came to dominate export earnings were of agricultural origin and met the needs of new manufacturing processes or of feeding a growing industrial workforce. Rising incomes in North America and Europe and changing patterns of consumption fuelled mass market demand for luxury tropical products. However, export growth between 1850 and 1912 did not lead to export diversification, and most countries remained reliant on one single commodity for revenue.

After 1850, foreign trade became intertwined with a new era of imperialism in which most commerce was controlled by just six countries. Great power rivalry took the form both of direct military interventions but also indirect political and economic domination. Latin America's role as a supplier of the commodities was maintained by the great powers according to the doctrine of comparative advantage in international trade, which suggests that a country will gain the greatest benefit in a trading relationship by concentrating its production on commodities that it can provide at a lower overall cost, either because these are found in abundance or they can be produced easily. Comparative advantage is the basis for many economists' belief in free trade and implies an international division of labour by which some countries stick to producing agricultural or mineral commodities to sell to those that produce industrial goods. Mexico's production of henequen on the Yucatán peninsula provides a good example of comparative advantage: production of this "green gold" grew dramatically in the nineteenth century with the increase in merchant shipping that reflected rapidly rising global trade (Wells 1998; Wilkins 1998).

In Europe and the US, agricultural and industrial productivity was enhanced by new technologies, growing populations that in turn fuelled urbanization, and rising real incomes that generated new demand for producer and consumer goods. Advances in transportation through steamships and new communication technology transformed shipping, trading and financial services.

Extractive sectors – agriculture, minerals and forest products – offered the new Latin American and Caribbean republics the only realistic path to prosperity (see Topik, Marichal and Frank 2006). Between 1850 and 1913, Latin American exports of primary products and exotic foods expanded tenfold. In return, European and US capital flowed into the region as did ideas, technology and, in countries such as Argentina and eventually Brazil, immigrants. Industrial processes, steam power and transportation, steel, refrigeration and wire fencing transformed the landscape, and land and labour themselves became commodities. The growing use of steam power drove the export-led development model, with Central American bananas, Amazonian rubber and Argentine beef all able to reach markets far away. Argentina's interior was agriculturally developed by immigrants from Europe who often had little knowledge of how to cultivate in new surroundings, causing environmental deterioration (see Sawers 2000).

The expansion of the commodity economy in this period has been referred to as the "Second Conquest" of Latin America and the Caribbean because of its impact on development and society and its relationship with foreign capital and markets (see Topik and Wells 1998). This perspective suggests Latin America's commodity history should be understood as part of a broader history of global interconnection in which states emerging from the turbulence and instability of independence and wedded to notions of national development eyed agricultural and mineral resources on lands hitherto under-exploited by their local populations in a form of "internal colonialism". Elites in this era were influenced by new ideas about race, progress and science (see Chapter 2). There was considerable variation between – and within – countries as to the extent and timing of their insertion into world trade networks, but without exception Latin American nations joined the global economy through their exports of primary commodities (see Wilkins 1998).

- ***Coffee***. The Industrial Revolution in Europe turned coffee into one of the main traded commodities by value during the nineteenth century, and it became the main export crop of nearly half the countries in Latin America. From 1850 to 1930, up to 95 per cent of the world's coffee was produced in the region, mostly for the US and Europe. Escalating demand turned coffee into a pioneer packaged, branded product for mass consumption in stores, restaurants and coffeehouses (see Wilkins 1998). Coffee cultivation had tended to create monocultural dependence on one export by the end of the nineteenth century, and by 1929 it accounted for the lion's share of exports in Brazil, Colombia, Guatemala, Haiti, Nicaragua, Costa Rica and El Salvador (see Topik 1998). Growing external demand caused important ecological changes in late nineteenth-century Brazil and the Andes. The coffee boom occurred on newly opening frontiers and involved expansion into uncultivated lands, forest clearing, the building of towns and the laying of roads and railroads (see Roseberry 1991; Monseff Perissinotto 2003).

- ***Sugar***. Sugar production transformed the environment of Caribbean countries such as Puerto Rico and Cuba. Efforts to modernize plantations in Puerto Rico were unsuccessful by the 1870s and the sugar industry survived only by placing more land under cultivation and increasing the exploitation of workers (see Funes Monzote 2008).
- ***Bananas***. Growing demand for bananas spurred economies of scale and farmers began to crowd plants together, spreading infections. To avoid this, US multinationals employed shifting plantation agriculture which drove them to buy up vast tracts of the coastal Central American floodplains and to clear forest and plant rapidly (Soluri 2004; Tortorelo 2004).
- ***Mining***. The industrial revolutions in western Europe and the US created new demand for base minerals. Copper, lead and zinc mines in Peru's Central Andes transformed the sub-region's fragile ecosystem and their US owners constructed roads, railroads, smelters, mining camps, dams, hydroelectric plants and *haciendas* (see Dore 1991). Mines consumed huge quantities of timber, causing extensive deforestation and erosion. Dams to provide energy for machinery flooded farmland in peasant communities far from mines. Land prices alongside railroads soared, replacing subsistence farming with livestock grazing and commercial agriculture. Smelters and refineries poisoned the air and water across large areas.
- ***Guano***. Guano – the accumulated waste of sea birds, produced by marine life off Peru's coasts, which served as a natural fertilizer – became the country's most important export and had a global impact on soil fertility from 1840 to 1870. British and US farmers imported vast quantities of the natural fertilizer, but by the 1870s the resource was becoming depleted, sparking a war in 1879 between Peru, Chile and Bolivia. The commercial exploitation of guano had a significant environmental impact in Peru and beyond. By doubling yields, it transformed agricultural productivity and meant farmers did not have

to rotate crops or fallow fields. This greatly increased the number of people that could be supported by agriculture on a global scale, with a consequent impact on human population.

- ***Oil.*** The most profound impact on Latin American economic development came as a result of oil production, which was initially financed with foreign capital and thereafter came under state control as a result of nationalism. Oil represented a new kind of commodity with a powerful political edge and would come to overshadow coffee or henequen. It was dominated by foreign corporations, generating large revenues for hungry states and spurring the creation of new sectors throughout the economy. The industry required exploration, drilling, refining, transportation and the creation of a huge infrastructure, requiring a willingness to mobilize large sums of capital and expertise, and it quickly began to have a profound impact on the environment (see Box 1.3). From the 1960s, oil would become the basis for the industrialization of Latin America (see Wilkins 1998).

The First World War devastated the global economy and demand for primary commodities collapsed in the early 1920s, ending Latin America's export boom. In the 1930s, the Great Depression lowered commodity prices and the share of primary products in output. New synthetic materials – nitrates, latex and textiles – displaced traditional products such as guano, rubber and cotton.

Economic growth from primary exports in Latin America and the Caribbean in the period 1850–1914 had several distinguishing features:

Environmental limitations. The possibilities and constraints of the natural environment shaped this phase of Latin American and Caribbean development. Varying conditions determined if and how resources could be extracted, or favoured certain products over others, and in turn the ways in which territories were integrated into the world market. At the same time, prevailing ideas about economic development, consumption, science and nature also shaped how the environment was exploited (see McCook 2002b; Chapters 2, 5). Disease and the response by exporters to it had an important effect on land use and the development of scientific knowledge.

Statebuilding. The key political development of the export era was the creation of modern, centralized states able to galvanize economic activity on a national scale – statebuilding (see Véliz 1980). Centralism

Box 1.3 Early oil production and the environment

By the 1920s, the oil industry was already leaving an indelible mark on Latin America's environment, and although its impact has not been well studied there is no doubt that it was profound. First, the oil companies amassed millions of acres of tropical forest, changing land-use patterns and traditional forms of subsistence agriculture. This led to shifts in land and resource tenure laws, changes in patterns of landholding and gradual dependence on the oil economy in some areas (Santiago 2006). In Mexico, for example, oilfields developed by the American Edward L Doheny in the tropical forests of northern Veracruz between 1900 and 1931 had a lasting impact on the environment and on the Huastec indigenous groups in the region. Doheny bought large tracts of land, and by 1917 his "jungle kingdom" totalled over 600,000 acres. Similarly, Weetman Pearson, an English engineer, reported owning about 600,000 acres of land over the entire Gulf coast (see Santiago 1998). Second, oil production caused serious pollution. In 1908, the Dos Bocas well exploded at San Diego de la Mar in Veracruz, Mexico causing one of the largest oil spills in history. Fires raged from 4 July to 30 August until the oil deposit had burned out, creating huge clouds of toxic gas. Nearly 90,000 barrels of oil flowed into the surrounding landscape, Tamiahua Lagoon and the Gulf of Mexico each day. In 1910, another blowout occurred at the Potrero del Llano No. 4 well in Temapache, a Nahuatl and Huastec area in Veracruz (see Santiago 1998). In Venezuela, the early oil boom damaged the ecosystem of Lake Maracaibo, which is located above that country's premier hydrocarbon basin, and damaged the health of local villagers (see Kozloff 2004). Catastrophic explosions in the area led to the first efforts to improve environmental regulation of the petroleum industry. Technology was rudimentary for decades, and repeated oil spills contaminated beaches and killed fish along the Pacific, forcing fishing communities to abandon their homes. Development in remote areas such as Colombia's De Mares concession in the Magdalena River valley had a lasting impact. Living quarters, utilities, terminal facilities, railways and refineries were built and roads opened through tropical forest.

has been at the heart of statebuilding in which the administrative structures inherited from colonial rule incorporated territory under central state control, often thereby enabling foreign capital to exploit natural resources. This incorporation, often termed "integration", was a familiar theme of nineteenth- and twentieth-century elite discourses about people and their environments aiming to encourage foreign investment and often overlooking basic environmental constraints (see Offen 2004). As a result, in Latin America and the Caribbean, states have been dominant actors in the extraction of natural resources and remain so in strategic sectors such as hydrocarbons.

Foreign influences. Foreign capital and markets drove the development of commodities, and this era exemplifies how globalization has been a longstanding feature of Latin American growth (see Passananti 2007). Foreign investors often created economic enclaves in mining and agriculture that operated beyond the writ of national governments. Foreigners dominated all the services and infrastructure required for these to function such as credit, transport, marketing and innovation; and foreign trade, insurance and financing structures, particularly those of Britain and the US, took the commodities to market. Foreign consumption patterns created the demand for these products. In turn, the primary export sector was vulnerable to price fluctuations determined in foreign stock markets. Foreign domination inhibited local diversification and governments often did not intervene to protect sectors lest this deter foreign investment. The control by US banana corporations of huge areas in sub-regions such as Central America inevitably generated political interference, creating the so-called "banana republics" in which companies maintained dictatorships and subverted governments hostile to them. Often countries were heavily dependent on just one product, such as sugar: by 1913, more than half the exports of 13 Latin American countries were concentrated in just one product, invariably exported to just a few countries – the US, Great Britain, France and Germany. While Britain was a source of finance for development for much of the nineteenth century, by the end of the century it was US entrepreneurs and corporations that were propelling the export economy. Backed with US military and diplomatic support, speculators created the first giants of corporate agro-industry (see Tucker 2000). Whole areas of production in Latin America and the Caribbean became dominated by large US corporations, with significant consequences for the environment. They cleared forests and displaced the production of indigenous and peasant communities with mono-crop export plantations, founded on the principle of private property that further diminished biodiversity (see Tucker 2000). US demand for beef reared in northern Mexico had significant ecological consequences and US demand for rubber and coffee drove ecological transformation in Brazil (see Brannstrom and Gallini 2004).

Political impact. Export-led growth and the influx of foreign capital had an important socio-political impact on Latin America and the Caribbean, generating forms of mobilization that would influence development in the twentieth century. The increase in commodity exports from Latin America and the Caribbean powered the development of industrial capitalism in the US and Europe – a driving force of global environmental change – and laid the foundations for the rise of capitalism in the region itself. The US became an important model of economic efficiency in Latin America and its rational forms of production using the latest technology and large, vertically integrated companies supplying growing domestic markets eventually established US consumer capitalism as a template for elites. Latin American economies had developed during the nineteenth century on the basis of agro-exports controlled by a small number of oligarchic landowners, a model that limited the emergence of industry and tied the fate of elites closely to the interests of external actors. In some societies, elements of this social structure persisted and by the time of the oil boom the agro-export economy had not overturned the rigid postcolonial social structure subordinating non-white majorities to inferior status, and landowners retained power. As capitalist markets expanded, they generated competition over access to resources, and territorial struggles fuelled by the desire to expand commodity extraction became a key source of conflict, often between central states controlled by liberal elites and indigenous peoples (see Chapter 2). Extraction invariably overlooked environmental limitations and had an impact on the sustainable practices of indigenous communities employing communal agriculture, who were marginalized or forced from the land (see Gallini 2004; Offen 2004). Integration into the world economy through the export of raw materials was sustained by liberal ideology by which elites pursued economic development on the basis of private property relations that outlawed the communal ownership of land. Commodity production also led to exploitation and a characteristic of societies with export-led economies was inequality.

Box 1.4 Banana spraying and organized labour

Environmental historians are sometimes criticized for examining the ecological impact of capitalism in ways that pay little attention to the role of workers, while at the same time historians who employ class relations as a framework of analysis rarely incorporate ecological change. Yet there is a close relationship between environmental change and changes in production processes, and organized workers have often been among the first environmentalists. One context that provides examples of this was the role played by pesticide workers in the Central American banana industry. Marquardt (2002) explores the use of biocidal agrochemicals in Latin America from 1938 to 1962 by the United Fruit Company, which required thousands of workers to hand spray its banana plantations to control sigitoka disease. Focusing on Costa Rica, he explores sprayers' relationships with the larger banana workers' union movement, and how together they forced fundamental changes in the pesticide programme. He demonstrates the importance of integrating labour into the study of environmental change in agricultural capitalism by showing that the fortunes of the Costa Rican banana unions were intimately linked to the environmental history of crop disease and pesticide technology.

Faber (1993), for example, calls attention to the emergence in sub-regions such as Central America of authoritarian *caudillos* from among the coffee elites, who manipulated politics and monopolized the economy using the coercive arms of the state. The main losers from Latin America's role in the international division of labour as a producer of agricultural goods and raw materials were poorly paid rural workers, many of whom headed for cities, fuelling urbanization. Early in the twentieth century, however, the pressures generated by export-led growth began to undermine the control of the oligarchs, who saw the need to incorporate urban middle classes and workers into the political process. Growing urban populations did not fit easily into the social hierarchy that had supported the development of large estates and ranches for export-led growth. As a result, Latin America's model of growth generated new class tensions, and in some countries, such as Mexico, revolution. The oil sector provides an example of how new commodities began to shape politics in this period. Oil workers became militant within a decade of the arrival of foreign companies because foreigners retained managerial positions, alienating native workers. Latin American states and political movements began to discover mutual advantage in assisting organized labour in its struggles against foreign employers, often under the banner of nationalism (Brown and Linder 1998). In some cases, the direct environmental consequences of unsustainable development served to radicalize social groups. In Mexico, indigenous Huastec and Nahuatl labourers recruited under pressure to fight the Potrero del Llano No. 4 oil well blowout in 1910 were politicized (see Santiago 1998). Biocidal agrochemicals in the Central American banana sector destroyed workers' health and led organized labour to take an interest in environmental conditions (see Box 1.4).

Industrialization

The export economy created the conditions for an early phase of industrialization to begin in some of the larger economies of Latin America after 1870, and industrialization proceeded on a limited scale in Argentina, Brazil, Chile and Mexico until 1913 as an offshoot of the export economy. In Brazil and Colombia, the coffee sector nurtured industrialization, but in El Salvador it occurred due to a dense, proletarianized population and national entrepreneurs. Industrialization in Latin America was also due to changing global terms of trade and imperial policy elsewhere in the world, with much of Asia and the Middle East in this era lacking the autonomy to pursue pro-industrial policies that an independent Latin America could benefit from. Latin American states in need of energy for new factories embraced hydroelectricity, aided by the development of reinforced concrete that made the construction of dams possible. By 1900, small, private hydropower stations had been established near several cities to benefit mostly local industries, with serious environmental consequences (see Chapter 4). Dams obliterated landscapes formerly used for agriculture and timber, redirecting rivers and displacing entire communities. The creation in 1927 of a large reservoir impounding the Pinheiros River was accompanied by the location at Cubatão of Brazil's largest generating plant, helping to turn São Paulo into Latin America's largest and most polluted industrial centre.

The principal phase of industrialization in Latin America and the Caribbean was conducted under protectionist trade policies of "import substitution industrialization" (ISI) between the 1930s and the 1970s. The Great Depression that followed the Wall Street crash of 1929 hit Latin America hard and forced countries to reconsider their relationship with the international economic system. Policymakers became aware of the need to reduce their reliance on the export of commodities and the import of manufactured goods, and in the 1930s most countries in the region began nurturing their own industries through ISI influenced by "structuralist" ideas that argued for state-led economic growth (see Chapter 5). This strategy laid the basis for inward-looking national development policies while allowing Latin America to take advantage of capitalist expansion elsewhere in the world that provided markets for its products (see Frankenhoff 1962). ISI policies in Mexico and the Southern Cone fuelled the growth of small classes of domestic industrialists and urban workers. In some parts of South America and in Central America, however, where traditional exporting elites retained considerable power, the state and other institutions such as the Economic Commission for Latin America (ECLA, later ECLAC to include the Caribbean) often played a more significant role in creating industry. Government policies biased towards helping new industries and ISI through protectionism became a cornerstone of development strategies until the 1980s. These policies enabled most countries in Latin America to produce basic goods, and a few countries successfully created heavy industries. Larger economies were able to diversify exports beyond a single traditional primary product. Manufacturing grew in importance as a proportion of gross domestic product (GDP), and one measure of this was the declining share of the labour force employed in agriculture between 1930 and 1980 (see Cardoso and Helwege 1992). However, by the end of the 1950s, the early phase of ISI was already becoming "exhausted" and new approaches were sought to develop non-traditional exports or promote new forms of agricultural development while stimulating new industrial exports. A shift towards more complex industrial products was hampered by a lack of access to investment and technology, and many governments began to welcome multinational corporations into their countries.

Industrialization had a significant impact on political development by nurturing centralizing and authoritarian states that took on an ever greater economic role. These states often acted in the interests both of traditional oligarchs and newly emergent groups such as urban trades unions and professional bureaucrats. The institutional structure of the state also grew much larger after the 1950s as ministries grew in size and new government agencies were created to promote manufacturing. Structuralist strategies invariably failed to take into account the need to ensure state interventions benefited the majority, and revolutionary activity in the 1960s prompted states to assert further control over society while assuming social welfare commitments. The state apparatus expanded and managers, bureaucrats, professionals and technocrats became more powerful and formed an important coalition underpinning the authoritarian regimes of the 1960s and 1970s. Military interventions throughout Latin America and the Caribbean coincided with the exhaustion of the first phase of ISI and a model of "bureaucratic authoritarianism" was developed by O'Donnell (1973) to account for the relationship between the military regimes and development.

Under ISI, states tended to manage society in ways in which class and sectoral pressure were divided horizontally through "corporatism" to alleviate class conflict and prevent the development of broad opposition coalitions. The industrializing state's need to maintain control over organized labour helps to explain why early ISI in Latin America was sometimes accompanied by "populist" alliances behind the banner of nationalism. Non-organized sectors of the population – in particular, the peasantry – were largely excluded from the benefits of industrial development.

ISI also entrenched inequality and transformed poverty from a rural into an urban characteristic by strengthening a tendency to disregard agricultural production. Credit was diverted to industry and public spending biased towards growing urban areas. Until the 1960s, there were only limited efforts to change the social structure of the countryside and landholding patterns, and large, unproductive estates persisted. The exclusion of large numbers of people from the benefits promised by industrialization and from the coalitions which it gave rise to fuelled unrest. Millions of peasants abandoned the countryside, swelling urbanization, and radical political alternatives developed outside the formal institutions of politics. The neglect of agriculture further reinforced a need to import food, and worsened contrasts between urban and rural populations. ISI also encouraged consumption patterns among an urban middle class that imitated those of industrialized countries, concentrating consumption in high-income strata and thereby increasing inequality and fuelling political tension. The poor are much less able to make choices that are not damaging to the environment, and poverty, alongside industrial production, was a significant cause of ecological degradation (see Chapter 4).

Later phases of ISI were heavily dependent on foreign investments, markets, technology and debt, greatly limiting national autonomy and deepening the relevance of economic ideas such as "dependency" (see Chapter 5). Dependency theory provides the potential for highlighting the role played by corporations from the North Atlantic world in unsustainable and environmentally destructive extraction of the region's natural resources (see Castro Herrera 2001). As much of ISI was built on easy access to large amounts of foreign debt, one of the most important consequences of this phase in development in Latin America and the Caribbean was the debt crisis after 1982 (see below). Loans in the 1970s from multilateral agencies and private banks had a significant impact on the environment, enabling states to fund megaprojects such as the Itapú dam in Brazil, which cost $20 bn (a fifth of the country's foreign debt). Weak states struggled to manage the environmental and regulatory impact of these huge infrastructure initiatives.

The model of industrial development in Latin America between the 1950s and 1970s had important consequences for the environment.

Agriculture. ISI had a profound impact on rural life and tradition by extending capitalist forms of agriculture across the countryside. "Modernization theory" suggested that the traditional agrarian cultural pattern in the region had to be dismantled if progress akin to that of the industrialized world was to be achieved, and so agrarian modernization was considered crucial by policymaking elites (see Larrain 2000). Key features of the transformation of agriculture in the late twentieth century were:

(i) Rural poverty, out-migration and urbanization

Under ISI, capital was directed to industry and agriculture was neglected, fuelling mass migration out of the countryside by peasants who went to the cities or the US. Worsening poverty led to deforestation and soil erosion (Roberts and Thanos 2003). Plantation and ranch owners, under pressure to keep down costs, maintained peasant workforces on subsistence wages that kept them poor. Machinery, pesticides and fertilizers made agricultural production capital intensive, meaning only a small proportion of the rural poor found wage work (see Dore 1996a; see also van Dooren and Zarate-Hoyos 2003). Small-scale farmers faced both a process of concentration of land by large capitalist farms and a decline in their own viability. This was very apparent during the so-called "Green Revolution" of the late 1960s in which technological developments along with machinery, pesticides and fertilizers transformed agricultural production and processing, encouraging the expansive use of land. The resulting growth in Latin America's cities engendered new environmental issues and strengthened the link between environmentalism and social justice (see Chapter 2). Urban pressure on resources such as water and pollution often catalyzed the development of environmental policies. Moreover, urban growth has not been confined to large cities and is also associated in coastal areas with the rapid expansion of tourism. In the Caribbean, cruise ships form a growing tourism sector, but cause environmental damage.

(ii) Commercial farming

Policies prioritizing industry and favouring urban centres fuelled the rapid expansion of commercial agriculture, encouraged by the Green Revolution. Agro-industries were generally mono-crop rural enterprises covering extensive landholdings – often from cleared forest in countries such as Brazil – and using vast amounts of chemical inputs.

The growth of agribusiness in Latin America, much of it controlled by multinationals, further moved the focus of production from local consumption to export and transformed the countryside.

- ***Attitudes***. Capitalist forms of agriculture altered attitudes towards land, resource use and consumption. Latin American producers now sought to take advantage of reversed seasons, allowing production to serve northern markets. Recently, agro-industry has pioneered the use of genetically modified crops (see Chapter 5). A continued reliance on exports has put pressure on governments to play down issues of sustainability (see Chapter 2). As early as the 1970s, a long-term lack of consideration for the environment was affecting some sectors (see Bulmer-Thomas 1994). For example, soil erosion in Haiti was preventing it from expanding exports; and the destruction of forests to make way for ranches was affecting the climate.

- ***Social relations.*** Corporate farming hit peasant producers and divided the rural sector between rich agro-exporting firms and smallholdings. The share of the labour force in agriculture fell dramatically as the use of machines and fertilizers grew (see Table 1.1). There was a large increase in landlessness and migrant seasonal workers moving between the rural and urban sectors in countries such as Brazil and in Central America. With these divisions came poverty and low productivity, which in turn caused environmental degradation.
- ***Deforestation and pollution.*** Intensive and expansive farming in Central America and the Caribbean caused deforestation, soil exhaustion and pollution. Coastal forests were destroyed to make way for the expansion of plantation crops such as cotton. Excluded peasant farmers often moved on to unfertile land unsuitable for slash-and-burn agriculture. Central America became the world's greatest per capita consumer of pesticides, contaminating water and soil (see Faber 1991; Díaz-Briquets and Pérez-López 2000).

Multinationals and foreign investment. In the post-war period the most dynamic sector of world production was of consumer goods such as cars, fridges and televisions, and this was dominated by large multinational corporations. Foreign capital flowing to Latin America and the Caribbean once directed at extracting raw materials now went into the production of consumer goods (see Larrain 2000). Latin American governments welcomed multinationals as providers of technology and capital. These quickly came to dominate whole areas of production such as auto manufacturing, greatly expanding the extraction of raw materials such as ores. In 1960, for example, Mexico was producing about 50,000 vehicles per year with limited domestic content; 10 years later it was producing 193,000 with mainly domestic content (see Franko 1999).

Over-production and consumption. Dramatic changes in the nature of production under ISI and the new technology and processes brought by multinationals transformed the scale of past extraction, with a huge impact on the environment. Mining offers a good example of this: by the 1960s, technological innovations had shifted mining from exploiting high-grade subterranean veins worked by individual

Table 1.1 Agricultural development indicators in Latin America and the Caribbean, 2008–12, selected countries

	Agricultural land, percentage of land area (1)	Employment in agriculture (2)	Fertilizer consumption, kg per ha of arable land (3)	Land under cereal production (ha) (4)	Permanent cropland (percentage of land area) (5)	Poverty headcount ratio at rural poverty line (percentage of rural population) (6)	Rural population (percentage of total population) (7)
Argentina	53.9	1	25.4	10.9m	0.4	–	8
Bolivia	34.2	32	6.1	0.94m	0.2	66.4	33
Brazil	32.5	17	125	19.21m	0.8	–	15
Chile	21.2	11	452.2	0.56m	0.6	12.9	11
Colombia	39.5	18	499.4	1.03m	1.7	46.1	25
Costa Rica	36.8	14	826.6	0.08m	6.5	29.3	35
Cuba	61.7	19	14.2	0.35m	3.7	–	24
Dominican Republic	50.6	12	65.3	0.19m	9.3	48.4	30
El Salvador	73.9	21	107.4	0.37m	11.1	46.5	35
Haiti	64.2	–	–	0.63m	10.2	–	47
Mexico	53.1	13	54.5	8.76m	1.4	60.8	22
Paraguay	52.8	26	66.4	1.54m	0.2	44.8	38
Venezuela	24.1	8	157.1	1.15m	0.7	–	6

Notes:

1. Agricultural land refers to the share of land area that is arable, under permanent crops and under permanent pastures.
2. Percentage of total employment, Argentina, Costa Rica, Paraguay, Venezuela = 2011; Bolivia, Brazil = 2009; Chile, Colombia, Cuba, Dominican Republic, El Salvador, Mexico = 2010.
3. 2009.
4. 2011.
5. 2011. Permanent cropland is land cultivated with crops that occupy the land for long periods and need not be replanted after each harvest, such as cocoa, coffee and rubber. This category includes land under flowering shrubs, fruit trees, nut trees and vines, but excludes land under trees grown for wood or timber.
6. Bolivia, Chile, El Salvador = 2009; Mexico = 2010; Colombia, Costa Rica, Dominican Republic, Paraguay = 2011. Rural poverty rate is the percentage of the rural population living below the national rural poverty line.
7. 2011

Source: World Bank, Agriculture & Rural Development data (http://data.worldbank.org/topic/agriculture-and-rural-development).

miners to extracting low-grade ores from surface deposits in open-cast mines using machinery (see Dore 1991). This came at a high environmental cost: entire mountains and valleys were destroyed and soil and water systems were poisoned over large areas. In the absence of effective competition, ISI was also marked by irrational overcapacity, with industrial plants being either more numerous or larger than required to meet domestic demand and operating at high costs (see, for example, Baer 1972). Multinationals pioneered new marketing infrastructures that greatly encouraged consumption among Latin Americans, exemplified by the car culture that now prevails (see Chapter 2).

Inefficiency and waste. The environmental impact of industrialization, and pollution controls, were often neglected during the pursuit of rapid development. Industrialization was promoted by ECLA and expanded to heavy industries such as steel mills, oil refineries and assembly plants. Brazil was a pioneer in creating heavy industry and its Volta Redonda steel mill, for example, badly damaged the forests and subsoils of Minas Gerais (Roberts and Thanos 2003). Nationally manufactured goods from Latin America often did not meet international quality standards because they had been developed under protective tariffs that meant companies were not forced by competition to become more efficient. Production processes were wasteful and there was little pressure on industries to clean up. Nor did industrialization foster a new entrepreneurial class in the region, generating instead a wasteful business class dependent on state protectionism for its existence. The services of infrastructure sectors such as energy or telecommunications were often underpriced to produce cheap inputs that would stimulate the growth of industry and the private sector. Underpricing generated losses in those sectors, preventing them from investing in cleaner and more efficient technology. Industrial policy was also supported through monetary and fiscal policies and the state gave companies generous subsidies and credit to nurture their growth. To create a market for products such as automobiles, governments controlled wages to enable people to buy cars. State enterprises also became engines of political "clientelism", giving politicians opportunities to offer jobs in return for support, and making it easy to turn a blind eye to poor environmental practices. Policy tools used to manage

Box 1.5 National development strategies and growth poles

Development strategies during the later period of ISI involved the construction of great industrial complexes, usually around mines, with serious environmental consequences. Petroleum and metal ore deposits, often in remote regions, were seen by politicians, bankers and lending agencies as offering the chance to create "development poles" (see Dore 1991). The first of these, established in conjunction with metal mining in Latin America, was in the Orinoquía region in Bolívar, Venezuela, where in the 1960s the government built a large iron and steel complex including open-pit mines at Ciudad Guayana. The development ignored the impact on the tropical rainforest, the river network was altered to meet its needs, and the Guri Dam flooded large areas. In Mexico in the 1970s, the exploitation of large oil deposits in the states of Tabasco and Chiapas transformed Villahermosa rapidly from a small river town into a city of a million people, with refineries, ports and pipelines. The government expropriated farmland for mining, and air and water pollution reduced the fertility of agricultural land that remained. In Brazil, the opening up of Amazonia as part of a development strategy led to widespread environmental degradation. In the early 1970s, Brazil's military regime resolved to open up the rainforest to development. The role of large private corporations in the area grew, and capital from southern Brazil and land speculators were lured there by tax rebates, subsidies and loans. Settlers flocked to the area, clearing lands and seeking work on ranches. Forest was burned to make way for cattle ranchers, aided by government financial incentives, and this damaged soil fertility. The destruction of natural resources accelerated and ranchers and small farmers were joined by mining corporations. One of the largest development poles in Latin America was Brazil's Grande Carajás Project, which in the 1980s began to convert Amazon rainforest into the world's largest industrial and agro-livestock centre and had a massive impact on regional ecosystems. Amazon development policies have also encouraged informal mining, in the form of prospecting. In the 1980s, about one million *garimpeiros*, or prospectors, responding to high prices on world markets for gold, flocked to pan the rivers of the rainforest using the roads and railroads installed for Grande Carajás.

ISI – import licences, investment permits and government contracts – encouraged corruption, strengthening the influence in policy-making of producers that has ensured the environment remains at the service of economic growth (see Chapter 5). From the 1950s until the mid-1980s there were few if any environmental restrictions on industry in Latin America and multinationals could, in effect, export polluting operations from the US and Europe to the region. Countries often pursued strategies based on vast industrial "growth poles" (see Box 1.5).

Neoliberalism

In most of Latin America and the Caribbean, state ownership in the economy expanded dramatically in the 1970s because of massive lending within international financial markets. Latin American governments grew over-exposed to foreign debt and, by late 1982, rising international interest rates and falling oil prices initiated the so-called debt crisis. This led to a "lost decade" of stagnation and painful recovery and, during the 1980s and 1990s, to radical structural reforms advocated by "neoliberals" who restated the ideas of economic liberalism (see Chapter 5). Reforms reflected an agenda among international creditors and multilateral institutions such as the World Bank and the International Monetary Fund that has been called the "Washington Consensus". This emphasized among other things trade liberalization, foreign investment, public-spending cuts, privatization, deregulation and property rights (Bulmer-Thomas 1994).

Neoliberalism threw open the region's economies to trade and investment, deepening its incorporation into the process of globalization that was accelerating after the Cold War ended in the early 1990s. Since then, attracting foreign investment has been a central plank of development strategy. In 2011, for example, ECLAC reported that $153 bn in foreign direct investment (FDI) flowed into Latin America and the Caribbean – 31 per cent more than in 2010 (ECLAC 2011b). Rising FDI has often been driven by high prices for key commodities such as hydrocarbons and metals, again highlighting Latin America's reliance on international markets, and large amounts of investment have headed for the mining industry in Peru, Chile and Colombia.

Neoliberals reduced the state's economic role through privatization and deregulation, nurtured the private sector and reoriented the focus of growth back to exports. In such circumstances, it was clear that it would be necessary to dismantle trade barriers and from the late 1980s governments across Latin America removed protectionist measures. Neoliberal policymakers institutionalized trade reforms through multilateral and regional "free trade" agreements. However, the ascendance of left-of-centre governments in Latin America and the Caribbean since the late 1990s has diluted some aspects of neoliberalism (see, for example, Kingstone 2010). Neoliberal reforms contributed to environmental degradation in several ways:

- ***Regulation***. The way privatization was carried out under neoliberal reforms has often been criticized for a failure to establish a strong regulatory structure to govern the activities of newly private utilities. Latin American countries also competed for limited sources of foreign capital by diluting their environmental restrictions.
- ***Growth and poverty***. Poverty is an important cause of ecological degradation because it intensifies pressure on the environment in many ways (see Chapters 4, 5). Neoliberal policies in Latin America and the Caribbean did not create a sufficient number of jobs to bring down unemployment or have a considerable impact on reducing poverty and inequality (see ECLAC 2004; World Bank 2009b).
- ***Trade reform***. By seeking to expand exports through private investment, governments pursued development strategies that made few concessions to sustainability, and exports of natural resources rose significantly. Although neoliberal reform left Latin American and Caribbean countries better placed to take advantage of a commodity boom that began in 2003, diversification did little to change a continuing reliance on some commodities. A report by ECLAC in 1999 concluded that emissions from the manufacturing sectors in Argentina, Bolivia, Brazil, Chile, Colombia, Costa Rica, Mexico and Peru rose significantly after the reforms of the 1980s and 1990s (Schatan 1999). Jenkins (2003) asked whether trade liberalization in Latin America created pollution "havens" whereby industries seek out countries where environmental regulations are seen as weaker (see Chapter 5). He found the cases of Argentina and Brazil indicate that liberalization has been associated with a shift towards greater specialization in polluting industries and a tendency for pollution to increase.

Continuities

Key themes shaping the role played by the environment and natural resources in Latin American and Caribbean development can be discerned, and these can help us to identify important continuities in the politics of the environment today. For example, some of the basic features that characterized sub-regions such as Central America centuries ago – foreign domination, political repression, poverty and inequality, popular rebellion, the forced removal of people from their land, ecological deterioration and the large-scale extraction and export of resources – have all been present in recent times (see Faber 1993).

Key continuities in the environmental history of the region have been as follows:

Imperialism, neocolonialism and dependence. A key driver of resource extraction since pre-Columbian times has been imperialism and the insertion of Latin America and the Caribbean into the world economy on terms that have been determined by external forces. However, imperialism in the region pre-dated the Spanish Conquest and unsustainable environmental practices were evident among pre-Columbian urban empires established by the Aztecs and Incas. These were centralized, conquering powers that demanded from subjects vast quantities of goods in tribute. Expansion represented an effort to push forward the frontier of production in response to growing tribute demands. In his comparative study of past civilizations that collapsed, Wright (2005) argued that resource depletion and unsustainable demands on the environment as these societies reach their peak of expansion have invariably played a causal role. Wright examined the collapse of the Mayan civilization, noting how a conservative leadership resisted reform after periods of over-expansion. The conquering Iberians, similarly, saw the Americas as a source of revenue to finance colonial expansion while allowing Spain to finance global trade. The mineral wealth of the Americas provided the foundation for the expansion of global commerce, the industrialization of Europe and ultimately the dominance of today's form of consumer capitalism. Extraction also shaped the socio-political topography of the Americas in ways that are still apparent: all the main colonial cities – Lima, Panama, Havana, Veracruz, Buenos

Aires, Rio de Janeiro – emerged out of the new trade in precious metals, in mining regions or on the route of the metals trade.

Independence in the nineteenth century set for scene for new, direct imperialist interventions in the region alongside the development of "neocolonial" relationships with emergent powers. Spanish colonialism ended in 1823, when the Monroe Doctrine staked out the Western Hemisphere as the domain of an ascendant US.

Direct military interventions in the region have generally been accompanied by an ambition to extract or control the trade in natural resources. In 1861, for example, Napoleon III intervened in Mexico partly because he coveted the silver that could be mined there. Similarly, the US military occupation of Cuba after 1898 led to the rapid consolidation of full control over the sugar industry. McCook (2002a) has examined how in Cuba and Puerto Rico the US shaped the course of agricultural development in this period in ways that reflected the importance it placed on sugar production. US military interventions or support for military coups in the region have often been against governments that have threatened its extractive interests (see Faber 1993). Latin American countries themselves also succumbed to imperial ambition during the export boom, sparking conflicts over resources such as the valuable and abundant sodium nitrate deposits in what is now northern Chile.

Neocolonial relationships reflecting the asymmetry in power between Latin America and the Caribbean and Europe and the US have also been a key feature of development. By ending the Spanish monopoly on trade, independence opened up countries in the region to European and then US businesses, and Latin America's economies after 1825 remained subordinate to European needs. US territorial expansion in the Caribbean Basin was accompanied by the expansion of its companies with the support of Washington. The control by foreign capital of key commodities such as coffee, and the nature of demand in the domestic markets that this capital hailed from, encouraged mono-crop production. Coffee was produced in Latin America and the Caribbean for consumption in other countries, and before 1930 at least 80 per cent of its coffee production was being sent abroad. Indeed, the US consumption of coffee was responsible for the clearance of vast areas of land in the Andes and was the key to ecological transformation in late nineteenth-century Brazil. Growing US and European demand for Brazilian coffee encouraged planters to abandon soils as they became exhausted for new land, consolidating a tradition of frontier expansion marked by deforestation and erosion.

The banana agro-export sector represents a good example of the extent to which foreign interests exercised neocolonial power in Latin American and Caribbean countries. While these countries hosted the production of bananas, it was US and European corporations that developed the marketing and transportation infrastructure to meet growing domestic demand.

Neocolonial alliances between local landholders and foreign interests reflect how independence and the eventual triumph of liberal ideas in Latin America that gave rise to the export economies of the nineteenth century generated a form of internal colonialism, by which elite alliances governing central states exploited weak, remote areas of their countries that were ethnically or racially distinct. These relationships often reflected the aspirations of local elites who believed it was necessary to replicate European and US political traditions and to rationalize Latin America's role in the international economy. They embraced liberalism and foreign ideas such as positivism and social Darwinism as tools of progress (see Chapter 2). They often sought to modernize their countries by giving foreigners concessions for mining, logging and energy production.

The export of commodities in Latin America and the Caribbean under neocolonial conditions during the nineteenth century established patterns of dependent development that shaped politics. The primary export sector was heavily dependent on foreign capital and markets, and vulnerable to boom-and-bust cycles. Foreign capital was essential to make extractive activities such as mining viable and to avoid deterring investment Latin American governments were not inclined to protect some sectors as the Spanish Crown had once done. Chicle (natural chewing gum) in Mexico's Yucatán Peninsula, for example, was developed by alliances between local entrepreneurs and US companies such as William Wrigley's (see Forero and Redclift 2006). Oil was also developed as a commodity entirely with foreign capital, almost exclusively that of the US and Great Britain. Faber (1993) argues that in the 1950s the US government assumed a more active role in expanding "dependent" capitalist development in Central America. Washington further enhanced its role with the creation in 1961 of the Alliance for Progress – in response to the Cuban Revolution – that aimed to promote stability in Central

America through the expansion of capitalist export agriculture and industry which, in turn, had a significant social and ecological impact. In El Salvador, Guatemala and Nicaragua, oligarchies used US economic and military assistance to develop large estates for the production of export crops such as coffee, cotton, sugar, bananas and cattle by clearing forests and peasant communities.

Foreign capital and political influence continue to be of paramount importance in how natural resources are extracted in Latin America and the Caribbean today. Some scholars argue that discussions of environmental politics add a crucial dimension to the study of empire precisely because they focus on the extraction of resources and the consequences of consumption (Paterson 2000; see also Dalby, 2004). In turn, taking empire seriously, and focusing on the importance of the flows of resources from the peripheries with their related conflicts, adds considerably to the possibilities for rethinking environmental politics (see Conca 2004; Box 1.6)

Statebuilding and institutional change. A second key theme that emerges from a survey of environmental history in Latin America and the Caribbean is the relationship between environmental management – particularly that of key commodities considered strategic to rulers and of status goods – and the evolution of centralized state institutions and rational policymaking, statebuilding.

In the pre-Columbian period, assertive policymaking often reflected the efforts of the imperial centre to control important resources. The Aztecs, for example, operated hydrological policies to control flooding and develop the *chinampa* economy. It was the centralization of authority in Aztec society that enabled the *chinampas* to spread from the Valley of Mexico's southern lakes to most of its lake and island cities. In the Andes, the evolution of Inca bureaucracy was closely tied to the expansion of tribute. Similarly, it was the subsequent effort of the Iberian imperial bureaucracies to maximize revenues from the American colonies that shaped the extension of metropolitan control over both production and property rights. Where central policies were not applied there could be costly environmental consequences. After Conquest, for example, the indigenous people of Mexico City continued to try and control the waters of Lake Texcoco for agriculture, but Spanish dislike of waterways and their insistence on extending the city on swampy ground meant indigenous mechanisms to control

Box 1.6 Imperialism and the environment

Crosby's influential book *Ecological Imperialism* (1986) deepened a debate among environmental historians about the relationship between empire and the environment. Many began to argue that the process of imperial expansion, whether in terms of direct conquest or indirectly through trading patterns or military interventions, fundamentally changed many ecological processes. Scholars have increasingly suggested that environmental matters have been more fundamental to imperial politics than is usually understood (see Grove 1997; Dalby 2004). The relationship between the US and Latin America and the Caribbean has long been characterized in terms of domination and resistance that reproduces traditional narratives of imperialism, making the region valuable to these debates. The theme of empire has considerable potential to advance scholarship in global environmental politics. Dalby (2004), for example, makes a strong case for the usefulness of an imperial conception of the world political economy with ramifications for how we study global environmental politics. He argues that it is important to focus scholarship on the geography of resource allocation and the modes of accumulation that drive how goods are distributed. Empires are complex supra-national arrangements for the extraction of resources and their consumption tied together by rules and trading relations that go beyond territorial states. Some scholars have also sought to understand imperialism in terms of culture and power and, for example, how the US has shaped production and consumption patterns in regions such as Latin America and the Caribbean (see Joseph, LeGrand and Salvatore 1998). The "consumption" of exotic landscapes under nineteenth-century imperialism, for example, may be reproduced in various forms of contemporary tourism, even "ecotourism" (see Chapter 6).

floods fell into disrepair. Increased soil erosion after Conquest caused by Spanish livestock or the felling of trees for construction silted up the lakes and raised water levels. The serious floods that resulted after 1555 eventually prompted city officials to conclude that it would be necessary to drain the lakes.

One reflection of the relationship between statebuilding and the exploitation of natural resources in the nineteenth century was the territorial struggle between centralizing elites and peripheral groups.

Many areas of Latin America were racked by conflict between the powerful class interests dominating nation states and indigenous communities, usually over access to resources. Territorial penetration and the appropriation of resources relied on both a repressive state apparatus and scientists such as cartologists and geologists (see Offen 2004; Gallini 2004). Incursions by the state were often justified by recourse to ideas of national development and racist theories that built on previous narratives about New World inadequacy and "determinism" (see Chapter 2).

From 1850 to 1930 the young states of Latin America and the Caribbean drove forward export booms in which agricultural and mineral production dominated policies while causing deforestation, soil erosion and pollution. The development of the state was, in turn, closely associated with the rise of powerful oligarchic interests linked to the export economy, such as the "coffee bourgeoisie" in Brazil's "First Republic" (1899–1930). In countries such as Venezuela, the development of the modern state was intimately related to the production of oil. This dependent relationship between a state and a key commodity has sometimes been called the "resource curse", a notion that attributes the sluggish development of other economic activities to tight control by a "rentier state" over one commodity. Statebuilding politicians sometimes even resorted to the use of environmental arguments against oil companies in order to extend state authority (see Kozloff 2006).

Two environmental factors in particular contributed to the development by states of policymaking structures and new institutions. First, extreme weather events and earthquakes are common in Latin America and the Caribbean and states often designed policies to prepare for natural disasters or respond to them (see Miller 2007). The Inca and Maya, for example, lived in fear of drought and their construction policies reflected this. In the colonial economy, storms in the Caribbean and Gulf caused serious damage to agriculture. Natural disasters can impose a severe burden on weak economies. The Caribbean hurricane season in 1780, for example, was the most disastrous ever recorded, with eight storms killing 27,000 people. Johnson (2011) has argued that the ecological crises of this period in the Caribbean both catalyzed the general adoption of free trade in the Americas and fuelled the sentiments that would give rise to the subsequent "Age of Revolution".

Second, a reliance on mono-crop commodities compelled states to create or nurture new scientific and regulatory institutions between the eighteenth and twentieth centuries. Fledgling states established bureaucratic infrastructures and scientific institutions for agricultural development, geographical and geological survey, meteorological forecasting and the census. Scientists developed new technologies or introduced new organisms that would magnify the impact of development on the environment, often in an effort to encourage production for export (see Chapter 2). In Puerto Rico, for example, Spanish imperial administrators sought to create an agrarian institute or model *hacienda* after the 1840s to prepare for the eventual replacement of the slave-based, single-crop plantation mode of production with a more diversified economy based on free wage labour.

In the twentieth century, expanding states began to fill roles within the export economy that had previously been undertaken by monopoly interests. In Brazil, federal and state governments came to finance much of the coffee trade and hold most of its stock. In Mexico, the increasingly interventionist revolutionary state under President Lázaro Cardenas (1934–40) took over the oil industry and created co-operatives to control the chicle labour force (see Forero and Redclift 2006).

Expanding state bureaucracies, in turn, fostered the development of new social classes and political tensions. Throughout Latin America and the Caribbean, workers in extractive sectors such as oil became dependent on wages and the state on export revenues, nurturing a common interest in greater state intervention in the economy though regulations and restrictions.

Social relations and conflict. The ways in which the environment was exploited shaped the relations between social groups that have determined political development, often by generating conflict over land and resources that could be exacerbated by pre-existing inequalities.

Onerous demands for tribute by Aztec nobles, for example, fuelled resentment among subject peoples, many of whom were ready for rebellion by the time of Spanish Conquest. Maya society was also strictly hierarchical and overpopulation, peasant rebellion and strife among the nobility may have weakened classical cultures, helping to explain their collapse in about AD1000.

Demographic collapse prevented the Iberians reproducing the colonial experience of Asia and Africa – whereby a small elite engaged in coastal trade but left indigenous culture intact – and turned the new colonies into political extensions of the European empire. Commodity production shaped social relations by generating conditions of exploitation within societies. The competitive production of certain crops consolidated new classes that made exploitative relations more likely. Entire new populations were created as a result of low immigration, the impact of disease on indigenous communities and slavery. In the eighteenth century, a colonial planter class created by sugar production, the extermination of the indigenous population and a pre-existing Atlantic slave trade gave rise to circumstances in which plantation slavery was introduced in the Caribbean to produce coffee. Coffee is often blamed for severe inequalities, harsh labour conditions and slavery. The development of coffee exports entrenched conservative and oligarchical relations in countries such as Brazil and hence delayed industrial development.

Everywhere, the export model and the new urban politics it began to foster entrenched inequality and increased the number of people in absolute poverty, generating political unrest. In turn, inequalities, heightened by ways in which the environment was exploited, generated conflict – and Latin American and Caribbean history is punctuated by struggles over land and resources deriving from indigenous resistance, labour mobilization and political conflict (see Box 1.7).

The environment and democracy. The condemnation of environmental degradation in Latin America and the Caribbean has often been accompanied by an assumption that political systems in northern societies are more mature and progressive. Yet much of the disparity in action and attitude between North and South can be explained by poverty and weak democratic systems. The ways states and elites in Latin America and the Caribbean have utilized resources over centuries, and the struggles that these have generated, reveal how a lack of democratic norms are important to the study of environmental history. As such, the region offers many examples by which to explore the relationship between environmentalism and democracy. Key features of politics there have been authoritarianism and centralism, and in Latin America and the Caribbean democratic development has proceeded in fits and starts. The military regimes that already held

Box 1.7 Export-led development and unrest

In Brazil, economic development in frontier areas was often a military exercise because forests were often populated by indigenous groups, enhancing the relationship between the military and national economic development. In Mexico, the export of chicle played an important role in the Caste War in Yucatán beginning in 1847 – an attempt by the Maya to recover control over territories they had failed to recover after independence in 1823. A key environmental resource over which social groups in Latin America have fought has been land, access to which was at the heart of the Mexican revolution (1910–20) and shaped state formation (see Baitenmann 2011). Agrarian conflicts remain common throughout Latin America, and in countries such as Guatemala a large number of small civil society organizations such as Church-based groups or non-governmental organizations (NGOs) assist peasants trying to resolve disputes over land and resources (see also Van Leeuwen 2010). Contemporary disputes often have historical environmental causes that play out over the long term. There has been recurrent resistance by peasants and social movements to the activities of large multinational banana corporations in South and Central America (see Striffler and Moberg 2003) In Nicaragua, the leftwing Sandinista revolutionaries implemented a wide range of environmental initiatives after 1979, distributing large tracts of unused national land to peasants who converted forests into farms in order to maintain political support. In Mexico, land was at the heart of a significant rebellion by the mainly indigenous Ejército Zapatista de Liberación Nacional (EZLN) in 1994 in the southern state of Chiapas (see Sabin 1998).

or took power across the region in the 1960s and 1970s, for example, merely followed earlier democratic interludes. In turn, transitions to democracy saw these regimes being replaced by elected civilian governments in the 1980s and 1990s. By 2000, most of Latin America could be described, on the basis of competitive elections, as democratic in some way, although undemocratic practices continue.

Authoritarianism has had important environmental implications, as most Latin American and Caribbean citizens long lacked political opportunities to exert pressure on their rulers to protect the natural resources on which they depend (see Roberts and Thanos 2003). In theory, authoritarian rulers do not have incentives to use resources sustainably, prioritizing rapid economic development to gain legitimacy and bolster security (Porritt 1984). As they control most of society's resources, this encourages them to reward supporters by pillaging the ecosystem because there is no real advantage in improving environmental quality (Bueno de Mesquita et al. 2003). They do not impose regulations to address environmental harm because they themselves would disproportionately pay the costs of any tighter rules; and they ignore the interests of future generations, because they will not be in power for the long term (Congleton 1992; see also Collier and Hoefler 2004).

The case for liberal democracy is often based on arguments about deliberation and debate by which concerned citizens can influence policymaking through the ballot box, pressure groups, social movement activity, the media and local political structures (Payne 1995; see also World Bank 2001; Silva 1996). Democratization gives a political voice to the poor, and if this alleviates poverty it may in turn enable a more sustainable distribution of resources (UNDP 2003). The lack of democracy in Latin America and the Caribbean has meant that citizens remained quiet in the belief that they could do nothing to change environmental policies, and in most countries individuals had no right to sue for environmental damages until recently. Democracy also offers the best guarantee of good "governance" because at its heart is the rule of law – which the failure to enforce has often resulted in environmental degradation (see Chapter 3). Democratic rights and participation is a key way of ensuring regulatory standards aimed at improving environmental conditions.

An important by-product of the democratic transitions in Latin America and the Caribbean since the 1970s and 1980s, as civil society groups began to assume a greater profile, has been the emergence of environmental awareness and pressure for regulation (see Volume 2). Nonetheless, the idea that there is a natural coincidence between democracy and environmental protection remains open to debate. While theory has suggested that liberal democracies should perform better than autocracies on the sustainable use of resources, the evidence remains unclear (see Ward 2008). The democratic transitions in Latin America and the Caribbean are also variable and incomplete, and policymakers and political elites routinely favour powerful corporate interests.

Conclusion

Territories, commodities and knowledge have emerged as themes of particular interest to scholars of environmental history in Latin America and the Caribbean. An understanding of the opportunities offered by the natural resources available in some territories – and the limitations of others – can help to explain many different forms of development in the region since pre-Columbian times. These opportunities and limitations have determined the degree to which, and how, communities have transformed their natural environment and, as a result, the social relationships that have emerged within them and nurtured a mosaic of political forms and boundaries. Territorial opportunities and limitations also determined which commodities were sought after and why – from the feathers paid in tribute to Aztec lords to the coffee harvested by African slaves in Brazil for a mass market in the US. The many ways in which the effort to control how these commodities have been used and distributed has been, and remains, the motor of political change. A key feature of the Latin American and Caribbean trade in commodities since Conquest has been how its international character and economic relationships on a global scale – today understood in terms of globalization – have been linking the region to far-flung countries ever more closely since the sixteenth century. Therefore, if it is fair to suggest that the most important factor influencing environmental change in Latin America and the Caribbean since pre-history has been human activity, it is also fair to argue that for the last 500 years this process has been driven largely by forces external to the region. While the achievement of democracy in recent years offers the majority of Latin American and Caribbean citizens the opportunity to influence environmental change for the first time, it must be set against that backdrop of globalization that ties them ever closer to the consumption patterns and political norms characteristic of those external forces. It is this reality that makes knowledge – the third theme of particular interest to scholars of environmental history in Latin America and Caribbean – such an important object of study. The ways in which nature has been understood and ideas about it have informed human interactions with the natural environment in the region are examined in more detail in the next chapter.

Recommended reading

Brannstrom, Christian and Stefania Gallini. 2004 "An Introduction to Latin American Environmental History", in Christian Brannstrom (ed.), *Territories, Commodities and Knowledges: Latin American Environmental Histories in the Nineteenth and Twentieth Centuries*. London: Institute for the Study of the Americas.

Castro Herrera, Guillermo. 2001. "Environmental History (Made) in Latin America", H-Net Humanities and Social Sciences Online (February-April). Available online at www2.h-net.msu.edu/~environ/historiography/latinam.htm [accessed September 2012].

Miller, Shawn William. 2007. *An Environmental History of Latin America*. Cambridge: Cambridge University Press.

Roberts, J Timmons and Nikki Demetria Thanos. 2003. *Trouble in Paradise: Globalization and Environmental Crises in Latin America*. London: Routledge.

Soluri, John. 2006. *Banana Cultures: Agriculture, Consumption and Environmental Change in Honduras and the United States*. Austin: University of Texas Press.

Topik, Steven C and Allen Wells (eds). 1998. *The Second Conquest of Latin America: Coffee, Henequen, and Oil During the Export Boom, 1850–1930*. Austin: University of Texas Press.

Useful websites

Biodiversity Heritage Library: www.biodiversitylibrary.org

Environmental History of Latin America, online bibliography, Stanford University: www.stanford.edu/group/LAEH/

H-Net, H-environment Historiography Series, H-Net Humanities and Social Sciences Online: www2.h-net.msu.edu/~environ/historiography/historiography.html

CHAPTER TWO

The environment in ideas

"NATURAL" LANDSCAPES are often the product of historical struggles over resources in which cultural practices have shaped production systems. The ways in which we understand and interpret nature obey cultural priorities but also the practical constraints of the environments in which we live. Just as the ways in which societies use natural resources begin with a culturally informed understanding of the natural world, nature also influences our systems of thought and knowledge. In turn, our knowledge of natural systems shapes how we use resources and the political competition that this generates. It is important to examine the relationship between the natural and social worlds, and to explore the different ways in which the natural environment has been understood and interpreted since pre-Columbian times. Those understandings have been influenced by religious and scientific interpretations of the position of humans in relation to nature alongside, and often reflecting, the dominant models of social and economic organization. They have been influenced by the evolution of political philosophy and social thought in countries far away from Latin America and the Caribbean with starkly different conditions. Some powerful myths about nature and human dominion of it that hark back to pre-Columbian times persist and continue to shape how politics in the region is understood. At the same time a contemporary, global consumer culture is leaving its profound mark on the environment in the region. Environmental ideas themselves, alongside growing recognition of the non-European, indigenous heritage of Latin America, are now also shaping the approach taken by states, citizens and corporations towards resource use.

Nature and culture

Our knowledge of the environment and how this affects our attitudes to its use have been important concerns to sociologists who have debated the relationship between the natural and social worlds. An early debate in geography concerned the degree to which the constraints and opportunities offered by landscapes simply determined human behaviour (environmental determinism), or whether these landscapes should in fact be studied as cultural *constructions* reflecting the human impact on them over time based on specific understandings of their role (see Sauer 1952; also Denevan and Mathewson 2009). The Amazon has been a fertile source of such debates, and in recent years a key question in several disciplines has been the character of the environmental constraints that this sub-region imposes upon its culture and economy (see Cleary 2001; Hames and Vickers 1983; Descola 1994). Ironically, such questions have been generated by concern among policymakers, scientists and activists about the fate of what they once saw as an untouched wilderness. However, it has become clear that human interventions in Amazonia have been carried out on a vast scale over a long time (see Chapter 1; see also Bahn 1993; Cleary 2001). Some anthropologists and archaeologists have taken deterministic positions by arguing that the natural characteristics of the Amazon limited social organization to small villages and shifting cultivation (see Meggers 1971). Others have rejected any distinction between the natural and the cultural, arguing that the relationships between Amazonian society and the environment are so multiple and complex that it makes deterministic positions speculative (Descola 1994; Cleary 2001). In short, given the forms of indigenous land management in Amazonia, it is difficult to distinguish clearly between "wild" and "managed" areas (see Rival 1998). Cleary (2001) points out that the problem here is how scholars researching Amazonia see a dualism between nature and culture, and suggests that one way forward is to employ a notion of landscape history: the term "landscape" can help to convey the transition from wilderness to manipulated environment in which nature *coexists* with culture. Another way to tackle this dualism is offered by Irwin (2001), who makes the case for a sociological approach to understanding the environment. Irwin argues that a central axis of debates about the relationship of the natural and social worlds has been between two schools of thought: realism and constructivism. The former consider the environment as external to social life as a form of "objective reality", while the latter considers it to be constructed by social relationships and forms of understanding. Although sociologists such as Irwin argue that neither the social nor the natural can be given a paramount status in this discussion, constructivism is of value when considering the environmental history of Latin America and the Caribbean. This is because it implies a sociological approach that considers, above all else, how and why societies invest meaning in the "natural".

At one level, this is common sense: natural resources are viewed and used differently by those who live in proximity to them and depend upon them for their subsistence to those who may have urban-based needs and goals (see, for example, Orlove 2002). The sociological approach allows the researcher to avoid a tendency to view the human-environment dynamic as uni-directional, which leads to perspectives that can either imagine people acting upon a passive environment, or a set of natural, ahistorical forces acting upon people – when in fact *both* are historically interconnected (see Soluri 2000). The emerging field of agroecology offers concepts that can be useful in developing such an interdisciplinary approach, by focusing on the fluid and permeable interactions between specific forms of agriculture and their surrounding environments. From a historical point of view, this debate requires us at least to place as much importance on the ever-changing role of nature in ideas, and in turn how those ideas have changed the natural environment.

The colonization by the Spanish and Portuguese of the New World after 1492 was a complex process that continued for more than 300 years until new republics were established in the region by elites influenced by ideas of revolution and independence who took advantage of events in Europe to fashion nation states founded on republican and liberal principles. This lengthy marriage between two European powers and vast new colonies on the other side of the world can be understood in several ways: as a geopolitical project by expanding empires; as a religious mission, in which the motivation for colonial expansion was the spread of the Christian faith; or as the encounter between radically different cultures and systems of thought and knowledge in which influence went in both directions.

Ideas about the natural environment of the New World play a central role in all these explanations for what occurred, shaping colonization itself and the response of the colonized, but also the form subsequently taken by European and ultimately global politics, economic development and culture (see De Acosta 2002). Theories of globalization often refer back to the global trade routes that were being established by European empires in the early modern period. Wallerstein (1974), for example, who conceptualized a single "world-system", initiated a series of historical debates by interpreting the sixteenth century as the founding era in the creation of a *global* capitalist system that encompassed both Europe and the Americas. Many scholars have extended such debates to incorporate the intellectual and cultural dimensions of globalization (see, for example, Stern 1998).

Such debates draw attention to the different ways in which encounters formally described as "imperial" can be explored. In particular, attitudes to nature and consumption and about how new territories and their inhabitants could be exploited formed a central axis in the endeavour of Conquest while simultaneously influencing the conquering power. The sheer novelty and abundance of the territories encountered by the Spanish and Portuguese forced them to search for new concepts and values by which to characterize and understand the new lands and people – and in the process changed how they themselves understood such themes. As a result, the conquest of the New World played a key role in transforming *global* attitudes towards nature, by representing a step towards the development of an ideology about human mastery over the natural world that originated in Europe between 1450 and 1750. This ideology, in turn, would bolster the emergence of scientific perspectives, the Industrial Revolution, the formation of the modern state and the ascent of capitalism.

Conquest and the colonial era

Nature and society in religion and cosmology. At the time of Conquest, both Christianity and the organized religions of the peoples encountered by the Spanish were implicated in imperial expansion. The fundamental changes in the environment that followed Conquest were facilitated by the ideology of the Catholic Church. Christian beliefs and the impressions of the conquistadors and missionaries and their earthly motives all combined to shape their attitudes towards the natural environment they encountered in the New World. Yet for both the Church and its congregation, religious belief concealed a motive of material gain behind their support for the enterprise of conquest.

However, the first significant empire the Spanish encountered, that of the Aztecs, had also used religion as a tool of imperialism aimed at material gain, creatively giving their rule sacred justification through the links the Mexica people claimed with the Toltec civilization that had pre-dated them (see Williamson 1992). The Incas, similarly, used religion to underpin imperial expansion in the Andes, with the Inca's authority conceived as of divine origin.

Despite these similarities between conquerors and conquered, a key distinction between Christian and indigenous cosmologies was the degree of separation they maintained between human spirituality and nature. In animistic beliefs – the attribution of spiritual dimensions to non-human entities such as animals and plants or features of the landscape – nature itself is a sacred realm that can be worshipped or praised. Christianity, by contrast, asserts that nature was created by God for the *benefit* of man, who possesses a spirit separated from an earthly, material realm. In pre-Columbian belief systems gods were found in nature; to Christians, God assumed the form of man, and the Catholic Church denounced the deification of nature as a primitive heresy (see Dore 1991).

This Christian separation of nature from spiritual questions was profoundly important, ultimately reinforcing the separation of society, as a sphere of human development, from nature, as a resource provided by God. It allowed the Church to accept the morality of Christians who exploited natural resources (see Pattberg 2007; White 1967). The Christian understanding offers an example of broader assumptions in western intellectual tradition that have conceptually divided the natural and social environments. Irwin (2001) has made observations about the contemporary period that help to illustrate the continuing potency of this perspective: issues of ecology, pollution and global environmental change, for example, have been considered as *outside* the competence of the social sciences, and indeed the natural environment has generally been presented as outside human agency.

Two positions found in environmental sociology are useful in understanding this early separation of nature from spiritual questions: a pioneering statement by Catton and Dunlap (1978) describing views about human exceptionalism: the assumption that people are fundamentally different from other creatures and therefore human society is not subject to constraints; and a more recent, interdisciplinary, argument that rejects the notion of a clear-cut nature–society duality, seeks to explore how nature offers a focal point for political, economic, social and cultural interconnections, and emphasizes the extent to which the categories of nature and society are continuously reconstituted through each other (see, for example, Macnaghten and Urry 1998). According to this second position, "nature" is an *idea* that resides in cultural understanding that is produced and transformed by specific social practices. Such a position stresses the need to examine discourses about nature – it is *discursive* – and is of clear value to the study of environmental history. The contemporary notion of an opposition between nature and culture, as historically and culturally specific to post-Enlightenment European thought, is likely to be discursive (Latour 1993; Strathern 1981; Williams 1980; Raffles and Winkler Prins, 2003).

In early colonial Iberian America, a reflection of this detachment between society and nature was the character taken by subsequent processes of urbanization that built on a pre-Columbian legacy. Urbanization has been an important characteristic of Latin America's evolution, and citizens in the region have held different attitudes towards the countryside and "wilderness" than in North America or Europe. Pre-Columbian empires in Mesoamerica and the Andes were founded on city states from which power was exercised over the countryside and subordinate cities according to socio-religious priorities. The Iberian conquerors extended this trait and their attitudes about the risks inherent in nature derived from their European experience and shaped the cityscape (see Tortolero 2004).

In pre-Columbian cosmologies, the natural environment was considered inseparable from the social order. These societies attributed to the natural world spiritual powers and existed in a mystical relationship with it, and landscapes often had sacred features. Taino, Aztec, Maya and Inca societies are often portrayed as proto-ecologists whose exploitation of nature was bound by rigid cultural rules derived from their beliefs. These combined animism and totemism and did not separate the sacred and material worlds, making people fear nature and respect its power. The links between cosmology and the material order reflected how survival was dependent on preserving ecosystems (see Dore 1991). A precarious climate reinforced fatalism and a belief in the contingency of civilization (see Shaw 2003).

Like the Iberians, cosmology and politics were intimately related in pre-Columbian societies and life-giving myths were linked to how power was administered. For example, a central metaphysical issue in Andean thought, motivating the rise of the Inca empire and embodied in its political structure, was how to control a cycle that linked death and the regeneration of life. Ritual also offered a practical way for the priestly and political elite to manage scarce resources such as water (see Gose 1993; Sherbondy 1998; Boelens and Gelles 2005; Gelles 1995). Such ideological control facilitated the extraction of resources through tribute, which was later reproduced by the Spaniards for their own purposes (see Gelles 2000). Even today, activities in many villages in the highlands of Ecuador, Bolivia and Peru are organized along similar lines.

Religious beliefs also influenced attitudes towards race and ethnicity that would have a profound impact on the landscape and how resources were exploited, and Conquest nurtured or reinforced interpretations of the relationship between race and the natural environment. It spawned myths that reinforced Spanish Christian attitudes of religious supremacism maintained by notions of blood purity, which became a principle determining status and underpinning landholding. The hierarchy and the system of oppression based on race and occupation that was established during the colonial era has been at the root of many environmental problems since in Latin America and the Caribbean. They established a legacy of skewed land ownership through the imposition of patterns of plantation or mono-crop agriculture, or from the withholding of vast tracts of land from production. Resulting rural poverty has been a significant source of soil erosion and deforestation (see Chapter 4).

The sense of superiority felt by the Spanish was reflected in a critical conquest myth influenced heavily by the advocacy of Bartolomé de las Casas on behalf of indigenous people: the so-called "Black Legend". Las Casas argued that Spanish persecution was at the root of the demographic collapse of indigenous society, and this notion was then embraced by Protestant Europeans during the Reformation to denounce Catholicism. These ideas later informed debates that compared America with the Old World (see Bacci 2008). A sense of disappointment about the New World could certainly be found among the early visitors to the region, including Columbus, and came to be shared by later scholars who suggested that human and animal life in the New World suffered from arrested development, and hence the American continent was in some way "inferior". Such ideas were important props of imperialism, helping to justify the inferior status of American-born ethnic Europeans, creoles, who were discriminated against in metropolitan Spain; and to strengthen Eurocentrism, which propelled European expansion elsewhere. Nonetheless, Iberian views towards the neo-tropics were diverse, and in reaction to these ideas other Spaniards and Portuguese who stressed the exuberance of American nature fashioned early patriotic discourses in the New World.

The noble savage and the "pristine myth". Intellectual developments in sixteenth-century Europe that were giving rise to the ideas that formed the basis of the Enlightenment and republicanism had an important impact on ways in which nature and its exploitation in the New World were understood.

The indigenous societies that the Spaniards and Portuguese encountered tested European attitudes to morality and property ownership at a time of philosophical innovation. For example, communities that gathered indigenous populations into hospital-towns called Repúblicas de Indios in order to control and convert them, were organized on principles largely derived from *Utopia*, a work of fiction published in 1516 by Thomas More depicting an imaginary New World society. This influential treatise envisaged a proto-socialist society in which there was no private ownership.

Similar ideas continue to inform debates about Latin America and Caribbean environmental and social history, and in particular what William Denevan (1992) described as the "pristine myth". This is the notion that in 1492 the Americas were a sparsely populated wilderness, largely undisturbed by humans, where nature reigned and human societies lived in a harmonious equilibrium with their environment. The pristine myth remains important to ideas about nature and attitudes to non-Western resource use, and has influenced views in modern, urban Latin America and the developed world about indigenous society and both its historic and contemporary relationship with the land.

First, the pristine myth has helped to legitimize external interventions since the time of Conquest that both seek to take advantage of nature (from extractive activities to mass tourism today) and to take the "side" of nature, such as contemporary environmentalism (see Miller 2007). The idea that indigenous people lived in harmony with nature helped revive the notion of the noble savage, and the writings of conservationists and indigenous rights advocates often echo the early chroniclers' assumption that indigenous people lived in conformity with their environment (see Redford 1991). This idea has been appropriated and adapted by indigenous organizations themselves and exercises influence over how we perceive nature and development in the Americas. Its corollary is that it was European conquest that transformed this benign indigenous landscape, a position advanced influentially by Kirkpatrick Sale (1990, 2000; see also Smith 2001).

Second, the pristine myth has shaped other social and political debates in the Western world and, in turn, how Latin America and the Caribbean has been studied. The vision of New World society that informed More has been extensively debated, but prominent among interpretations of his work is the view that it was an attempt at mythologizing indigenous cultures at a time when their role – and the role of countries such as Spain and their monarchies in God's "divine plan" – was being debated within the Roman Catholic Church itself. The Church was coming to terms with the influence of scientific enquiry and such debates would inform the subsequent Age of Enlightenment.

The pristine myth has also informed other ideological positions, such as nationalism and anti-imperialism. Notions of mystical primitivism and of a contrast between a natural world and human civilization are at the heart of debates about "ecological anarchism", for example (see Volume 2). Primitivists interpret "civilization" as inherently destructive and believe ideas of progress are merely a smokescreen to justify ecological degradation (see Smith 2007). The myth can also absolve Latin Americans themselves from historical culpability for environmental damage. More broadly, the pristine myth has also influenced a vision of ecological history, increasingly challenged, that assumed much human experience was exempt from

Box 2.1 Property relations

The pristine myth draws attention to the different ways in which property and consumption were understood by pre-Columbian peoples and the Christian newcomers. A concern with property relations underpinned the myth of the noble savage, and chroniclers of the New World and social thinkers such as Jean-Jacques Rousseau (1712–78) noted the lack of private property among the natives and the emphasis their communities placed upon equality (see Redford 1991). Yet, although ideas about property and consumption in Aztec and Inca society differed from those of the Europeans, there were also similarities, and some pre-Columbian societies were divided on the basis of class and ethnicity, were legalistic and were sometimes litigious over issues of possession. Consumption among high-status groups could be excessive, and elite attitudes by the time of Conquest in the case of the Aztecs were becoming materialistic. Consumption patterns were also the main hierarchical markers among the Iberian settlers, who used resources and property, particularly precious metals and landholding, to signal social standing. The Spanish disregarded indigenous land claims and expropriated holdings on a massive scale, made easier by demographic collapse and the inability of their jurisprudence to accept indigenous property concepts, in particular communal ownership.

natural constraints and that the ecological consequences of our past deeds could be ignored (see Worster 1990; Jones 1991). It has been of great significance to the evolution of perspectives on the Amazon (see below). As we have seen, there is substantial evidence that the landscape encountered by Europeans in the early sixteenth century had been shaped by human society throughout the region, and there are examples of the pre-Columbian over-exploitation of resources deriving from a desire to amass property (see Box 2.1).

Cultural fusion and visions of nature. By the middle of the sixteenth century, in the main cities of the New World centres of learning and bureaucratic life had created a small secular cultural elite alongside the religious scholars who had chronicled Iberian American life. Eulogies to the lives of the conquistadors and praise for the grandeur of the region exemplified the first stirrings of a patriotism that began to challenge European ideas such as the Black Legend. One theme that developed in literature and the arts was that of civilization and its juxtaposition with barbarism. Alongside, a physical and cultural intermingling – *mestizaje* – was fusing peoples and traditions and becoming the distinctive trait of popular culture. Increasingly, indigenous culture has been reappraised in ways that examine Columbian and European features in combination. Murals in the Augustinian cloister at Malinalco in Mexico, for example, reveal a significant convergence of ideas and symbolism about Mexican flora and fauna. For example, the Garden of Eden converges with Tlalocan, an Aztec paradise, and Tamoanchan, conceived in Mesoamerican cultures also as an earthly paradise (see Peterson 1993).

The tensions implied by cultural fusion reflected highly diverse societies where no single vision of man and his relationship with nature prevailed, but in which rival visions competed according to a social group's position in the hierarchy. In such a mix, the Crown and Catholicism were among the only shared points of reference and both were conservative institutions that limited the exposure of Iberian American society to influences that were transforming the outside world such as the Reformation, Counter-Reformation, mercantilism and the Industrial Revolution. One result of this was the growing assertiveness of the Creole elite in Hispanic America in opposition to the imperial, metropolitan identity asserted by Spain itself. Creole thinkers and religious figures began to portray their lands as favoured by God and to identify with the glories of indigenous antiquity in what has been called "proto-nationalism" (see Brading 1985). Subsequent thought began to challenge the triumphalism of Spain and praise the splendours of the New World's natural environment and indigenous achievements (see Chasteen 2008).

Empire and conservationism. Conservation policies in both the pre-Columbian and colonial eras responded to dwindling resources, demographic change and imperial policymaking.

Evidence that in some instances the large pre-Columbian societies consumed resources at unsustainable levels comes from the existence of conservation policies in the region prior to Conquest. Elites in all the large pre-Columbian societies imposed policies to conserve some resources and imposed environmental regulations and standards.

Following Conquest, the demographic collapse of indigenous society, the limited scale and slow progress of Iberian settlement, the prohibition of non-Iberians from the new territories and Crown restrictions on certain economic activities limited the impact of colonization on the environment. Some Crown policies were aimed at or resulted in conservation in some extractive sectors, and both Spain and Portugal legislated to protect forests, game and fisheries in the New World. Tight restrictions on immigration driven by xenophobia and religious differences further alleviated pressure on the land and forests.

While some Spanish ranching practices were also beneficial to the environment, such as the burning of pasture to remove pests and flooding in lowland areas, settlers had different attitudes to the use of resources and mostly abandoned pre-Columbian practices aimed at conserving them (see White 1967). Iberian ideas had, in some cases, a direct impact on the landscape (see Box 2.2).

Issues of conservation were addressed most explicitly by imperial figures when the competition for resources – especially among elites – grew pressing, as occurred in the smaller countries of Central America and the Caribbean (see Funes Monzote 2008). However, measures to restrict trade and conserve some resources for economic reasons were eased as pressures for Independence increased across Latin America. Between 1778 and 1796, trade through the American ports was liberalized by the Spanish Crown, and it increased significantly prior to the Independence revolutions after 1806.

In the later colonial period, new scientific perspectives and forestry methods influencing policy in countries such as Britain would filter through to Iberian America. These were reflected in the development of ideas about the need to conserve resources such as forestry in the Caribbean colonies. The experience of Barbados, where deforestation represented a direct economic cost but also reduced stream flows, caused soil erosion, raised temperatures and reduced rainfall, galvanized British colonial officials to revise attitudes towards tropical nature. The "desiccationist" doctrine arguing that trees attracted rain and improved the climate, and theories about the role of vegetation in purifying air, prompted them to create forest reserves. Such scientific approaches to natural resources management gave rise to early conservationism. The Iberian colonial authorities responded to these ideas in 1800 by introducing more comprehensive forest legislation in both Spanish and Portuguese America.

Box 2.2 Water in Mexico

Spanish political imperatives and cultural attitudes to water resulted in the draining of basin lakes in New Spain. In central Mexico, water had been a valued resource crucial to the productivity of Aztec agriculture. Despite saturated ground, Cortés built his capital upon Tenochtitlán, and buildings soon began to sink. Indigenous efforts to control the lake waters for agriculture faltered after their society collapsed, mechanisms to control floods fell into disrepair and the *chinampas* were abandoned. Lakebeds silted up, raising water levels, as soil erosion increased following the abandonment of indigenous fields, new livestock trampled the ground and the Spanish felled trees for piles. The Spanish discharged sewage into the lakes and Aztec dikes and causeways now became devices to control pollution. Between 1555 and 1607 serious flooding returned to Mexico City and authorities decided to drain the lakes, eventually constructing a vast canal and tunnel, but to little effect. While the waterways around Mexico City remained an aesthetic asset into the late nineteenth century, as the population grew, the lake and its canals were increasingly identified with disease, prompting the dictator Porfirio Díaz to hire foreign contractors using steam shovels and dredges to drain Lake Texcoco in the 1880s (see Tortorelo 2004). Draining the lake had serious environmental and social consequences: it exacerbated subsidence within the city, and during the twentieth century Mexico City sank by up to 7.5m. As the population grew, wells were sunk to tap underground remnants of the lake for drinking water and once saturated soils began to contract. The great canal itself sank , reducing its gradient and capacity. Draining the lake also destroyed many lakeshore communities who had relied on it for food, as fish died and waterfowl disappeared. *Chinampas* that had survived since Aztec times dried up to be replaced by irrigated fields. The Mexican conservationist Miguel Ángel de Quevedo was a vocal critic of lake drainage policies. Displaced lakeshore communities were ready recruits to the revolutionary movement that would later topple Díaz in 1910, an issue that would become a burning concern to the modernizing states of Latin America during the 20th century (see Baitenmann 2011). Land reform, and the agrarian institutional infrastructure formed by states in response, has had a dramatic impact on the environment throughout the region.

Independence

In the eighteenth century Jesuit thinkers influenced by the Enlightenment inaugurated a new era of political thought that sparked the turmoil of the Independence era. This was an early example of an important phenomenon in the intellectual history of Latin America and the Caribbean: political ideas have often been imported. Following independence, the ties that would develop between the new republics and the international economy have since been the most important factor shaping political development in the region. This is important, because the main ideologies of the last 150 years have been generated by the impact of the Industrial Revolution on northern European social structures. They have derived from different circumstances with no counterparts in Iberian tradition. In Latin America, industrialization would occur much later without similar changes in social structure, and imported ideologies were highly influential, with modernity itself conceived of as a European or US phenomenon. As the independent republics began to stabilize in the nineteenth century, European political ideas began to have an important impact on the Latin American and Caribbean environment.

Liberalism and capitalism. The most important ideological development in nineteenth-century Latin America and the Caribbean was the growth of political and economic liberalism (see Véliz 1980). In the agro-export economies that were beginning to take part in nascent globalization, liberal ideas about progress and possessive individualism had profound implications for land use. Independence initiated radical changes in the structure of agroecosystems in the region in favour of market demands (see Worster 1990). The expansion of agricultural exports required access to new lands, and this could only be achieved by opening up virgin territory or expanding into communal lands controlled by indigenous or peasant communities. For this reason, liberals often advocated the disentailment of "corporate" property held by the Church or indigenous communities. From the mid-nineteenth century on, liberal elites endeavoured to dismantle all forms of communal property in favour of private ownership. Many of the huge estates in El Salvador and Guatemala, for example, were established from the alienation of communal lands after 1870 as the liberal state promoted coffee production.

This process was further influenced by technological change and new markets. Rising incomes in Europe and the US created a new demand for "tropical luxuries" such as coffee while increasing demand for traditional staples. As capitalism developed, it transformed economic attitudes by envisaging an economy in which transactions were freely undertaken for the purpose of maximizing profit. This had important implications for Latin America, by substituting for a motive of subsistence that of personal gain. Export capitalism also changed how people related to nature by creating, for the first time, a general market in land: "land" became a commodified abstraction and could be traded for the first time, with significant environmental implications (see Worster 1990). New forms of production also began to simplify local ecologies by reducing the number of species found in an area. New markets and transportation possibilities influenced the way in which production was planned by encouraging farmers to specialize in producing an ever smaller number of crops to sell for profit, and monoculture prevailed. In Cuba, for example, devastating hurricanes in the 1840s and 1850s induced producers to switch from growing coffee to sugar and tobacco (see Pérez 2001). Castro Herrera (2001) argues that an examination of capitalism in the environmental history of Latin America and the Caribbean must acknowledge several unique axes of development:

- capitalism developed in the context of a destructive use of natural and human resources akin to a "pillage mentality";
- the relationship with nature developed under the domination of foreign capital, meaning that it was subordinated to the interests of North Atlantic societies;
- the North Atlantic capitalists shaping the world market found well-organized political counterparts in the form of oligarchies throughout Latin America and the Caribbean. These were landlords eager to associate with foreign capital and offering abundant land, resources and labour in exchange for investment and access to the world market.
- the process that created the basic conditions for capitalism in the region occurred through the violent expropriation after the 1850s of the land and labour of non-capitalist sectors.

Castro Herrera argues that these characteristics unique to the development of capitalism in Latin America and the Caribbean had important implications for attitudes to nature in the region, and help to explain the coexistence of two very different, almost antagonistic, ways of relating to it and of understanding its role in social life. A North Atlantic and oligarchic vision of nature would reign until the contemporary era and exclude alternative visions elaborated among non-capitalist sectors of society such as indigenous, *mestizo* and Afro-American groups. The consequence was that oligarchic elites in the region appropriated for themselves the role of representatives of civilization destined to lead society towards progress in opposition to a "backward" realm of nature.

A renewed emphasis upon ideas derived from liberalism became evident in the period inaugurated by the Mexican Revolution (1910–17) as the new classes generated by rapid economic change demanded inclusion. Although the liberal pause would slowly come to an end between the Second World War and the period of military authoritarianism in the 1960s and 1970s, economic liberalism has become the orthodoxy in Latin America and the Caribbean.

Science, progress, modernity. The first scientific explorations of Latin America and the Caribbean took place during the colonial era and these shaped many subsequent attitudes towards the region and had an important influence on culture and society.

The discovery of America acted as a stimulus to intellectual enquiry and influenced European scientific culture by introducing such concepts as the "tropical" into post-Enlightenment thought. For many years it was the local New World officials who explored the region's geography, metals, species, fruit and social systems. Nature was not a focus of systematic study and most attention was given to the human dimension of conquest – how indigenous peoples had been treated. What mainly concerned the Crown was the practical issue of good administration in its new lands, distracting attention from the natural environment. When nature did become the object of scientific study, it was under the auspices of the imperial state in pursuit of revenue. In some cases, such as spices like ginger, the crown even subsidized cultivation and trade in a form of state-sponsored "colonial botany" (see De Vos 2006; Pugliano 2009; Cooper 2007). This established a technocratic relationship between science and the demands of statist economies that has been much in evidence since. The goals of botany began to coincide with the goals of empire to identify and categorize new and useful plants.

Scientific ideas and their application to the problems of agriculture would stimulate a trend towards the radical simplification of production on *haciendas* and plantations (see Worster 1990). Latin America was also an important laboratory for medical research into diseases such as malaria, yellow fever and Chagas (see Gade 1999; Peard 1999). After 1800, science, transportation and industrial technology came together with new disciplines such as agronomy to change the way that entrepreneurs looked at nature, which was seen increasingly as a resource to be exploited.

The initial classification of the natural world in the region was largely a non-Latin American affair conducted against the backdrop of European imperial competition over resources (see McCook 2002a, 2002b). Science equipped the European powers to survey Latin America for imperial expansion, and alongside the ships sent to map the coastlines came agents and scientists from Kew Gardens and the Royal Geographical Society (see Ellis 2001).

The notion of a distinctive tropical nature was tied to empire and the geopolitical concerns of competing European powers. In Panama, for example, studies on the geography and nature of the Isthmus began to increase during the mid-nineteenth century at the time of the French and North American initiatives for the construction of a canal. Castro Herrera (2008) argues that the construction of the railway in Panama after 1850, which opened up previously isolated areas, had an important influence on the category of the "tropical" in North American culture (see also Frenkel 1996; Arnold 1996).

The discipline of natural history itself, with its emphasis on collecting and classifying species from across an increasingly accessible globe, was propelled by ideas spawned by the work of influential geographers and naturalists such as the French botanist Aimé Bonpland, the German naturalist Alexander von Humboldt and the English zoologist Charles Darwin. Initially Europe's desire to exploit New World plants did not generate conflict, but as the nineteenth century progressed the newly independent states of Latin America began seeking to commercialize their natural patrimony. Brazil, Peru, Bolivia and Colombia took steps to prevent the export of valuable native plants, although they did not stop Europeans from taking rubber and cinchona to establish plantations in Asia. Kew Gardens played a key role in what today would be described as "biopiracy" (see Kawell 2002).

Scientific progress remained in step with imperial designs. Davis (2001) has examined the rise of meteorology alongside the extension of European empires in the nineteenth century and how early meteorological science portrayed a cruel and unpredictable nature that could easily be blamed for hunger, allowing grain merchants to avoid responsibility for disruptions to global patterns of food production that were the main contributing cause of famines. Dalby (2004) points out that environmental science has been tied into the thinking of empire especially when it has provided support for "neo-Malthusian" arguments about overpopulation, nature and disasters in "far away" places (see Stott and Sullivan 2000). The evolutionary biology of Darwinism shaped the dominant nineteenth-century paradigm of environmental determinism (see above) in the disciplines of geography and anthropology. By arguing that aspects of physical geography such as climate influence the characteristics of human groups and so shape culture, European and US scholars could assert that tropical climates caused laziness or promiscuity in stark contrast with a northern "work ethic". In Argentina, Darwinism became influential in the mid-nineteenth century at a time when debates about how to organize the nation were shaping perceptions of gender and consumerism. Later classic works about Latin American nationalism such *Ariel* (1900) by the Uruguayan essayist José Enrique Rodó and *The Cosmic Race* (1925) by the Mexican thinker José Vasconcelos reacted against the harsh, utilitarian implications of natural selection by trying to recover the role of spiritualism, harmony and beauty.

Liberalism also underpinned the practice in the later nineteenth century of compiling botanical inventories for each nation. Between 1885 and 1935, governments throughout Latin America and the Caribbean financed the publication of national floras and began to establish botanical institutions. These national flora helped states establish a sense of control over the natural world and incorporate it into the new, national political and economic order. Much of Latin America's real and potential wealth in this period lay in its plants, and botany offered a way of increasing exports (see McCook 2002a). Foreign researchers also played a key role in this process. In Costa Rica, for example, foreign influences on scientific explorations had an important impact on institution-building that have continued to the present day (see Evans 1999).

Conservationism and environmentalism. Political turmoil in the new republics following Independence largely silenced early calls for conservation and the few, limited policies aimed at protecting resources such as timber inherited from the late colonial era fell by the wayside. Independence gave elites the ability to overturn restraints on trade and to raise international capital for the expansion of export production, with British capital flooding into sectors such as mining. The first undercurrents of environmentalism in this era responded to extensive destruction of forestry resources and the impact of this on society. Sugar mills consumed vast quantities of wood wastefully, and when firewood ran out this often caused stoppages. Coffee production denuded forests above Rio de Janeiro after 1800 and reduced the city's water supply, and by the 1840s other urban areas were experiencing water shortages for similar reasons. Desiccationist doctrines holding that reforestation could solve water shortages spread in the Iberian colonies (see above), and in countries such as Brazil scientists began to argue against the destruction of forest because of its economic, social and medicinal uses. Brazil gained its independence under a monarchy and enjoyed relative stability and continuity that enabled its emperor to maintain some colonial policies: Brazilwood remained a monopoly, other timbers were protected until the end of the nineteenth century, and reforestation policies were introduced. In Cuba in the 1860s and 1870s, woodland engineers began criticizing those who opposed controls on deforestation and argued that loggers were indifferent to the public interest. In Mexico in 1861, President Benito Juárez (1858–64) decreed the country's first national forest law, and in 1865 the government set aside a significant area of forestry west of Mexico City, Desierto de los Leones.

Pressures for conservation grew in direct relation to a resource's level of exploitation and the implications of this for future production. By the late nineteenth century, the demand for some resources generated by decades of economic growth during the export boom accelerated efforts to safeguard them. By the 1890s, soil exhaustion was beginning to affect coffee production in Costa Rica, El Salvador, Guatemala, Haiti and Venezuela and cacao production in the Dominican Republic, Ecuador and Venezuela. Disease threatened banana production in Costa Rica, Guatemala, Honduras and Panama. In Venezuela in 1917, a law was passed limiting the collection of egret feathers to the breeding season. In Peru after 1906, the government regulated extraction of depleted guano reserves.

Positivism, race and national identity. The notion of a distinctive tropical nature reinforced new European theories on race to legitimize discrimination, dispossession and slavery. Sensitivity towards race and ethnicity is important in the study of environmental history because landscapes have often been transformed as a result of colonization by different ethnic groups (see Young 2005). In the nineteenth century ideas encompassing a belief that human evolution had reached a "positive" stage in which scientific method could be used to discover truth contributed significantly to racial theories and reflected the commitment of liberalism to pursue progress regardless of cultural or religious obstacles. Encouraged by the development of scientific ideas, "positivism" was influential throughout Latin America, promoting social order, stability and economic growth. Positivist ideas greatly influenced emerging disciplines such as anthropology, empowering scientists to order humankind into a natural hierarchy and assisting the enterprise of empire. In Latin America, they allowed the assertion of authoritarian instincts and appealed to elites who sought to justify their privileged social position and affinity for European culture. European racial ideas drove internal colonialism whereby expanding states pursuing national development policies dispossessed indigenous people (see Carneiro da Cunha 1992; Henley 1996). Attitudes by white, Europeanized elites towards indigenous people have had a profound influence on the latter's marginalization from politics, excluding them from decisions over resource use. In contemporary Latin America the proliferation of technocrats – highly educated policymakers with a preference for technical solutions to social and economic problems – attests to the continuing tendency by elites to seek "scientific" solutions in policymaking. Positivism also influenced literary developments by allowing writers to depict progress in a romantic, yet backward, state of nature (see Bethell 1998).

Liberal modernists reliant on foreign capital to develop their economies often embraced ideas about progress through capitalism brought by foreign corporations and scientists. Commercial expansion by US agro-export corporations in Latin America and the Caribbean was accompanied by ideological assertion, with foreign executives claiming to bring civilization to backward peoples and productivity to an unproductive nature (see Tucker, 2000; see also Joseph, LeGrand and Salvatore 1998). Banana corporations such as United Fruit promoted ideas of enlightened management by which they constructed model labour camps to discipline workers' lives in a lax tropical environment. Such ideals were informed by past prejudices about the inferiority of the New World and its peoples and the benefits of "scientific" high-input farming techniques (see Soluri 2000). In Cuba and Puerto Rico, the US shaped the role played by science in agricultural development between 1898 and 1930 largely because of its importance to sugar production (see McCook 2002a). Castro Herrera (2008) argues that in Panama US officials believed they had successfully realized a central ideal of nineteenth-century liberal culture: the triumph of progress through man's control over nature.

Independence in Latin America and the Caribbean also established the foundations for potent, and in global terms pioneering, discourses about nationalism. Nationalism has had an important influence on how the environment has been exploited and has been a source of the assimilationist and integrationist discourses by which central elites marginalized indigenous peoples (see Garfield 2001). Even today, nationalist official positions, influenced by capitalist priorities, construct the identity of marginalized indigenous groups such as the Mapuche in Chile in specific ways (see Richards 2010). The strength of nationalism in Latin American countries may help to explain the absence of romantic inclinations towards nature comparable to North American notions of wilderness (see Pérez 2001).

Industrialization and the rise of consumer culture

A latent tension in Latin American and Caribbean development during the era of export-led growth existed between indigenous tradition and the pursuit of modernity by elites influenced by foreign models. This tension was most evident during the main period of industrialization from the late 1940s into the late 1970s as the Cold War between the US and the Soviet Union and their allies presented the region with a stark choice about the ideal model of development: capitalism oriented towards a mass consumer culture, or statist socialism.

The limited industrialization that began in the late nineteenth century reflected admiration for northern industrialism, the economic and social belief advocating the development of industry, usually in urban factories. However, this perspective was weak in Latin America, where elites gained their power from large landholdings and agro-exports. But, in the early twentieth century demographic growth, the rise of cities and the political advantages to corporatist parties of an organized working class concentrated in urban areas, fuelled industrial growth (see Chapter 1). Later structuralist ideas in Latin America and the Caribbean that advocated state-led industrialization can be seen as a rejection of influential ideas derived from "modernization theory" in the industrialized world about how agrarian societies developed into modern industrial economies. Modernization theory, sometimes called linear-stage or stages-of-growth theory, assumed that the industrialized countries had also once been underdeveloped agrarian societies, and so development could be understood as a series of successive stages through which all countries pass. This perspective has been highly influential in US universities and presented development as a linear evolution away from traditional societies shaped by communities to those based on individual values akin to what had taken place in the developed world (see Parsons 1954; Rostow 1962). The US itself put this philosophy into action in Puerto Rico through Operation Bootstrap, an industrialization policy pursued after the Second World War that lured labour-intensive industries to the country, causing serious air and water pollution (see Berman Santana 1996). Perspectives originating in modernization theory have been highly influential in shaping both how development is understood within Latin America and the Caribbean and the attitudes of the industrialized world towards the region. These attitudes have a benign view of industrial capitalism and explain development in terms of the characteristics of the US and Europe, and it is for this reason that modernization theory has sometimes been criticized as "ethnocentric".

The import-substituting model of industrial development in Latin America and the Caribbean went through transitions as the region's place in the world economy changed, and ultimately gave way in the 1980s to a new round of export-led growth that stoked yet more pressures on the region's natural resources (see Chapter 1). The new industries that manufactured products formerly imported from the industrialized world gave millions of Latin Americans access to affordable consumer products for the first time. An emergent consumer

Box 2.3 Consumer culture

The term culture refers to values, beliefs, traditions, symbols, norms and institutions that determine human behaviour and shape how we understand reality. The framework of dominant ideas and assumptions in a society is sometimes called a paradigm, and in the developed, industrial world the cultural paradigm is consumerism. The culture of consumerism is a product of economic development and capitalism, and it drives every aspect of life through mass consumption. Consumerism has been promoted for centuries by the needs of capitalism and is constantly reinforced by governments, businesses, the media and educational bodies that work to expand markets for new goods and services. Norms are often spread from the industrial world to developing countries as part of a broader phenomenon, sometimes referred to as "cultural imperialism" or "cultural globalization". Changes in European society in the late seventeenth century created the foundations for the emergence of consumerism, and by the twentieth century this cultural paradigm was reflected in the work of institutions everywhere. The evolution of mass communication technologies, sophisticated advertising techniques, transnational corporations and television and the internet enabled these institutions to spread consumer values across the world. A key feature of capitalist development has been the development of norms that associate personal gain and consumption with progress and modernity: consumerism makes people everywhere associate greater consumption with well-being and success (Assadourian 2010a). Multilateral bodies representing the developed world such as the Organization for Economic Cooperation and Development (OECD) reinforce this assumption, gauging the well-being of countries in terms of the degree to which private consumption drives growth (see Jackson 2011). Consumption patterns globally are increasing consistently to the point where they are generally held to be unsustainable. The debate that consumerism has nurtured among environmentalists has focused on resource use and the theme of sustainability. Ecologists and the climate change lobby have argued for a rapid cultural shift in order to ensure human survival, while others have asked whether abandoning consumerism is desirable or, indeed, possible (see, for example, Luke 1998). Conca (2001) argues that changes in the global economy are giving new importance to how the question of consumption is linked to environmental degradation (see also Conca, Princen and Maniates 2001).

culture, in turn, was shaped by the activity of foreign and particularly US corporations in the region, which oriented production according to marketing philosophies prevalent in their domestic economies (see Box 2.3). A key aspect of the debate over the environment today is how it is influenced by our attitudes to consumption.

The US has played a dominant role in accelerating the development of consumer culture in regions such as Latin America and the Caribbean (see Joseph, LeGrand and Salvatore 1998). First, the globalization of sourcing for the expanding US consumer market after 1850 reached into almost every corner of Latin America, where in turn it influenced local social relations and cultural development (see Tucker 2000). Second, since the nineteenth century, the US has encouraged Latin American societies to adopt its cultural norms and institutions – what has been called "the American way of life" (see Igelsias Utset 2011). An idea that prevailed was that modernity was something essentially North American or European (Larrain 2000; Garcia Canclini 1989). Today, US-led mass culture continues to influence consumption patterns throughout Latin America and the Caribbean, and behaviour associated with "Americanization" can be found everywhere. This has led to cultural homogenization with US foods, fashion, music, leisure, architecture and even styles of humour found throughout the region (Roberts and Thanos 2003). The influence of the mass media has played an important role in this cultural evolution. Consumer values have changed the cultural norms and structures of even the most traditional communities (see Colloredo-Mansfeld 1999).

Conservation and the greening of the discourse

It was not until the twentieth century that ideas about conservation began to have a meaningful impact on resource use, and a common early response by governments to the warnings of conservationists was to establish national parks. States often imitated foreign models, especially that of the US, where Yellowstone National Park was established by the federal government in 1872. However, in Latin America, political disagreements over federalism limited progress and it was in a new US protectorate, Puerto Rico, that the region's first national park was established at El Yunque in 1903. Over the next 50 years, protected areas spread and gave rise to the first environmental institutions. Latin American and the Caribbean countries today are enthusiastic champions of national parks, and, according to the World Database on Protected Areas, the percentage of terrestrial area protected in the region rose from 9.7 per cent in 1990 to 20.3 per cent in 2010; and the percentage of territorial waters up to 12 nautical miles protected rose from 2.7 per cent in 1990 to 10.8 per cent in 2010 (IUCN/UNEP-WCMC 2011). The progress of conservationist ideas was influenced by many factors which meant that an awareness of environmental issues could be a by-product of either nationalist and authoritarian positions, of a pluralistic or democratic sensibility, of a revolutionary analysis of dictatorship or oppression, or of a recognition of the legitimacy of land claims by marginalized peoples. However, in general, the environmentalism in Latin America and the Caribbean that conservationist arguments gave rise to has evolved in a close relationship with state discourses as well as those of international financial organizations and has weak links with society and the public interest (see Castro Herrera 2001). An example of the contradictory roles nationalism can play as a source of conservationist ideas can be found in the Dominican Republic. The dictator Rafael Leónidas Trujillo (1930–61) recklessly logged forests to enrich himself and after he was assassinated in 1961 deforestation accelerated. Yet his successor, Joaquín Balaguer (1960–62, 1966–78, 1986–96), who inherited Trujillo's authoritarian state and kept much of it intact, had a lasting impact on the country's natural environment. His ecological policies turned him into something akin to a green authoritarian (see Box 2.4).

The period from the late 1950s until the mid-1980s was distinguished in Latin America and the Caribbean by growing authoritarianism in a climate of polarization among social classes and growing anti-communism. Conservationism was sometimes able to take advantage of political closure because conservationists could claim a patriotic objective in their efforts to protect natural patrimony without the same risk of repression faced by class-based actors. A shared commitment to a "national" environment sometimes allowed conservation groups to mobilize under authoritarian regimes. In Chile, for example, the environmental movement emerged in a context in which politics was heavily dominated by debates about class, limiting the popular appeal of environmental discourses. Early environmental initiatives were launched by figures with valuable

Box 2.4 Green authoritarians

The conservative anti-communist leader Joaquín Balaguer left a lasting imprint on the landscape of the Dominican Republic (see Diamond 2005; Miller 2007). The motives of his predecessor Trujillo had been oriented by personal gain as a key figure in the country's logging operations, and after his assassination in 1961 logging resumed under the control of powerful families and squatters occupied land and resumed slash-and-burn deforestation. Initially, Balaguer was unable to stop this, and when his successor President Juan Bosch (1963) came into conflict with loggers they allied with other opposition interests and overthrew him. After his election in 1966, Balaguer cracked down, banning all commercial logging and closing sawmills. He handed responsibility for forest policy from the agricultural ministry to the military, branding illegal logging a crime against security. Both poor squatters and rich agri-businesses were forcibly removed from forests and luxury homes built by wealthy people in the Juan B Pérez National Park were bulldozed. Balaguer reduced domestic demand for timber and charcoal production. He expanded the national park system, set aside some of the first marine reserves and protected shorelines, river margins and wetlands. In the interest of protecting biodiversity, Balaguer banned hunting and signed the Convention on Biological Diversity (CBD). He also pressed industries to reduce pollution, taxed mines heavily, opposed the construction of some dams and vetoed environmentally damaging road construction projects. Balaguer also founded an aquarium, botanical garden and natural history museum in Santo Domingo, and rebuilt the national zoo. One of his legacies was to institutionalize a domestic environmentalism relatively free of foreign influences. Some of the first Latin American and Caribbean NGOs dedicated to nature conservation were created in the Dominican Republic in this period, beginning with the Sociedad Dominicana de Orquidiología (Dominican Orchidology Society) founded in 1966.

North American connections or who had studied in the US. In 1973, a military coup ousted the democratically elected Marxist President Salvador Allende and installed General Augusto Pinochet (1973–90) at the head of a repressive regime. However, the ecology movement was able to organize in a climate of political repression by taking advantage of the aftermath of the United Nations Conference on the Human Environment in Stockholm in 1972 to gain access to government officials. In 1974, a number of ecologists established the Instituto de Ecología under Dr Juan Grau, who subsequently headed Chile's environmental authority in the latter part of the Pinochet government.

Other cases illustrate the ambivalent relationship between conservationism and authoritarianism. In Brazil, it was the modernizing face of military rule – based on nationalist ideas of developmentalism (see Box 1.5) – that both damaged the environment through megaprojects such as dams but also gave some impetus to environmental initiatives. Mexico's political system was also authoritarian for much of the twentieth century, although power was exerted through a corporatist party, the Partido Revolucionario Institucional (PRI, Institutional Revolutionary Party), which limited opposition by exercising control over social groups. It was from within this "corporate authoritarianism" that environmentalism gained its first political expression during the 1980s. The Partido Revolucionario Institucional, responding to the growth of opposition and its loss of legitimacy, and in response to growing discontent among the urban middle classes about the quality of life in Mexico City, nurtured an ecology movement that it attempted to link to the party. In Cuba, a key asset of the environmental movement was the open support it received from the authoritarian president Fidel Castro, who made environmental protection a prominent theme of policymaking in response to the Rio Conference on the Environment and Development of 1992 (see Houck 2000).

A more revolutionary nationalism was also the source of environmental ideas and policies pursued in countries such as Nicaragua after the victory of the leftwing Frente Sandinista de Liberación Nacional (FSLN, Sandinista National Liberation Front) in 1979. The long rule of the Somoza dynasty in Nicaragua had given foreign corporations such as the US-owned Nicaraguan Long Leaf Pine Company significant freedom to exploit natural resources such as timber (see Miller 2007). The Sandinista revolutionary movement represented a coalition and elements of the government it formed, such as the radical priest Father Ernesto Cardenal – a poet whose work expresses patriotic ideas about Nicaragua's landscape and nature – linked environmental degradation with poverty in order to advance ecological policies.

The interaction between nationalist arguments and environmental perspectives is still evident in Latin America and the Caribbean. In Costa Rica, which has set aside a quarter of its national territory as national parks, environmentalism was fostered by members of the political elite such as President José María Figueres (1994–98) to become a key element of national identity (see Evans 1999). Nationalism remains a strong political reflex in the diplomacy of countries such as Brazil, where it is often used to resist foreign interventions in the debate about development in regions such as the Amazon, and in Argentina, where it has been evident in an environmental dispute with neighbouring Uruguay over the Botnia pulp mill.

However, although the first stirrings of conservationism came during the authoritarian period, it was authoritarianism itself that fuelled the growth of environmental politics. A key feature of popular environmentalism in Latin America and the Caribbean has been its relationship with the process of democratization (see Chapter 1). Authoritarianism generated either armed insurgencies, often by broad cross-class revolutionary coalitions, or pressures from within civil society for greater pluralism during the 1980s and 1990s. Conservationist voices were just one among many in civil society seeking a political transition. The damage to the natural environment that had been caused by the export economy, the excesses of oligarchic landowners and industrialization generated pressures for conservation from within an awareness of how powerless ordinary citizens were to influence policymaking. These pressures coincided both with growing consciousness of environmental issues after the early 1970s and with the demands of broader movements for radical political reform. Nonetheless, there was little popular mobilization around environmental concerns throughout Latin America and the Caribbean in the 1970s and debates were confined to government officials, professional associations and within environmental non-governmental organizations (ENGOs) linked to groups in the industrialized world (see Mumme and Korzetz 1997).

Civil society actors were also influenced by ideological changes taking place elsewhere in the world which amounted to a reaction against consumer culture (see above). In the 1960s, a sea change in attitudes to the environment gave rise to the first international environmental initiatives and popular movements of the 1970s and

1980s. The 1972 Stockholm Conference initiated the modern system of international environmental management; launching discussions about the link between environmental protection and development that eventually spawned the notion of sustainable development (see below); and pioneering new forms of public participation in the UN system (see UNEP/IISD 2005). The state in Latin America and the Caribbean was the first to respond to these developments, albeit not in response to popular pressure. Policy responses to environmental problems have proliferated since in the form of environmental legislation, often modelled on US initiatives or agencies such as the Environmental Protection Agency (EPA), or responding to an international agenda. In 1971, for example, Mexico became one of the first Latin American countries to respond to the US air and water acts by passing its own Ley Federal para Prevenir y Controlar la Contaminación Ambiental (LFPCC, Law for the Prevention and Control of Pollution) and, in response to the Stockholm Conference, establishing its own agencies based on the EPA.

The environmental movement itself began to emerge as the product of a complex interaction of factors associated with post-Stockholm environmental laws and institutions and the growing dissemination of ecological themes in the media. Although political liberalization gave momentum to their development in Latin America and the Caribbean, environmental organizations were not highly influential in the movement for democratization, with the possible exception of Brazil, and were primarily beneficiaries of it. Nonetheless, by the late 1980s, environmental awareness was growing and green activists were beginning to achieve policy successes and find representation in government as a result of the movement's contribution to democratic transitions.

In Mexico, environmental organizations began to develop in the 1980s, and by the 1990s the country had about 1,000 private groups. In Chile, article 19 of the 1980 constitution made pollution unconstitutional and placed a duty on the government to ensure the preservation of nature, but the inclusion of environmental issues in political debate occurred definitively upon the return to democracy in 1990 (see Silva 1997; Muñoz 1997). In Brazil, environmentalist positions stretch back into colonial history, but a coherent new environmentalism emerged in the 1970s in response to the destructive impact of rapid economic growth under the military (see Pádua 1987). By the mid-1980s,

Brazil's green movement was growing rapidly and influencing policy (see Viola 1997). The evolution of the Brazilian movement illustrates several trends.

Diversity. A key theme in the development of the environmental movement in Brazil after the mid-1980s has been its involvement with other social groups, trade unions and NGOs, which has generated the perspective of "socioenvironmentalism" (see Volume 2). Environmentalism also expanded from strongholds in the south of the country to become a fully national movement, drawing attention to the diverse character of environmental activism and the issues pursued in different regions of one country.

Institutionalization. Growing awareness of environmental problems has led to institutionalization by which green movements became a stable presence in civil society and policy circles. During the deliberations for Brazil's constituent assembly in 1987–88, environmentalists systematically lobbied representatives for the first time and, as a result, the country's 1988 constitution was one of the most advanced in the world in terms of environmental protection. At the same time, they created the Partido Verde (PV, Green Party), and other political parties began to respond to environmental issues. The example of Costa Rica, which enjoyed largely uninterrupted democratic politics during the second half of the twentieth century, can also help to illustrate the subtle relationship between democracy and the institutionalization of environmental ideas (see Box 2.5).

Professionalization. Institutionalization has occurred alongside professionalization of the environmental movement and by the mid-1980s organizations were moving away from volunteerism to develop a professional profile emphasizing efficiency (see Viola 1997). This created distinctions between professional environmental organizations and a proliferation of smaller activist groups. As the media has become more important to raising public awareness about environmental issues, the role of non-professional organizations has decreased. Growing professionalism also reflected the establishment of Brazilian branches of international NGOs such as Friends of the Earth, the World Wide Fund for Nature and Greenpeace. Professionalization has an important impact on environmental groups, often transforming their objectives from creating awareness to formulating alternative

Box 2.5 Costa Rica's environmental ethic

Evans (1999) has traced the conservation history of Costa Rica which has developed around an extensive network of national parks. He has asked whether an existing national environmental ethic led to the development of national parks, or whether the establishment and development of national parks were a catalyst for the development of an environmental ethic. The country is unique in Central America for having a largely uninterrupted democratic tradition and for being free of the violent civil conflicts that plagued the sub-region between the 1960s and 1990s. However, Evans argues that Costa Rica's uniqueness does not account for the surge in environmental awareness in the last decades of the twentieth century. He believes that although scientists and conservationists have played a formative role in developing the nation's environmental consciousness, legislation in 1969 in the form of the Ley Forestal (forestry law), which established the basis to create national parks, was a key factor. Once the parks had been created, they became a source of national pride that inspired Costa Ricans to demand more protected areas and other environmental policies. Evans argues that by the mid-1980s most Costa Ricans had become "patriotically proud" of how their country was becoming a world leader in tropical conservation, and the country was also seen as a model throughout the developing world.

policies. Leadership began to adopt more pragmatic approaches to objectives and outcomes. In Brazil, larger environmental associations began to abandon an identification with the radical democracy of the political transition and to promote greater efficiency.

Internationalization. A key factor in the development of the environmental movement in Latin America and the Caribbean has been the internationalization of ecological solidarity through the establishment of links between groups in the region itself and environmental organizations and academics in the developed world. In most Latin American countries, the emergence of the environmental movement has been influenced both by domestic and international pressures (see Hochstetler and Keck 2007). International solidarity has been crucial for many organizations, especially in smaller countries such as those of Central America (Faber 1993).

This may help to explain why since the early 1990s and beginning with the United Nations Conference on Environment and Development (UNCED) in Brazil, Latin America has played a prominent role in the development of the international ecology movement. Environmental groups and politicians in the US and Europe have been at the heart of this process. In the US, major environmental organizations such as Greenpeace, Earth Island Institute, Earth First!, National Toxics Campaign and Friends of the Earth have recurrently supported activism in Latin America and the Caribbean. US conservation goals and strategies have also been a model for many Latin American movements and subsequent policy developments. This has had implications for how environmentalism has evolved in Latin America. The global environmental movement has tended to prioritize the debate about resource use over that of dominant social relations and property norms. Moreover, many international perspectives instinctively draw upon an Edenic narrative of paradise lost that articulates concern about the destruction of nature through the loss of "biodiversity". The international environmental movement has played a transformative role in raising the profile of the Amazon rainforest in discourse (see Box 2.6).

Growing consciousness of environmental issues has now made these a prominent concern in politics throughout Latin America and the Caribbean, and environmentalism has emerged as a key strand of opposition politics. Environmental themes are now present in all forms of media coverage and education. The emergence of popular environmentalism reflects an important change in attitudes towards nature in the region, which is increasingly seen as a victim of human excess.

The Latinobarómetro survey, an annual analysis of attitudes in Latin America and the Caribbean, provides valuable insights into levels of environmental awareness. Since the late 1990s, Latinobarómetro data has reflected dramatic changes in the level of importance attributed to environmental protection. In 1998, for example, 37 per cent of Latin Americans indicated that in the trade-off between economic development and environmental protection priority should be given to the economy; by 2011, however, only 17 per cent of people believed that economic growth should take priority (Latinobarómetro 2011). Moreover, 48 per cent of Latin Americans believe environmental protection is among the economic and social rights guaranteed in

Box 2.6 The Amazon in environmental discourse

The fate of the Amazon rainforest has become an international political concern since the late 1980s when media reports of large areas of forest being burned attracted global attention. Deforestation in the Amazon has since driven the growth of green politics in Brazil and beyond, and has forced politicians to admit a broad range of environmental concerns on to the agenda and try to co-opt environmentalists to their platforms. In Brazil, for example, the ruling Partido dos Trabalhadores (PT, Workers' Party) has incorporated a number of senior Partido Verde (PV, Green Party) figures in successive governments. While the Amazon has had a positive influence on the awareness of environmental issues in Latin America and the Caribbean, this has been disproportionate. One result is that Amazonian issues have monopolized funds for sustainable development while most people in the region confront environmental challenges that attract little international interest. Debates have also focused on deforestation itself and ignored broader development processes and how development and conservation in the area might, in fact, be reconciled (see Furley 1994). The Brazilian Amazon has become a symbol of environmental destruction because huge areas are being cleared, but, by Brazilian and international standards, it remains relatively intact (see Box 4.4). More than three-quarters of deforestation in the Brazilian Amazon has occurred in the last 40 years, yet deforestation also accelerated in Central America, coastal Ecuador and Chile (see Ryan 1991). Debates about the Amazon bring together some of the most potent themes in environmentalism and have changed over time. In 1970, discussion about development in the area concerned how to modernize it and all sides favoured clearing the forest (see Dore 1996b). Yet, by 1990, concern about irreversible deforestation and the destruction of Amazonian biodiversity was coinciding with a growing global narrative about climate change. Similar debates continue today in other countries with Amazon territories, such as Peru (see Walker 2012). However, one aspect of these debates that has changed remarkably little since the colonial era is the vision of the Amazon as a pristine wilderness inhabited by noble savages (see Cleary 2001; Raffles and Winkler Prins 2003; Slater 1996; Henley 1996). A long genealogy exists in which scientific and popular narratives have also depicted the area as a space of nature independent of human society (see Nugent 1993; Raffles 2002; Cronon 1996). Such an emphasis can make it difficult for local activists and sympathetic scholars to draw attention to social issues.

Figure 2.1 Economic development versus care for the environment, Latin America and the Caribbean 2011*

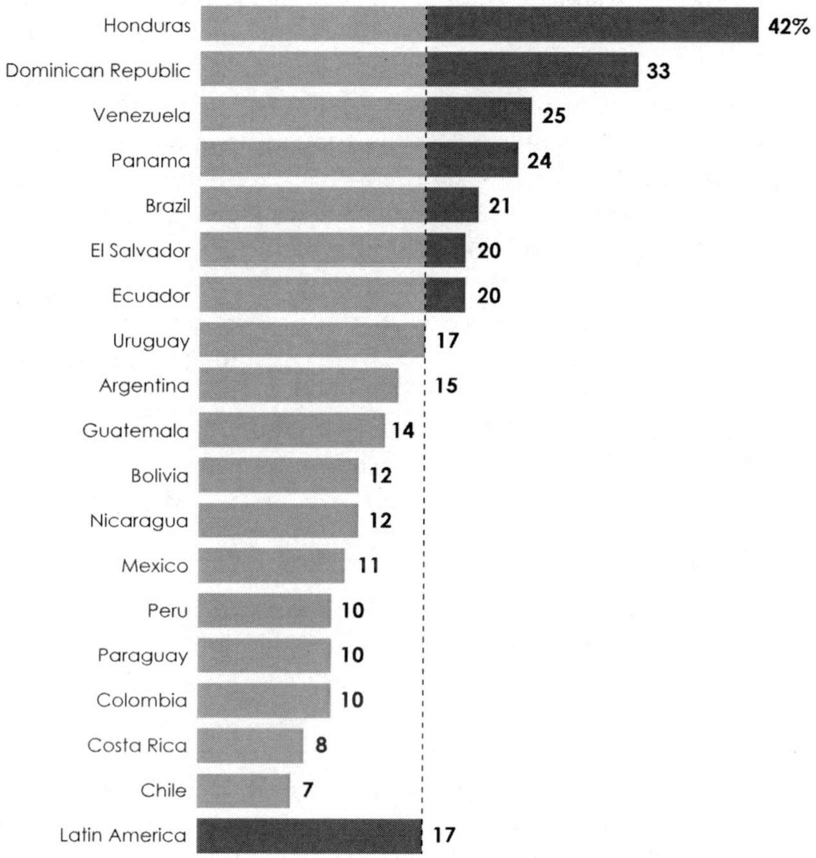

* When asked: "With which of the following phrases are you most in agreement: priority should be given to economic development even if it means damaging the environment; priority should be given to protection of the environment, even if it means slower economic development", those who answered "priority should be given to economic development even if it means damaging the environment".

Source: Latinobarómetro, *Informe 2011*. Santiago: Corporación Latinobarómetro (www.latinobarometro.org/latino/latinobarometro.jsp).

their countries. According to Latinobarómetro, Chile's population has the highest level of environmental commitment in the region and that of Honduras has the least (see Figure 2.1). A large and growing majority of Latin Americans also believe climate change is already affecting them (Latinobarómetro 2011).

Many factors have contributed to the development of environmental consciousness and a significant consensus has formed since 1992 around the reformist notion of sustainable development (see Chapter 6). The discourse of sustainable development has its origins in debates concerning the economic challenges faced by Latin America and the Caribbean during the "lost decade" of the 1980s following the debt crisis (see Chapters 1, 6). Multilateral lending agencies also began to adopt and promote the theme of sustainable development, generating an environmental critique that changed the discourse of major lending agencies such as the World Bank.

The notion of sustainable development reflects the attempt to reconcile old developmentalism with the new idea of environmentalism. As Dore (1996a) has pointed out, sustainable development is not about transforming capitalism; it is about reforming the status quo to make capitalism more eco-friendly. Environmentalists themselves often advanced sustainability in terms acceptable to multilateral financial agencies, thereby embracing their agenda of export promotion, free markets and a reduction in the role of the state. By the 1990s, some environmentalists were arguing that the rhetoric of environmentalism itself was being used to legitimize economic policies that obstructed sustainable development or were potentially destructive (see Sponsel 1995).

Nonetheless, the notion of sustainable development represents an advance in environmental politics in Latin America and the Caribbean by incorporating broader developmental concerns into ideologically informed debates about production and consumption. It exercises minds on such issues as how to change the paradigm of consumerism and the real purpose of economic growth (see Assadourian 2010a). The experience of Cuba provides a concrete illustration of how the absence of consumer culture and an emphasis on sustainability can contribute to rapid changes in attitudes towards the environment and public policies that promote sustainable development (see Box 2.7).

The focus on sustainable development, given urgency by concern about the impact of climate change, has contributed to an important reassessment of ideas about nature in Latin America and the Caribbean. The region now finds itself pioneering new environmental concepts that are starting to influence policymaking such as Earth jurisprudence – by which the Earth itself is attributed fundamental rights that human laws must incorporate. In 2008, for example,

Box 2.7 Cuba's Special Period and organic revolution

After 1970, Cuba's main trading partners were the Soviet Union and the communist bloc, and the Caribbean island became closely tied to the Council of Mutual Economic Assistance (CMEA), a socialist economic union based on barter trade. The dissolution of the Soviet Union and the disappearance of the CMEA in the early 1990s confronted the Cuban economy with its most serious crisis since the imposition of an embargo on the island by the US. In 1990, the then president Fidel Castro declared that the country had entered a "special period" of austerity and Cubans experienced falling per capita income, blackouts, rationing, factory closures and shortages of essential goods (Saney 2004; Ludlam 2009). Agriculture went into crisis – exacerbated by the country's inability to import pesticides and fertilizers. Cuba responded with what Miller (2007) has called the largest ever experiment in organic agriculture (see also Morgan 2006). Farmers reverted to using oxen in the fields and noted some advantages over tractors: oxen did not compact the soil, could be used in any season, permitting a third crop annually in some areas, and their manure could be used as fertilizer. Cubans revived experiments in biological pest control with organic pesticides such as neem extract, and established centres to breed predatory insects and parasitic wasps that protect plantains and sweet potatoes from weevils. Cuba responded to a lack of fertilizers by gathering manure from oxen, pigs and chickens; recycling biomass from sugar processing; using earthworms to boost compost (vermiculture); producing micro-organisms to fix nutrients in soil; and developing new rotational and intercropping systems and raised beds (Miller 2007) Authorities encouraged urban agriculture and city dwellers began to plant in patios and on rooftops; co-operatives created farms on baseball fields and car parks; and factories and schools employed unused space to grow food. By the late 1990s, organic production had grown considerably and Cubans were producing more food per square metre than under industrial agriculture (see also Díaz-Briquets and Pérez-López 2000).

Ecuador incorporated into a new constitution the declaration that nature, or "Mother Earth", has the right to exist, persist, maintain and regenerate its vital cycles, structures, functions and evolutionary processes. Such ideas are shifting Latin American and Caribbean policymakers slowly towards developing different, distinctively local ways of measuring human progress (see Tauli-Corpuz 2010). The relationship between ecological protection and human development has also drawn attention to the *systemic* character of environmental degradation in Latin America and the Caribbean. The many varied symptoms of excessive consumption are often treated separately but are in fact systemically linked (see Chapter 4). A systemic approach implies that in order to create sustainable societies overarching cultural changes are required to consumption and production patterns that challenge dominant external models upon which lifestyles have hitherto been based. Indicators such as the "Ecological Footprint" offer tools for the conceptualization of overconsumption and put in stark relief the consistent trend in human development of continuous and unsustainable growth (see Pollard 2010; also Chapters 4, 6). The focus on consumption is at the heart of debates about "ecological citizenship", which advocates new norms on which to base the individual's relationship with society and his or her attitudes towards the common good (see also Dobson and Bell 2006; Sáiz 2005). Finally, the focus on sustainable development and new environmental concepts and debates about citizenship have together given significant impetus to a potent re-evaluation of indigenous culture and knowledge within Latin America and the Caribbean.

Indigenous resource attitudes

Indigenous peoples have long been neglected by governments and international agencies, and since the nineteenth century they have been marginalized in the region in favour of urban, industrial, market-led growth. However, democratization has also transformed attitudes towards indigenous people and since the early 1990s considerable attention has turned to their relationship with sustainable development. In Latin America and the Caribbean, indigenous consciousness has grown significantly and their organizations have gained prominence.

There is no universally accepted definition of who is indigenous but in general indigenous peoples are the descendants of the original pre-Columbian inhabitants of the Americas who survive in ways distinct to dominant Western culture and society through ecosystem-specific cultural practices. This means they tend to practise small-scale, labour-intensive, sustainable forms of mainly rural production that require little energy and produce little surplus. They organize their lives around communities and, in general, share common ethnic markers – language, religion, clothing – as well as a relationship to a particular territory. Often, indigenous people have a cosmology and moral values that express a custodial, non-possessive attitude to land and natural resources (Sobrevila 2008).

The growing prominence of indigenous people in Latin America has been fuelled by the interaction of international efforts to recognize indigenous identities since the 1970s and the human rights movement, which has given rise to an "international indigenism" (see Niezen 2003). The new prominence of indigenous peoples arguably reached its peak in 1992 at the Rio Earth Summit, when an indigenous delegation wrote the "Indigenous Peoples Earth Charter" that identified issues of most concern to them, including: human rights, lands and territories, biodiversity and conservation, development strategies, and culture, science and intellectual property (Sobrevila 2008). Nonetheless, this international prominence is still a recent development and it was only in 2007 that the UN Declaration on the Rights of Indigenous Peoples – a universal instrument encouraging protection of the rights of indigenous peoples – was adopted by the General Assembly (Wessendorf 2011).

A key feature of the growing attention to indigenous people in Latin America and the Caribbean has been the development of the discourse of multiculturalism and its anchoring in law, which has important implications for the nation states of Latin America and previous ideas about state-led national development (see Sieder 2002). Multiculturalism reflects recognition by states of indigenous rights, which have also been systematically incorporated into international environmental law. Multilateral agencies and international and local NGOs now run many international programmes to help strengthen indigenous cultures (Wessendorf 2011). Multiculturalism has implications for the role of the environment in political discourses because development policies that national states pursue in the context of neoliberal globalization have generally favoured extensive, private land use and welcomed foreign investment in extractive industries such as mining and logging (see Horton 2006). Underlying the debates surrounding multiculturalism are often claims for greater political participation among marginalized groups seeking to protect their access to natural resources within their territories.

Struggles over resources. The relationship between indigenous people and non-indigenous societies since the colonial era has been distinguished by struggles over lands and resources and by indigenous resistance to the destruction of their cultures and ecosystems (see Coates 2004; Reitz 2001). Many of these struggles have lasted centuries and shaped attitudes and the institutional responses of national states towards indigenous land and resources. An instance of conflict was the Chiapas rebellion in 1994, when a mainly indigenous guerrilla army, the EZLN, launched an insurgency in southern Mexico. The Zapatistas articulated an array of indigenous and political demands reflecting existing competition for resources as well as the then climate of political opposition to one-party rule in the country (see Berger 2001). Nonetheless, there was an environmental dimension to this struggle generated by the strains caused by deforestation in the Lacandón jungle caused by an emphasis on resource extraction (see O'Brien 1998). While states continue to promote the development of natural resources, indigenous peoples, on whose lands most of these resources can be found, continue to suffer from the encroachments of multinational companies. What is sometimes called "development aggression" in the form of logging, mega-dams and other land development projects remains the main challenge facing indigenous peoples. In recent years, Peru has struggled with the tensions between state efforts to open indigenous territories to development and the need to protect indigenous culture (see also Box 5.7; Wessendorf 2011).

Sustainable development. A second explanation for the new prominence of indigenous identity in global politics relates to the attitudes towards nature that are attributed to indigenous groups and their millennial adaptations to ecosystems (see Sponsel 1995; Roosevelt 1994). The indigenous way of life often sits at the very heart of issues of development and biodiversity preservation, explaining their potential for playing a key role in executing policies of sustainable development. In the historiography of colonial Latin America, there has been considerable debate about the degree to which continuity – as opposed to rupture – characterized the "moral economy" of established rural communities for hundreds of years following conquest (see Cope 2010; Cook and Cook 2007). A large body of research into human anthropology and ecology implicitly contrast the materialist forces of economic globalization with the cosmologies and traditional knowledge of indigenous peoples. One result of this is that many scholars and observers also depict indigenous people as the moral core of opposition to capitalism (see Mander and Tauli-Corpuz 2006; Hall and Fenelon 2009).

We can gain important insights about the new value placed upon indigenous cosmology and knowledge by non-indigenous society from the approach of multilateral financing agencies towards projects aimed at preserving or enhancing it as part of sustainable development strategies. International treaties such as the CBD have recognized the close dependence of many indigenous and local communities on biological resources (see GEF 2010). Agencies, including the World Bank, UNDP, Inter-American Development Bank and African Development Bank all have their own policies and strategies on indigenous peoples, and these communities have been the focus of a broad range of projects funded by the Global Environment Facility (GEF). These programmes have focused on the co-management of protected areas and on maintaining biodiversity, which lies at the heart of the role attributed to indigenous society for two main reasons:

- indigenous communities play a significant role in conserving areas of high biodiversity, which forms a key part of their culture (see Sobrevila 2008). They have played a crucial role in domesticating biodiversity (see Chapter 1; MacNeish 1992; UNEP 2010).
- a key feature of indigenous peoples globally is their cultural diversity (see Wessendorf 2011). Diversity can reflect different forms of resource use in different ecosystems and lies at the heart of debates about indigenous knowledge of nature and the role this can play in sustainable development (see Box 2.8).

Indigenous communities are also now the focus of sustainable land management projects. Most of the lands now lying within South America's national parks are indigenous and community lands. In recent years there has been a global trend to divest public lands to traditional communities and it is thought that up to half of the forestlands in developing countries will be communally owned or administered by 2015. World Bank studies show that empowering indigenous peoples to manage biodiversity in their own territories has resulted in a more sustained and cost-effective way to protect biodiversity (Sobrevila 2008). Agencies such as the World Bank believe that by advancing

Box 2.8 Traditional knowledge

It has been recognized that indigenous knowledge may have the potential to contribute to *scientific* discourses on environmental management. There have been efforts to ensure indigenous knowledge is incorporated into the scientific work of the Intergovernmental Panel on Climate Change (IPCC) (see Tauli-Corpuz 2010). Indigenous knowledge and management systems are also increasingly being seen as a critical yet untapped resource in global conservation (Sobrevila 2008). The Convention on Biological Diversity recognizes the value of indigenous communities to conservation and the sustainable use of biodiversity. The World Bank, for example, has operated a number of projects involving indigenous communities that build on traditional knowledge (see World Bank 2010c). Despite a long history of colonization and displacement, many indigenous peoples still live in ancestral territories and have survived largely as a result of their detailed knowledge of local landscapes (Roberts and Thanos 2003). Indigenous peoples' knowledge of their resource base has been extensively documented by scientific research (see Posey 1999). This has shown that traditional knowledge provides the basis of resource management systems that have sustained indigenous societies for millennia (see Silvius, Bodmer and Fragoso 2005). Moreover, Western science has long looked to peoples considered primitive as a source of information about botanical resources (see Crosby 1972). Concern in the developed world about the loss of biodiversity is now linked to recognition of the damage caused by the loss of traditional agricultural practices and knowledge (see Nabhan 2002; CBD 2006; Maffi 2002).

sustainable forms of development indigenous peoples can also play a key role in climate change mitigation and adaptation. Global efforts are now being made to ensure that indigenous people themselves benefit from the application of traditional knowledge. Indigenous peoples have engaged in negotiations for an international legal regime on ABS (access and benefit-sharing) (Tauli-Corpuz 2010).

Yet, although indigenous groups have found themselves in the vanguard of the sustainable development agenda, they continue to be sidelined as economic policies result in the exploitation and extraction of their resources and ancestral lands (Sobrevila 2008).

Institutional inertia marginalize indigenous peoples even as they are increasingly invited to participate in the management of biodiversity. Most biodiversity funding still goes to government agencies, NGOs and Western scientists (see Bruner et al. 2004). Moreover, the growing prominence of indigenous people has also not been without critics, who point to historical discourses among non-indigenous peoples such as the pristine myth (see Redford 1991). In some cases, poverty and dominant market norms can also have the same impact on indigenous approaches to nature as among non-indigenous people (see Bebbington 1996; Alexander 1996). Townsend (1996) examined indigenous women settlers in Mexico's Lacandón forest and suggested that women may be just as keen to cut down trees as men where it represents the only solution to hardship (see also Sabin 1998). Redford (1991) has argued that indigenous people are not "natural conservationists" and pursue sustainable patterns of land use only under conditions of low population densities and abundant land.

Conclusion

Latin America and the Caribbean offers many examples of how knowledge of nature and religious and philosophical positions towards it have been important factors in shaping the environment since pre-Columbian times. These positions determine the many ways in which societies use nature and distribute its resources by providing a basis for attitudes towards consumption, conservation and hierarchy. A development of great significance in the last 40 years has been the emergence of environmental consciousness, which is making green issues prominent concerns in politics and altering traditional ideas about development and human progress. Those concerns frequently come up against the pressing need for development in a region where levels of poverty have been high. The emergence of a popular environmentalism suggests that there are many citizens who believe that the price paid by nature for a form of development that has been unequal has been unacceptably high. A consensus has formed in official circles since the early 1990s around the notion of sustainable development, which seeks to balance the need for growth with protection of the environment for future generations. Among other things, this notion exercises minds about the impact of consumerism and the *purpose* of economic growth. It has coincided with a re-evaluation of indigenous knowledge of the natural world and the contribution this can make to conservation.

Recommended reading

Assadourian, Erik. 2010. "The Rise and Fall of Consumer Cultures", in Linda Starke and Lisa Mastny (eds), *2010 State of the World. Transforming Cultures: From Consumerism to Sustainability*. Washington, DC: Worldwatch Institute.

Cleary, David. 2001. "Towards an Environmental History of the Amazon: From Prehistory to the NineteenthCentury", *Latin American Research Review*, Vol. 36, No. 2, pp. 64–96.

Davis, Mike. 2001. *Late Victorian Holocausts: El Niño Famines and the Making of the Third World*. London: Verso.

Evans, Sterling. 1999. *The Green Republic: A Conservation History of Costa Rica*. Austin: University of Texas Press.

Tucker, Richard P. 2000. *Insatiable Appetite: The United States and the Ecological Degradation of the Tropical World*. Berkeley: University of California Press.

Williams, Robert G. 1986. *Export Agriculture and the Crisis in Central America*. Chapel Hill: University of North Carolina Press.

Useful websites

Comité Nacional Pro Defensa de la Fauna y Flora (CODEFF), Chile: www.codeff.cl/

International Union for Conservation of Nature (IUCN): www.iucn.org

International Work Group for Indigenous Affairs (IWGIA): www.iwgia.org

Ramsar Convention on Wetlands: www.ramsar.org

United Nations Environment Programme (UNEP)-World Conservation Monitoring Centre (WCMC): www.unep-wcmc.org/

Wildlife Conservation Society, containing valuable information on conservation initiatives in individual Latin American countries: www.wcs.org/where-we-work/latin-america.aspx

World Database on Protected Areas (WDPA), a joint venture between the United Nations Environment Programme-World Conservation Monitoring Centre (UNEP-WCMC) and the International Union for Conservation of Nature's (IUCN) World Commission on Protected Areas (WCPA): www.wdpa.org/

CHAPTER THREE

Political legacies and challenges

THIS CHAPTER INTRODUCES STUDENTS to some of the main themes by which the politics of the environment in Latin America and the Caribbean can be studied – institutions, policymaking, political parties and social movements, and ideology – all of which are examined in more detail in Volume 2 of this title.

The study of democratic politics in Latin America and the Caribbean has shifted its focus from the transition from authoritarian rule to the nature of the institutions in which legitimate power is vested as well as institutional structures formally outside government within "civil society" such as educational bodies, businesses and the media. These institutions shape and deliver policy, but while considerable academic energy has been focused on the content of public policy in Latin America and the Caribbean and its consequences, there has been less attention paid to the policymaking process itself. Public policy – a government's response to public problems – is of fundamental importance to the study of the politics of the environment, not least because it determines among other things the distribution of "public" goods. In the study of the environment, one key area of policymaking is foreign relations because environmental change can test traditional concepts of sovereignty, and hence the very notion of the nation state. Although there are often common responses in Latin America and the Caribbean to the powerful forces of globalization – and although many of the environmental problems faced by countries in the region are similar – there also remain considerable differences in how the environment is dealt with in the foreign relations agenda of each country.

The most important factor shaping the development of institutions and public policy in Latin America and the Caribbean since the 1980s and 1990s has been democratization, which spawned new green parties throughout the region. Political parties are crucial components of democracies, but in Latin America and the Caribbean they face specific constraints that derive from the region's unique political history. There are common elements to the emergence of green parties within the wider process of democratization, some of which have become solidly established, yet also crucial local differences that often reflect the diversity of the region. Alongside parties, environmental activism in Latin America and the Caribbean has taken place largely outside the formal realms of politics among citizens brought together in diverse social groups. The shifting mosaic of environmental activism and the many networks and alliances that comprise it has been studied through the notion of "civil society". Parties and social movements are driven by ideas, and political ideas are of great importance to the environment and have played a key role in shaping the natural landscape of Latin America and the Caribbean. Since the 1970s, ideologies of environmentalism have gained ground throughout the region, whose natural environment has also generated considerable anxiety in the developed world (see Chapter 2). More recently, attention has turned to the ideas and traditions of indigenous people throughout the region, and how these might contribute to efforts to protect the environment. This focus has been sharpened by the emergence of a dominant official emphasis by governments and multilateral bodies on the need for "sustainable development".

This chapter examines the emergence of environmental institutions in Latin America and the Caribbean, factors that influence environmental policymaking, and in particular how the environment influences Latin American foreign policy. It provides an overview of the emergence and characteristics of green parties and alongside them the social movements campaigning on environmental issues and NGOs that are considered integral to the idea of civil society. Finally, it looks at how the environment fits into some of the main ideological themes that have influenced political development in the region.

Institutions

Strong, stable, representative institutions are crucial for a healthy democracy and institutions provide stability in policymaking. If they are weak this can foster uncertainty and scepticism about politics, leading to immobilism, lack of government authority and conflict. Institutions are also crucial for managing the relationship between national and international bodies working towards environmental sustainability. Environmental institutions have also been at the forefront of raising awareness about environmental issues. But governing institutions in Latin America and the Caribbean have often been shaped by factors that have hampered their effectiveness and obstructed the development of democracy such as personalism, authoritarianism, revolution, illegality, populism, corporatism and dependency. Until recently, institutions such as congresses have served merely as window-dressing for dictatorships or oligarchic rule. One way of approaching the study of institutions is to employ the concept of environmental governance, which is now being given considerable attention by multilateral bodies (see Box 3.1; Lemos and Agrawal 2006; UNEP 2012). This phrase has been used to refer to the general approach taken by public institutions to managing environmental issues and as a normative concept to promote best practice. In Latin America the notion of environmental governance emerged during the 1980s as a neoliberal concept emphasizing a way of managing natural resources that limited the role of state institutions and encouraged the participation of private enterprise. The resulting policies often included the privatization of natural resources such as water, forests and land, which had a significant environmental impact (Liverman and Villas 2006).

Environmental management in Latin America and the Caribbean has developed considerably over the last 20 years and governments have incorporated green concerns into public administration through a dynamic process of institution-building. Environmental regulatory frameworks and ministerial departments or agencies to establish and implement policy were created throughout much of the region during the mid-1970s (Acuña 1999). The evolution of environmental ministries has often been tied to that of agricultural, fisheries, mining and energy ministries safeguarding the economic contribution of natural resources and addressing public health issues. Environmental

Box 3.1 Environmental governance

Environmental governance refers to diverse areas of policymaking and delivery within both the formal structures of government but also civil society and business to manage the natural environment and public goods such as the atmosphere, climate and biodiversity sustainably. The concept refers to the rules, practices, processes and institutions – both formal and informal – by which the environment is managed, from conservation to the exploitation of natural resources. It has been the subject of much debate and critics say global environmental governance has been unable to solve problems because of fragmented institutional structures, obstacles to co-ordination, conflicts with economic priorities and divisions among countries. Yet environmental governance has made clear inroads in some areas: in enabling civil society to participate in decision-making; in fostering co-operation between states; and in scrutinizing bodies unrestrained by states, such as multinational corporations.

agencies themselves often evolved out of the creation of protected areas established to conserve forestry resources. Scientific institutions have also played a key role in environmental institution-building in Latin America and the Caribbean, influencing economic policies and providing an early source of environmental activism. The evolution of environmental governance at an international level has also influenced institution-building. The Rio Declaration at the 1992 Earth Summit, for example, gave significant impetus to this process, especially where agencies had not yet achieved ministerial representation in cabinet. Today most Latin American and Caribbean countries have dedicated ministries of the environment (see Volume 2).

Democratizing governments in Latin America and the Caribbean often inherited administrative systems characterized by bureaucratism that limited the ability of environmentalists to influence policy. Traditionally, the region has been seen as one with large yet weak states whose capacity was hampered by the absence of stable, professional civil services. Moreover, the bureaucracy has often been seen as a resource at the disposal of politicians by contrast with an ideal type distinguished by meritocracy (see Weber 1947; Stein et al. 2005).

Alongside the formal institutions of public administration, political institutions – presidencies, cabinets, legislatures, judiciaries and parties – are crucial policy actors. In developing regions such as Latin America and the Caribbean, formal political processes have played a key role in shaping both the emergence of environmentalism itself and subsequent environmental reforms (see Hochstetler and Keck 2007).

- ***The executive***. Presidentialism is the norm in Latin America and presidents are the key actors in policy formation and although their personal motivations affect how they govern this is also influenced by institutional norms. Presidential powers also vary considerably: his or her constitutional powers determine the relationship between executive and legislature, in particular how a president mobilizes support for policy; partisan powers relate to the level of support a president may have in congress (see Volume 2). Most of Latin America is distinguished by multi-party systems, meaning that the capacity of governments to form and maintain coalitions is a key factor affecting stability.
- ***The legislature***. The policy role of legislatures is growing in Latin America and the Caribbean, but their effectiveness depends on presidential and their own institutional powers. A number of factors determine how legislatures behave including the committee structures within them and the electoral formula which influences the characteristics, preferences and stability of policymakers and can also affect fundamental aspects of political life such as the motivations and integrity of lawmakers.
- ***The judiciary***. The judiciary's role as an arbiter is important to the policy process and, while it acts mainly as a source of veto, it can also nurture co-operation and foster a climate in which political actors shape policy that is stable and adaptable. Democratization is strengthening the judicial system's involvement in the policymaking process and has informed a debate among scholars about the "judicialization" of politics: the expansion of the province of the courts at the expense of politicians or public administration (see Tate and Vallinder 1995).

Constitutionalism is a key aspect of Latin American and Caribbean legal and political culture, rooted in legalistic traditions inherited from Spain and Portugal by which great importance is placed upon codified rules of political conduct. Constitutional change has driven the institutionalization of environmental management in the region.

Most constitutions compel a government to ensure that its citizens enjoy fundamental rights, such as the rights to life, justice and, increasingly, to a clean and healthy environment, which are then implemented through legislation. Potentially, constitutions provide a powerful tool for individuals or groups seeking to protect the environment. However, even where constitutions do not formally place an environmental duty on the state, courts across Latin America have often recognized environmental rights and duties under other constitutional provisions.

Today all Latin American countries acknowledge in their constitutions environmental protection in some way and the recent constitutional texts in countries such as Venezuela (1999), Ecuador (2008) and Bolivia (2009) requires these states to ensure legal, political and economic pluralism to reflect natural and sociocultural diversity (see UNEP 2010). Bolivia's "Law of Mother Earth" of 2011 aimed to establish parity between human and natural rights (see Box 3.2).

In general, the pattern of extending public administration to the environment has followed similar lines of top-down change, typically beginning with a new constitutional provision to protect the environment and then by the establishment of a comprehensive general framework law and a strategic policy, from which further detailed legislation flows thereafter. Yet, the environmental ministries and agencies of Latin America and the Caribbean operate in new democracies that remain weakly institutionalized, meaning environmental institutions in the region face a range of problems:

- ***Rapid institutional change***. Institutional structures in Latin America have in the past been prone to rapid and ill-planned changes that can disrupt their work and obstruct ambitious proposals from being acted upon.

- ***Lack of authority and legal clarity***. While environmental ministries in Latin American countries have generally codified violations of the law and the sanctions that will be imposed on offenders, they often lack the resources and authority to enforce these.

- ***Regulatory capture***. Environmental reform can be a sensitive political process in which policymakers come under pressure from powerful economic interests. A key risk facing environmental institutions is "regulatory capture" in which an agency responsible for developing and enforcing regulations is dominated by commercial interests and ends up advancing these against the public interest.

> **Box 3.2** Bolivia's Law of Mother Earth
>
> In 2010 Bolivia passed the world's first laws stating that nature has equal rights to humans with the so-called Ley de Derechos de la Madre Tierra (Law of the Rights of Mother Earth) which proposed 11 new rights for nature including: the right to life and to exist; the right to continue vital cycles and processes free from human alteration; the right to pure water and clean air; the right to balance; the right not to be polluted; and the right to not have cellular structure modified or genetically altered. The law also stated that nature has a right to not be affected by large infrastructure and development projects that threaten ecosystems and communities. The law formed part of a restructuring of the Bolivian legal system following the changes to the constitution in 2009 and was, above all, a statement of principles lacking legal force.

- ***Institutional overlap and co-ordination***. There may be significant unevenness in how environmental law is applied within one country.
- ***Funding constraints***. Obstacles to the establishment of effective institutions include funding limitations, and the financing of environmental protection by Latin American states has been erratic.
- ***Corruption and the rule of law***. Large corporations are drawn to countries with natural resources and may be tempted to leapfrog environmental regulations limiting extractive activities or imposing costs on them through corruption. Corruption among politicians, law enforcement officials and public officials open to bribery is a problem everywhere and Latin America and the Caribbean is no exception.
- ***Popular participation and accountability***. Popular pressure has not been a principal driver of institutional development in Latin American environmental management but has grown in importance. Institutionalizing participation in environmental decision-making has risen up the agenda in Latin America and the Caribbean.

Public policy

Environmental policymaking begins with the reality that natural resources are "public goods" that, in effect, belong to the entire community. Given this, it is the community that bears the cost if natural resources are depleted by minority interests. One of the main roles of environmental policymaking is to ensure that those interests shoulder the costs of using these resources and do not deplete them for future generations. Nonetheless, those interests will try to protect their use of resources, often in unison, and society may find it hard to counter this. At the same time, many environmental problems are complex and linked to other policy issues, such as trade or development strategy, which do not permit of simple solutions. The main trends shaping the context for environmental policymaking in Latin America and the Caribbean have been:

- ***Economic reform***. Reforms have enhanced the role played by transnational and local capital in economic policymaking and resulted in cuts to social spending and environmental policies, placing increasing pressure on nature and its resources. The export of raw materials remains the main driving force of environmental degradation in Latin American and the Caribbean.
- ***Diversity and rural–urban integration***. An emphasis on modernization combined with a lack of policies to promote rural development have led to neglect of the countryside. This, in turn, has fuelled the growth of urban populations while giving greater prominence to new stakeholders such as indigenous peoples (see Volume 2).
- ***Globalization and regionalization***. Policymaking in nation states is constrained by the forces of globalization (see Chapters 2, 5). Latin American and Caribbean countries are increasingly interdependent and address inequities of the global trading system by pursuing integration.

The way policymaking elites approach environmental issues is, in general, governed by the "traditional policy paradigm" that tends to give priority to economic growth over environmental protection (see Carter 2010). The traditional policy paradigm is reinforced by key features of Western systems: business (producers) enjoy a privileged position; governments have a sectoral structure; and elites dominate policymaking.

Producers. Today, in Latin America's most dynamic economies, business has emerged as a dominant interest that can manipulate the policy process. The discourse of producer groups has arguably been strengthened since the early 1990s by elements of the sustainable development agenda (see below). In Argentina, for example, an alliance between powerful biotechnology producers and a state that

Box 3.3 GM producer power in Argentina

The Argentine case – where biotechnology corporations operate in a context in which there is strong state support for them alongside an absence of popular opposition to what they produce – offers one example of the potential power of producer interests within the "traditional paradigm" of economic growth. Argentina has become one of the world's leading cultivators and exporters of genetically modified organisms (GMOs), accounting for more than a fifth of global genetically modified (GM) production, and is an influential player in the politics of biotechnology globally alongside the US and Canada (see James 2006). Successive Argentine governments have maintained a commitment to promote biotechnology, which played a key role in the country's economic recovery after its damaging 2001 debt crisis. One reason Argentina has embraced this technology, according to Newell (2009), is the power of agro-food corporations in the country and their role in sustaining what he terms "biohegemony". Newell argues that this biohegemony is sustained by an alliance of interests that includes big agribusiness producers and traders, Argentine exporters, multinational biotech firms, commercial banks and Argentina's state.

has embraced this technology for reasons of food and economic security means that the country has not experienced the protests seen in other countries that produce genetically modified products (see Newell 2009; Box 3.3).

Sectoral administration. In Latin America in the 1980s and 1990s, a technocratic perspective on environmental policymaking fostered the creation of ministries and agencies that treated the environment as a discrete policy area, yet gave these limited power in relation to other ministries. Technocratic perspectives can reinforce the way governments often divide responsibilities into distinct policy areas: "sectoral administration". This has tended to reproduce a policy climate which encourages economic expansion that is harmful to the environment in the long term.

Policy elites. A key concept in the study of environmental politics is that of closed policy networks or "communities" through which producer interests can enhance their influence. These networks may comprise public and private actors dependent on each other for information, funding, expertise or legitimacy. Influential actors within them seek solutions to problems that do not question principles shared by the policy community. Closed policy communities are common in sectors where environmental issues affect economic interests and the government has ties with producer groups.

The way policymaking is conducted will vary according to factors such as the profile of the main actors, the institutional structure, the sector in which policy is being developed, and the strength of the traditional policy paradigm and sustainability discourses. Three main elements shape how the power of policy elites is exercised – agenda-setting, advocacy coalitions and exogenous change:

- ***Agenda-setting.*** Levels of public and media attention to the environment fluctuates, and interest groups, the media and politicians engage in "agenda-setting" to control the policy process. Throughout Latin America growing public interest in environmental protection is reflected in an increase in news coverage of green issues.
- ***Advocacy coalitions.*** Shared ideas and information may create coalitions that compete to dominate the work of a policy community, especially where an issue is technically complex or politically contentious (see Sabatier and Jenkins-Smith 1993). In Latin America and the Caribbean, where ideas and information have overturned existing policy communities, these have often originated from outside the region.
- ***Exogenous change.*** Natural disasters or new issues such as climate change for which the dominant members of a policy community have no response may provoke radical change. Changes in international conditions – such as new treaties or economic recession – can disrupt a policy community's work. Privatization in Latin America and the Caribbean in the 1990s, for example, disrupted previous policy norms.

The complex interactions of participants in a policy process will also be shaped by institutions and political practices, which affect the roles, incentives and transactions of these actors in different ways. Policy formation is determined to a significant extent by the political institutions of a country and such factors as the nature of relationships between the executive and legislature, electoral rules, the federal structure and the judiciary's level of independence.

As the countries of Latin America have developed their environmental agendas, they have refined an array of policy tools. Policy instruments used to address environmental problems can be classified as: regulatory; managerial; economic; social; and climate change tools.

- ***Regulatory tools***. The bedrock of environmental policy in Latin America and the Caribbean is the system of general framework laws from which regulations are derived.
- ***Managerial and administrative policy tools***. Latin American governments use a wide range of managerial and administrative tools in environmental policy, with the basis of all policymaking being environmental impact assessments. "Environmental accounting", for example, is growing in importance as a planning tool, and concepts such as the "Ecological Footprint" have been taken up enthusiastically by countries and cities developing sustainable development strategies.
- ***Economic policy tools***. Support for the use of economic instruments as a more efficient alternative to regulation has grown in recent years and a range of tools can be employed to protect the environment, from traditional government spending to sophisticated instruments that harness the behaviour of the market, market-based instruments (MBIs) (see Chapter 6). However, Latin America has relatively little experience in using these instruments.
- ***Social policy tools***. Policymaking can seek to change attitudes with the long-term aim of nurturing more sustainable practices, and governments can use a range of social policy tools to achieve this, such as extending participation.
- ***Climate change policy tools***. Climate change has significant implications for policymaking and Latin American and Caribbean governments have begun to develop their own distinctive analysis of climate change and how to respond to international initiatives seeking low-carbon development (see De la Torre, Fajnzylber and Nash 2009). Given the strong tradition of government intervention in economic decision-making in Latin American and the Caribbean, governments in the region have been expected to take the lead in confronting climate change. They have gained a prominent international profile in negotiations (see Volume 2).

Foreign policy

The character of environmental degradation in Latin America and the Caribbean and how environmental governance has developed have both been influenced by the region's relationship with the outside world, making international relations a key theme in the study of environmental politics. Any discussion of the foreign policies of Latin American and Caribbean states cannot begin without acknowledging the traditional importance of the US. Relations between states in the region for most of the twentieth century were conducted under the umbrella of US predominance. A key factor in the recent evolution of those relations was the Cold War, which limited the ability of Latin American states to act autonomously in international arenas. The end of the Cold War and democratization greatly expanded the opportunities open to countries to co-operate, and since the 1990s, key themes steering foreign policymaking in the region have been autonomy, integration and globalization, often enshrined through membership of supra-national bodies such as the World Trade Organization (WTO). Since 2000, US influence in the region has declined and the creation in 2010 of the Comunidad de Estados Latinoamericanos y Caribeños (CELAC), which excludes the US and Canada, is a potent symbol of this. Enhanced activity by multilateral institutions, non-state actors and transnational corporations, social movements and NGOs have further complicated a picture of relationships traditionally based on sovereign nation states. The effects of globalization have been uneven and processes of regional integration are widening differences. A central question in globalization research is whether it leads to the convergence of political institutions, policies, the legal order and societal structures, or whether domestic responses to global challenges will continue to be determined by existing national structures. Research suggests that the diffusion of environmental policy innovations across borders occurs regularly (see, for example, Busch et al. 2005). But although many of the problems faced by Latin American and Caribbean countries are similar, there are considerable differences in how the environment is dealt with in their foreign relations agendas.

Key themes in the analysis of Latin American international relations that have an important bearing on understanding how the environment influences foreign policy include the following:

- ***Sovereignty***. Globalization is changing traditional understandings of sovereignty that reject outside interference in the domestic affairs of a nation state. Political scientists have debated the implications for the nation state of global environmental change (see Box 3.4). This is likely to transform politics in Latin America and the Caribbean.
- ***Multilateralism***. In the 1990s, following the end of the Cold War, there was a global shift in favour of multilateralism, an approach to issues in which states collaborate based on shared interests. Multilateral co-operation today includes *environmental multilateralism* – the extension since the 1970s of international environmental agreements to which Latin American states subscribe.
- ***Regionalism and integration***. Regional integration is a cherished aspiration of Latin American political elites and is an important theme in local relations. With the end of the Cold War a new spirit of continentalism was evident and its latest manifestation is the creation of CELAC and, most recently, the Pacific Alliance (Alianza del Pacífico)

Box 3.4 Environmental change and the nation state

The concept of the nation state has been inherited from the nineteenth century and has been increasingly challenged by international institutions and forms of global governance. While these do not threaten the continued existence of nation states, they limit their capacity to act in isolation. This challenges established notions of sovereignty and tests the methodological norms of disciplines such as international relations in which the nation state is the building block of the inter-state system. Global environmental change adds considerably to the challenges facing the nation state. Biermann and Dingwerth (2004) argue that global environmental change challenges the nation state in two ways: first, it adds to stresses on nation states by increasing the demand for adaptive and mitigative activities that reduce their resources and hence their administrative, organizational and technological capacity. This diminishes a state's ability to fulfil basic functions such as guaranteeing security, protecting civil rights and ensuring political participation, stretching the capacities of developing countries in particular. Second, the transboundary nature of global environmental change reduces the ability of nation states to act without the co-operation of other states and/or non-state actors – businesses, NGOs and scientists – which have assumed a prominent role in environmental politics.

aiming to create a free trade zone between Chile, Colombia, Mexico and Peru. Trade has driven integration, but the desire for greater influence in a multipolar world has also become key to this process.

- ***Natural resources and security.*** Multilateralism has eased military competition and bilateral strains in Latin America and the Caribbean, although territorial and maritime border tensions have not disappeared and there are disputes over natural resources
- ***The transboundary nature of environmental issues.*** Environmental problems do not respect national frontiers, meaning conservation strategies must emphasize co-operation. The cross-border nature of environmental issues in Latin America is also reflected in the creation of transboundary protected areas. These are examples of a contemporary challenge to the notion of sovereignty, demand new forms of co-operation, and can even help in resolving disputes.
- ***The transnational environmental movement.*** International ENGOs have played an important role in the policy response of governments in Latin America and the Caribbean to the environmental agenda, and have extended their activities throughout the region (see below; Kaimowitz 1996). A regional environmental movement has also emerged.

The trend toward globalization has reduced barriers to growing international trade and investment flows. Trade policy has huge implications for the environment because most economic activity originates in natural inputs (metals and minerals, soil, forests and fisheries). However, the environment and trade represent two distinct bodies of international law, with environmental law embodied in multilateral agreements and as national and sub-national regulations and trade law embodied in such structures as the WTO and regional and bilateral agreements. These are interacting and overlapping: increasingly, international environmental law defines how countries structure economic activities and trade law defines how they design domestic policies in areas such as investment and environmental protection (UNEP/IISD 2005). A key feature of trade opening in Latin America has been the proliferation of regional integration initiatives such as NAFTA. Since NAFTA came into force in 1994, countries in the Americas have included environmental provisions in many bilateral and sub-regional trade agreements (FIDA 2008). While the relationship between free trade and the environment remains contested, there is recognition that policy imbalances favour the interests of large corporations at the expense of environmental protection. However, the WTO has gradually been giving more attention to climate change and refining its rules on the environment (see WTO/UNEP 2009). The structure of international environmental regimes follow several core principles:

- ***Prevention***. It is expensive and difficult to rectify environmental damage once this has occurred so it is better to avoid it in the first place.
- ***Subsidiarity***. Decision-making should occur at the lowest level of government or political organization that can act effectively.
- ***Common but differentiated responsibility***. Not all countries are equally to blame for past environmental damage, and they have different capabilities for tackling it.
- ***"Polluter pays"***. Polluters should pay for the environmental damage they cause.
- ***Precaution***. While Latin American and Caribbean countries must often make environmental policy in the face of uncertainty, a lack of scientific evidence cannot justify inaction.
- ***Openness***. Transparency and public participation in policymaking are necessary for good environmental management.

Environmental law is a large and growing area of national and international jurisprudence and some of the basic principles of this branch of law are:

- ***Sovereignty***. Ideas about sovereignty in international environmental law relate principally to resource use. The Stockholm and Rio Declarations assert that states have "the sovereign right to exploit their own resources pursuant to their own environmental policies" but requires them to ensure this does not damage their environment or that of other states (see Clemons 2009).
- ***Co-operation***. States have a duty to co-operate on environmental issues and to be good neighbours. The duty to co-operate is a key principle underlying international water law, for example, without which it would be impossible for states to fulfil obligations under treaties.
- ***Equitable utilization***. Environmental diplomacy has been dominated by questions of equity, yet this concept is contested and at the

heart of haggling over such as issues as binding emission-reduction targets. Equitable utilization is the cornerstone of international law on transboundary watercourses.

- ***Precaution***. Global environmental politics has strengthened the importance of the precautionary principle that instruments such as the Cartagena Biosafety Protocol and those on ozone and climate change have applied to problems still characterized by scientific uncertainty. The precautionary approach does not halt harmful action but lowers risk.
- ***Sustainable development***. This has become an important concept in international environmental law, asserting that states have an obligation to develop in a way so as to preserve resources for future generations (see Chapter 6).

Green parties

Parties exist to compete for power, are the main agents for representing social interests and offer citizens the ability to hold governments to account for what they have done (see Scartascini et al. 2011). Parties influence policy by aggregating interests in society, impose order on competing groups and demands, offer voters a choice between rival policies and enable communication between a government and society. In legislatures, they organize business and influence the conduct of representatives. They act on the policymaking process by advancing political programmes and influencing relations between executive and legislature (Scartascini et al. 2011). In Latin America and the Caribbean, democratization provided the context for the emergence of green parties by permitting new political forces and activism to converge, especially around the 1992 Earth Summit in Rio (see Hochstetler and Keck 2007). Democratization put parties at the centre of political activity in most of Latin America and the Caribbean.

Green parties began to emerge in Latin America during the processes of democratization that began in the late 1970s. In some of the larger countries, such as Mexico and Brazil, they rapidly became a feature of the political landscape, and in some cases have had a significant impact on politics. Yet their fortunes have wavered, and in most of the region green parties remain minor or yet to obtain legislative seats. Nonetheless, greens have become potent advocates of environmental protection and sustainable development. Moreover, despite their size and hitherto marginal role, Latin America's greens have been at the heart of co-operation among ecology parties globally. The formation of green parties remains a recent development in the politics of most Latin American and Caribbean countries. In some countries, such as Brazil and Mexico, their development has been stable and grounded in social activism. In countries where a few dominant, traditional parties coexist alongside a large number of smaller and provincial parties and electoral alliances, such as Chile, Uruguay and Argentina, it has been more difficult for green parties to take hold nationally. New parties either struggle to survive or are still being launched and these small parties are often concentrated in one region or city and extend their reach nationally only gradually.

The forms in which green parties developed can help to explain their different characteristics and how their positions vary, and a number of factors have contributed to their emergence:

Foreign and regional models. Green parties in Europe offered models for Latin America at a time when authoritarian regimes were beginning to crumble. Party formation has sometimes gone hand in hand with involvement in regional groups such as the Federación de Partidos Verdes de las Américas (FPVA, Federation of Green Parties of the Americas) created in Mexico City in 1997.

Social movements. The main impetus for the creation of green parties in Latin America came from social movements concerned about the environment that had their origins in civil society mobilization against authoritarian rule (see below). However, the transition from movement to party is a complex process and moving from demonstrations to formal party structures with democratic decision-making processes is difficult (see Rabelo 1998).

Political reforms. The reform of laws and rules to establish or reinforce democratic politics has been an important feature of political development in Latin America since the late 1970s and was a factor in the emergence of green parties. Easing obstacles to party registration and removing penalties that exist for poor performance in elections encourages the formation of new parties.

In Latin America and the Caribbean parties formed by indigenous communities to advance their interests and distinctive world view incorporating ecological principles must also form part of any discussion of political ecology. Parties representing indigenous people have emerged in a number of countries in the region and have had an important influence on politics.

Green parties in Latin America and the Caribbean share a commitment to sustainable development and equitable social policies that are put forward by similar parties elsewhere. Beyond their ecological commitments, support for democracy and criticisms of development models, several features recur in their platforms:

- ***Political centrism***. Traditionally political debate in Latin America and the Caribbean has been shaped by disagreements influenced by social class. In many cases green parties have originated among urban social movements whose leadership has been in the hands of middle-class activists and scientific ecologists taking advantage of a political opening and the decline of class-based politics. Just as the objectives of social movements were often local or confined to a single theme, in many cases green positions did not fit neatly into established left–right divisions.

- ***Alternative politics***. The reluctance of green parties to position themselves on a traditional left–right spectrum has been heavily influenced by ideas from Europe, especially by the "new left". In the 1970s, this term sought to distinguish the reformist positions of leftwing parties and movements from earlier, mainly Marxist organizations motivated by a rigid class-based understanding of society. Reformist parties adopting the new left position have aimed to capture the support of minorities marginalized for reasons that cannot obviously be explained by class, such as women and indigenous or black people.

- ***Ecology***. Issues of ecology help to explain the origins of the social movements that gave rise to green parties in Latin America and the Caribbean, but have not always dominated their programmes. One reason for the greens' limited focus on environmental issues is that parties are often formed around locally specific issues, and this can pose difficulties when they need to take a national approach.

- ***Economic equality and sustainable development***. Green parties such as the PV in Brazil have tended to assume "red–green" positions that combine a socialist or social-democratic vision of greater equality with environmental protection.

- ***Localism***. Localism is a prominent theme in the platforms of green parties. This focus on the local sometimes supports the promotion of participative democracy. Brazil's PV, for example, advocates participative democracy through national, regional or local referendums, and extensive policies to educate citizens in ecological values (Partido Verde Brazil 2011).

Incomplete democratization coupled with the constraints of economic development has limited the extent to which environmental parties can influence politics, complicating the organizational, institutional and ideological obstacles faced by greens when they try to mobilize in systems dominated by class-based parties. Other political factors continue to constrain the growth of green parties, not least the development by mainstream parties of their own green platforms. Significant divisions have sometimes developed within and between green parties, and in some countries several ecology parties have competed for representation. The merits or demerits of party formation can be clearer when considered alongside the general level of environmental awareness in a country. In some cases, the high profile of environmental issues themselves can limit the growth of political environmentalism. Costa Rica's Partido Verde Ecologista (PVE Green Ecological Party) has struggled to establish its presence in a country where environmental awareness is high and the mainstream parties have all developed green agendas (see below). Moreover, having a party may not be essential to advance the cause: even in the absence of a party or electoral success environmentalists can still influence policy. A number of formal and informal limitations on political expression and mobilization handicap efforts by environmental groups to mobilize support:

- ***Regulations and thresholds***. Political parties have to obey regulations that affect their behaviour and performance which are included in constitutions, statute laws, electoral codes and even executive decrees. A key issue in the development of green parties has been the level at which thresholds for parties to register have been set. Although Latin American thresholds are not highly restrictive, the most well-established green parties in Mexico and Brazil have nonetheless both fallen foul of registration procedures.

- ***Seat allocation formulas***. Formulas for allocating seats – the ratio of votes to seats for each party – can work alongside thresholds to constrain small parties. Where a formula awards seats to parties winning small proportions of the vote, this should promote the formation of new parties and improve their electoral performance, but where a formula favours larger parties this is likely to inhibit them.

- ***Voting systems.*** Proportional representation (PR) is more likely to encourage new and minority parties than majoritarian systems because it lowers obstacles to them entering the system and increases choice for voters. PR is used throughout Latin America, usually in mixed systems in which half of the legislature's lower chamber is elected in a single-member district (see Van Cott 2005). However, voting systems have in practice tended to constrain minor parties.
- ***Decentralization.*** Levels of decentralization vary throughout Latin America and the Caribbean but most countries hold direct municipal or regional elections. Decentralization has created conditions more favourable to the rise of green political groups and the creation of new electoral districts can also encourage the formation of indigenous parties.
- ***Censorship.*** The abandonment of formal censorship has been a key indicator of political liberalization in Latin America but direct and indirect forms of censorship, self-censorship and bias persist and can limit environmental mobilization.
- ***Political violence.*** In Latin America the candidates of minor parties and environmental activists can be at risk of violence and intimidation. In Brazil, for example, in 2011, in the Amazonian state of Pará, at least eight environmental activists were murdered by gunmen.

Social movements and NGOs

In the last few decades Latin America and the Caribbean has experienced new levels of mobilization outside the formal institutions of politics as social movements have become a focus of activity. A key characteristic of civil society is diversity and social movements today range from environmental groups and organizations of indigenous people to human rights organizations and feminists. Although civil society played a significant role in democratization, its political role has since become more complex and some scholars have suggested that it is now more limited in its ability to influence politics (see Foweraker 2001). A key theme of debate has been the relationships betweens social movements and political parties, which have often sought to control them as a source of competition. It has also been suggested that social movements may be at an advantage over parties in areas such as the environment because they can identify problems, suggest solutions and mobilize without the need for a formal political infrastructure. Pressure from civil society and organized social movements has made environmental awareness an important part of the language of governance in Latin America and the Caribbean. Governments are also more willing to enforce strict regulations to ensure that corporations extracting natural resources do not harm the environment. Social movements have generated a theoretical literature because they do not easily fit the traditional understanding of protest in terms of factors such as class or ideology (see Slater 1985; Tarrow 1994).

The context within which social movements emerged is important for understanding them. The economic crisis of the 1980s and ensuing neoliberal reforms had a significant impact on marginalized groups. At the same time, Latin American states were undergoing democratization leading to greater inclusiveness and freedom to organize. This context of diminishing economic opportunities alongside the strengthening of rights to participate shaped social movement activities (Roper, Perreault and Wilson 2003). Key social movements characteristic include:

- ***Rejection of traditional political structures***. Social movements operate outside institutionalized channels and challenge traditional definitions of citizenship, democracy and participation; traditional forms of rule by dominant classes and political interests; and traditional hierarchies.
- ***Formation of transnational networks***. The evolution of social movements has been determined by the emergence of a global civil society, and they often forge transnational links (Brysk 2000). Environmental campaigns in Latin America have often been transnational, reflecting alliances between national organizations across frontiers and the cross-border nature of many environmental disputes.
- ***Cultural discourses***. Study of new social movements has often focused on identity and cultural politics (see below and Volume 2). These organizations have sometimes articulated a form of solidarity linked to identities such as ethnicity or gender.
- ***Neoliberalism and globalization***. Globalization has often been associated with social movement mobilization because the pressure to become integrated into global markets affects diverse social sectors.

> Popular mobilization in Latin America and the Caribbean can often be understood as a response to the impact of global economic forces because rural populations experience neoliberalism in terms of decreasing access to land or environmental destruction.

During the 1970s, incipient environmental mobilization at the grassroots level was occurring in just three Latin American countries – Brazil, Mexico and Venezuela – but by the 1980s mobilization was extending across the region (Viola 1997). The profile of environmental movements has grown as part of the democratization process, often in a relationship with indigenous movements, although the ideas of these two groups do not always coincide. Key issues facing the environmental movement today are its heterogeneity, disagreements among groups over values, expectations and demands, and a lack of consensus about policy priorities. Some groups argue that economic globalization and social inequality are the main causes of environmental degradation. The term "environmental justice" – which brings together broader issues of global injustice and local concerns about the environment – has grown in use as a way of addressing ideas that link inequality and environmental degradation in Latin America and the Caribbean (see Carruthers 2008b). Environmental social movements are intrinsically multi-sectoral, fostering linkages between a large and diverse number of indigenous, peasant, public health, labour, student and urban popular groups.

Environmental NGOs (ENGOs) also form an important part of the landscape of green movements in Latin America and the Caribbean. NGOs are private organizations funded either by voluntary contributions through membership, donations from larger organizations or self-financing (Foweraker, Landman and Harvey 2003). They have played a crucial role in shaping attitudes towards the environment and pushing issues up policy agendas (Torres 1997). NGOs often transcend traditional political and class boundaries by incorporating participants from diverse backgrounds and relying on a diversity of benefactors. They tend to be pragmatic and more inclined to co-operate with government than to oppose it, and, by linking ecological and economic concerns in Latin America and the Caribbean, they have attracted participants who were previously not interested in ecological issues (see Price 1994). In Latin America and the Caribbean early ENGOs originated as conservation groups. ENGOs have been studied according to several typologies and research has differentiated between those that work for change within governance institutions and those that adopt a more confrontational stance.

Indigenous movements have become an important focus of study in the politics of Latin America. About 50 million people within 800 linguistic groups maintain indigenous lifestyles in Latin America which are often communitarian and rural. Most indigenous communities live in peasantized, agricultural areas such as Mesoamerica and the Andes and all of them exhibit high levels of poverty and inequality (see Hall and Patrinos 2005; World Bank 2005). Indigenous groups have been mobilizing to demand recognition of land rights since the nineteenth century, but since the 1970s a more politically self-conscious movement has emerged across Latin America and forged international links. Rising indigenous consciousness has pushed issues such as cultural diversity and autonomy up the political agenda. In recent years indigenous people have played a prominent role in environmental protests, articulating common responses to the unsustainable extraction of natural resources and putting forward new perspectives on development. Indigenous movements combine material and cultural demands as part of a broader opposition to economic and political exclusion (Foweraker, Landman and Harvey 2003). They have often provided a unifying focus for other organizations and non-indigenous groups, particularly those on the left, around shared goals. Today they are motivated by several issues, from self-determination to political reform. The emergence of the indigenous movement has had important implications for politics in Latin America:

- ***The state***. Indigenous mobilization represents more than just a demand for greater inclusion and often amounts to an effort to redefine *statehood* (see Kay 2004). Official recognition of indigenous identity in law has implications for governance and the characteristics of democracy, implying the need for policies that meet the needs of excluded groups.

- ***Multiculturalism and national identity***. Indigenous mobilization poses dilemmas for national identity by raising questions about the past understanding of nationhood and advancing a manifesto for multiculturalism.

- ***Individual versus collective rights***. Indigenous mobilization in Latin America has generated debates about the relationship between individual and collective or social rights.

- ***Relations with formal politics, other social movements and NGOs.*** Indigenous organizations have forged significant relationships with three types of non-governmental organization: ENGOs; those addressing humanitarian and socioeconomic development concerns; and those involved in the provision of credit (see Roper, Perreault and Wilson 2003).

Environmental groups use a variety of conventional and unconventional methods to gain resources, allies and influence. Studies of the environmental movements show that they employ a broad repertoire of tactics which vary over time but found that the most frequent forms of behaviour are contacts with the media and efforts to mobilize public opinion (see Dalton, Recchia and Rohrschneider 2003). There are several potential explanations for how movements behave:

- ***Resource mobilization.*** Resource mobilization theory argues that the behaviour of social movements will be dependent on organizational resources, so resource levels differentially affect their activity (see McCarthy and Zald 1977). Having a paid staff, for example, prioritizes organizational maintenance over confrontation, meaning that resource-rich or professional organizations might tend to undertake low-risk, conventional activities while poorly funded groups relying on volunteers might engage in protest-based tactics. This suggests that ENGOs with small budgets and staffs may be more likely to undertake confrontational activities, yet data indicates that protest is more common among groups with larger staffs and budgets (see Dalton, Recchia and Rohrschneider 2003).
- ***Ideology.*** Ideology shapes how organizations understand environmental problems and respond to them, making some types of activity more likely than others. Environmental groups emphasize their ideological distinctiveness and independence from larger networks and their positions may as a result isolate them, making it more likely they will engage in unconventional activity such as civil disobedience and demonstrations.
- ***Political opportunity structures.*** Political opportunity structure theories which places an emphasis on the institutional context in which social movements exist suggest a movement will choose the most effective way of exerting influence depending on the circumstances. Several factors influence the choice of activity such as levels of democratic development, access to allies within government and a country's level of development.

Green ideology

Latin America and the Caribbean has, overall, been mainly an importer of ideas, ideology and social theory, and the Western heritage of its elites and the ties that have developed between its republics and the international capitalist economy have shaped the ways in which political thought has developed. Most of the main ideologies of the last 150 years were generated by the impact of the industrial revolution on northern European societies then superimposed upon the Iberian tradition. The character of political ideas in Latin America and the Caribbean has been shaped by several formative local themes such as centralism, liberalism, positivism and corporatism. Political culture in the region has been influenced by two broad sources of struggle: the conflict between left and right based on a loose understanding of politics as a competition between socio-economic classes; and social contestation based on identities that provide inherent or imagined sources of difference between groups. Both have important implications for the development of environmental ideas in the region.

The clash between leftwing and rightwing ideas has had an important influence upon Latin America's political evolution, and an important development since the end of the Cold War has been the effort by competitive parties to develop a centrist politics that challenges the rigidity of the former left–right spectrum. In recent years, the left has shifted towards social-democratic positions and the right towards greater acceptance of democratic pluralism, and there has been a convergence of ideas in the mainstream "centre". This decline in the force of traditional left–right poles has been a key factor in the development of environmentalism, offering the prospect of a politics that transcends past divisions that can confront non-class issues once considered marginal. In Latin America the relationship between the environment and class is more nuanced than in Europe, with evidence suggesting that in sub-regions such as Central America the causes of environmental degradation often have their origins in social relations (see Painter and Durham 1995).

There have often been strong links between the left and ecology parties, and similar views on social justice, democratization and equality have encouraged both to explore the potential of rainbow alliances and "red–green" coalitions. Overlapping but nonetheless distinctive strains of thought have emerged in efforts to reconcile positions.

The concept of human rights has become the most important theme in Latin American jurisprudence in terms of highlighting environmental degradation and seeking the enforcement of regulations. Struggles with an environmental component often take the form of efforts by marginalized groups to assert their human rights. A concept that has been of clear relevance in Latin America and the Caribbean is that of environmental justice, and the environmental justice movement built on the discourse of rights in the 1990s as democratization gathered pace. The concept of environmental justice has been understood in different ways, but what all definitions share is a concern for equity – equal rights to participate in environmental policymaking and to benefit from the distribution of environmental goods (see Box 3.5; Kütting 2004).

In developed nations – where ecologism is often driven by the ways in which modernization and development have alienated citizens from nature – environmentalism tends to emphasize conservation and quality of life issues, whereas in Latin America and the Caribbean, where environmentalism is motivated by the dependence on nature of peoples for their survival and where many environmental disputes are as much about *access* to resources – clean water, fertile land, forest resources – as about saving them, the struggle to protect nature has often been linked to the struggle for economic and social justice (see Faber 1993; Roberts and Thanos 2003; Carruthers 2008b). This marriage between the language of social justice and environmentalism often fuses imported notions with local, indigenous ideas or experiences to give rise to what has broadly been called "socio-environmentalism". In recent years the issue of climate change has provided another focus for demands for environmental justice, sometimes called "climate justice", especially among developing countries such as Bolivia (see Athanasiou and Baer 2002; Angus 2009; Building Bridges Collective 2010).

Environmental awareness in Latin America has grown alongside both the "pink tide" that has brought leftwing leaders with a more assertive social agenda to power throughout the region, and the rise of the indigenous movement, which is often associated with ideas about sustainable development. It would be surprising if there had not been attempts in the region to build bridges between socialism and

Box 3.5 Environmental justice

Schlosberg (2004) has examined different meanings given to environmental justice and argues that understanding this solely in terms of distributive justice is insufficient. Justice itself has many meanings and concentrating merely on distribution cannot encompass the diverse demands made by the global environmental justice movement, which include the recognition of cultural identity and full participatory democratic rights. Rather than seek to understand environmental justice solely as a theoretical concept, Schlosberg looks at how it is defined in practice by social groups within the highly diverse "environmental justice movement". Schlosberg argues that the justice these demand is in fact threefold: equity in the distribution of environmental risk; recognition of diversity; and participation in the political processes that create and manage environmental policy. Carruthers (2007) examined the effort to apply the language, tools or assumptions of the US concept of environmental justice in Latin America both as a discourse of popular mobilization and as a set of principles for analysis, interpretation and policy. He suggests that although there are problems applying this in countries such as Mexico, local and regional organizations and advocacy networks have successfully employed the language, images and direct-action strategies of other environmental justice campaigns and this notion offers a potent opportunity for transnational advocacy (see also Carruthers 2008a).

ecologism, and a second discernible strain of thinking that links social and environmental concerns is "eco-socialism" (see Pepper 1993). Several political experiments have aimed to marry environmental and socialist ideas, beginning with what has been called the "revolutionary ecology" of Nicaragua's Sandinista government in the 1980s (see Faber 2002). More recently, eco-socialist ideas have been attributed to the leaders and activities of socialist movements or parties that place a strong emphasis on environmental issues, such as Evo Morales in Bolivia, Rafael Correa in Ecuador and Hugo Chávez in Venezuela.

Identities provide inherent or imagined sources of difference between social groups and have also been a key source of political struggle in Latin American and the Caribbean. The region's history as one conquered and colonized by European settlers who coexisted with large indigenous and imported slave populations has always made questions of personal and group identity prominent in political and social thought. Activity motivated by identification with a national idea, ethnicity and race, or gender has become an important theme in the study of politics. Several sources of identity have been prominent in Latin American and Caribbean history:

- ***Nationalism***. Nationalist doctrine is malleable, able to coexist, inform and mine other ideologies, and environmental discourses may adopt a nationalist flavour to appeal to latent sentiments of identification (see Evans 1999). Environmentalism has the potential for coinciding with nationalist ideas that build on a sense of patriotism and the need to defend sovereignty.
- ***Religious identities***. Political ideas are often shaped by religious and cultural traditions, and there is broad recognition of the important role these play in influencing attitudes to the environment and supporting the notion of sustainable development or deterring consumerism (see Assadourian 2010b).
- ***Ethnicity and race***. Ethnic and racial themes have been prominent in Latin American thought since Conquest, and many of the great debates of the twentieth century have related to agrarian issues and, by extension, to the indigenous question. The relationship between race and the environment has grown in prominence as a theme in Latin American social movements. Some scholars such as Sundberg (2008) have even argued that the environment has been fundamental to the formation of systems of racial classification.

At heart of green politics in Latin America and the Caribbean lies the tension between environmental protection and economic development. The concept of sustainable development suggests that it is possible to enjoy growth and development while also protecting the environment. As a reformist doctrine, it is attractive to policy-makers and has become the dominant "official" discourse promoted by multilateral agencies despite ambiguity that can make it hard to translate into practical policies (see Carter 2007; World Bank 2001). It is premised on the well-established notion that environmental goods and services – such as the Earth's oceans and atmosphere – are global "commons", public goods whose consumption or use by one individual does not or should not reduce availability of that good to another or their right to use it. An important role played by the concept of sustainable development has been ideological, by broadening the popular appeal of environmentalism. The Rio Declaration of 1992 outlined 27 principles for the achievement of sustainable development (see Stoddart (2011). Key principles that inform global governance for sustainable development are:

- ***Equity***. The overarching concept of sustainable development established by the Brundtland Commission was equity: intra-generational equity (fairness to living people) and inter-generational equity (fairness to future generations). These oblige the international community to reduce inequality between and within countries and to ensure future generations have sufficient natural resources to sustain themselves (Martin 2003).
- ***Precaution***. The precautionary principle was enshrined in the Rio Declaration in 1992 and emphasizes that officials need to take a cautious approach in environmental management in order to prevent harmful activities: developers who wish to undertake a specific action must prove that their activities will not harm the environment. This principle is crucial by providing a means of overcoming the scientific disagreements inherent in environmental policymaking because it implies that a lack of certainty should never be used as a reason for postponing measures to stop the environment being damaged.
- ***Democracy and participation***. Sustainable development emphasizes the importance of democracy and participation in solving environmental problems: its requirement for equity means that as the poor shoulder a disproportionate share of the costs of environmental damage they should have access to the political process in order to address this (see Carter 2007). In Latin America and the Caribbean, the notion of democratic control of resources through sustainable development has been embraced by the left and social movements.
- ***"Polluter pays"***. This principle makes those who cause environmental pollution responsible for paying the costs of rectifying the damage and was first articulated in 1972 by the OECD. Principle 16 of the Rio Declaration obliges states to ensure environmental costs are "internalized" by polluters. The principle has important implications for the responsibilities of states and for funding solutions to environmental problems.
- ***Common but differentiated responsibilities***. This notion was broadly accepted at the 1972 Stockholm Conference but became established at Rio and refers to the need for each state to play its role in achieving

sustainable development at a global level, but also establishes that this role is different for each country according to their economic and technical capacity and past contribution to environmental degradation.

Conclusion

Strong institutions are essential for good environmental management, but too often in Latin America and the Caribbean ministries and agencies, and the political institutions that formulate and interpret policy, have been bedevilled by problems, sometimes enabling powerful corporations to dominate them with damaging consequences for the environment. Regulatory capture is a significant problem for environmental policymaking in Latin America and the Caribbean, where abundant natural resources create huge incentives to weaken environmental regulations. Although today environmental issues are routinely taken into account in development policies, green policies have generally been insufficient to halt ecological destruction in the region. This is, first and foremost, because policymakers do not generally call into question economic models based on the export of raw materials and the pressure these place on natural resources. Also, although Latin American and Caribbean countries have access to the same environmental policymaking tools available throughout the world, distinctive political, legal and administrative constraints limit what they can do in practice. International factors have played a formative role in the economic and political development of Latin America and the Caribbean and have driven environmental management in the region. Participation in global trade and the expanding reach of international environmental law enshrined in multilateral and bilateral agreements have also transformed the context in which national policy is made.

In their effort to influence policymaking, green parties in Latin America and the Caribbean face a unique set of political circumstances that can make it hard to survive. They are often small and hampered by their local origins, lack of funds and political rules designed to ensure stability between two or three large parties after many years of authoritarian rule. Alongside parties, social movements and NGOs have been key actors in the evolution of environmental politics in Latin America and the Caribbean. The heterogeneity of environmental and indigenous groups can be a strength, particularly if it enables organizations to mobilize a broad constituency of support and on that basis attract international attention. But it can also represent a weakness, providing a source of disagreements among groups over values and demands and hence a lack of consensus on policy. Differences often derive from the ideas that motivate these groups and their members. Modern political evolution in Latin America and the Caribbean has been shaped by the contest between leftwing and rightwing ideas based on the underlying motif of class and fashioned by struggles over development strategy. These ideas, in turn, have been informed by the politics of identity in a region of considerable diversity, where the emphasis has been upon nationhood, religion or ethnicity and race. Coherent modern ideologies that have ecology as their main focus are, relatively speaking, newcomers to the region's ideological landscape. This means environmentalism has had to evolve and coexist with the dominant themes of class and identity that, in many instances, continue to sideline it. However, growing attention to environmental problems globally has created opportunities for champions of environmentalism to influence public opinion. One indication of the success they have had has been the way in which multilateral agencies and governments have embraced the agenda of sustainable development, which has become something of an orthodoxy in governance at every level.

Recommended reading

Barcena, Alicia, et al. 2011. "Sustainable Development in Latin America and the Caribbean 20 Years on from the Earth Summit: Progress, Gaps and Strategic Guidelines", LC/L 3346, August 2011, 2011-457. New York: United Nations. Available online at www.eclac.org/rio20/noticias/paginas/9/43799/REV.Rio+20-Sustainable_development.pdf [accessed March 2014].

Barkdull, John and Paul G Harris. 2002. "Environmental Change and Foreign Policy: A Survey of Theory", *Global Environmental Politics*, Vol. 2, No. 2 (May), pp. 63–91.

Baud, Michiel, Fabio de Castro and Barbara Hogenboom. 2011. "Environmental Governance in Latin America: Towards an Integrative Research Agenda", *European Review of Latin American and Caribbean Studies*, 90 (April), pp. 79–88.

Chambers, W Bradnee and Jessica F Green (eds). 2005. *Reforming International Environmental Governance: From Institutional Limits to Innovative Reforms*. Tokyo: UN University Press.

Dangl, Benjamin. 2010. *Dancing with Dynamite: Social Movements and States in Latin America*. Oakland, CA: AK Press.

Díez, Jordi and Susan Francheschet (eds). 2012. *Comparative Public Policy in Latin America*. London: University of Toronto Press.

Hochstetler, Kathryn and Margaret E Keck. 2007. *Greening Brazil: Environmental Activism in State and Society*. Durham, NC: Duke University Press.

Peet, Richard and Michael Watts (eds). 1996. *Liberation Ecologies: Environment, Development, Social movements*. London: Routledge.

Useful websites

Asociación Interamericana para la Defensa del Ambiente (AIDA, Inter-American Association for Environmental Defense): www.aida-americas.org/front

Climate and capitalism online ecosocialist journal: http://climateandcapitalism.com/

Comisión Centroamericana de Ambiente y Desarollo (CCAD, Central American Commission on Sustainable Development): www.ccad.ws/

Commission for Environmental Co-operation (CEC) (North American countries): www.cec.org/

Comunidad de Estados Latinoamericanos y Caribeños (CELAC): www.celac.gob.ve

Earth System Governance Project: www.earthsystemgovernance.org/

ECOLEX database on environmental law (FAO, IUCN and UNEP): www.ecolex.org

Ecosocialist International Network: www.ecosocialistnetwork.org/

Federación de Partidos Verdes de las Américas (FPVA, Federation of Green Parties of the Americas): http://fpva.org.mx/

Foro Interamericano de Derecho Ambiental (FIDA, Inter-American Forum on Environmental Law): www.oas.org/dsd/fida/

Fórum Brasileiro de ONGs e Movimentos Sociais para o Meio Ambiente e o Desenvolvimento (FBOMS, Brazilian Forum of NGOs and Social Movements for the Environment and Development): www.fboms.org.br

Foundation for Deep Ecology: www.deepecology.org/movement.htm

Global Greens: www.globalgreens.org/

Indigenous Knowledge and Peoples (IKAP): www.ikap-mmsea.org/index.html

Instituto do Homem e Meio Ambiente da Amazônia (IMAZON, Institute for the People and Environment of Amazonia): www.imazon.org.br/

International Institute for Sustainable Development (IISD), Latin America and Caribbean Regional Coverage: http://larc.iisd.org/

International Network for Environmental Compliance and Enforcement, Directory of Web Sites of Environmental Agencies of the World, Americas and the Caribbean: www.inece.org/links_pages/onlineresourcesEnvironmentalagencies.html

International Work Group for Indigenous Affairs (IWGIA): www.iwgia.org/environment-and-development/sustainable-development

REDD-monitor.org: www.redd-monitor.org/tag/cdm/

Rio+20 Institutional Framework for Sustainable Development: www.earthsummit2012.org/conference/themes/institutional-framework-for-sd

Stakeholder Forum, an international organization working to advance sustainable development and promote stakeholder democracy at a global level: www.stakeholderforum.org

UN Commission on Sustainable Development (CSD): www.un.org/esa/dsd/index.shtml

UN Non-Governmental Liaison Service (LIN-NGLS): www.un-ngls.org

UNESCO Decade of Education for Sustainable Development 2005–14. http://unesdoc.unesco.org/images/0014/001416/141629e.pdf

UNFCC: http://unfccc.int/2860.php

Vitae Civilis (the Vitae Civilis Institute for Development, Environment and Peace): www.vitaecivilis.org.br/

Worldwatch Transforming cultures blog: http://blogs.worldwatch.org/transformingcultures/

CHAPTER FOUR

Development and globalization

THE NATURAL ENVIRONMENT in Latin America and the Caribbean is highly diverse and abundant, and, like every part of the world, confronts many problems, most of which are different from those of other regions only in terms of scale and detail. The environmental conditions that prevail in the region – and the specific challenges that it faces – can mostly be attributed to the forms taken by economic development over centuries, a defining feature of which, particularly since the nineteenth century, has been its relationship with the global economy. Today, the term "globalization" often provides a way of characterizing the many trends and problems buffeting all societies and economies (see also Chapter 5). Globalization poses multiple environmental challenges in the developing world and prompts questions about the degree to which these are made more difficult to address by their specific relationship with the global economy and the rapid changes they have undergone in recent decades (see Díez and Dwivedi 2008). There is no doubt that globalization has incalculable implications for Latin America and the Caribbean. International trade and financial flows mean that its economies have become progressively more integrated with the global economy with dramatic consequences for the issues that require an environmental policy response by governments such as land use, agricultural practices, biodiversity and infrastructure development. Globalization has spurred a massive movement of species between and within regions of the world, and is influencing every aspect of environmental management, putting governments under pressure both to resist measures that they consider may be obstacles to growth yet to subscribe to an agenda on sustainability increasingly addressed by multilateral arrangements. Moreover, globalization – or, at least, the global frame of reference that it provides for the critical debate about climate change – can also be a valuable way of approaching the many complex environmental issues that prevail in a region such as Latin America and the Caribbean. Climate change offers a single prism with which to understand regional ecological challenges in a *systemic* way. This chapter examines some of the main environmental challenges facing Latin America and the Caribbean in key thematic areas – land-use and forests, biodiversity, water and marine environments and urban stress and air pollution – then turns to climate change and how it is likely to affect these existing challenges.

Land degradation

Land degradation is the result of soil erosion, exhaustion or the loss of nutrients, and the accumulation of toxic substances, often because of changing land-use patterns and bad management. The Global Assessment of Land Degradation and Improvement (GLADA) project estimated that nearly one-quarter (24 per cent) of the world's land area was undergoing degradation, as measured by a decline in ecosystem function and productivity, over the period 1980–2003 (Bai et al. 2008; CBD 2010). According to GLADA, 14 per cent of the world's land degradation occurs in Latin America and the Caribbean, affecting about 150 million people. The problem is most serious in Mesoamerica, where it affects 26 per cent of the land, while in South America degradation has affected 14 per cent; Guatemala has the highest proportion of degraded land in the region (more than 51 per cent of its territory) followed by Uruguay (49 per cent) (UNEP 2010). Every country in Latin America and the Caribbean is affected by soil degradation and this is aggravated by droughts and floods. Some of the worst affected areas are on the agricultural frontier in fragile ecosystems, such as the edges of the Amazon forest, and the result of human activities such as deforestation, livestock-raising and gold mining. GLADA data from 1982 to 2002 suggest that if degradation trends continue until the end of the century 66.3 per cent of the territory of Paraguay, 62 per cent of Peru and 57.2 per cent of Ecuador will become degraded (ECLAC 2010). In the Caribbean, seasonal variations in rain and droughts followed by torrential rains exacerbate soil erosion. On Hispaniola, there has been extreme land degradation and loss of biodiversity, especially in Haiti, where population pressure is heaviest (ECLAC 2007a; UNEP 2010). Degradation ranges from desertification in low-lying tropical areas to severe damage caused to arid soils in the altiplano at high altitude (see Box 4.1).

Land degradation can compromise extensive areas rapidly and is mostly irreversible. Poor irrigation, deforestation, excessive grazing, poverty and political instability can all make land less productive. Loss of plant cover due to changes in land use produces microclimatic effects and increases the vulnerability of communities to natural disasters, extreme weather events and climate change (Lambin, Geist and Lepers 2003; UNEP 2010). Intensive land use has had a significant effect on biodiversity and land degradation also removes a crucial means of removing carbon dioxide (CO_2) from the atmosphere (see Bai et al. 2008). The way land is used is influenced by a complex interaction of factors.

Agriculture and forestry. One of the most important processes driving global environmental change is changing soil use associated with agriculture. Worldwide, agricultural production for human food and animal feed has tripled since 1961 (FAO 2007a). This has generated two trends: deforestation as land is brought under cultivation; and the abandonment of marginal agricultural land that can promote the recovery of ecosystems in areas with poor soils. Nearly 30 per cent of all land in Latin America and the Caribbean is suited to agriculture, although total cropland, excluding pastures, represents less than 10 per cent of the total area (UNEP 2007, 2010; Canziani and Diaz 2000). Agriculture remains a crucial source of export income, occupies up to 40 per cent of the economically active population and is essential for food. Brazil and Argentina have the most land devoted to agricultural production, which is dominated by intensive agro-industrial farming that has led to considerable degradation (Seixas and Ardila 2002, ECLAC 2007a). Tropical areas such as the Amazon have been significantly affected by farming (Lambin, Geist and Lepers 2003). Some countries over-use their land: in Mexico, about 19 per cent of national territory is suited to agriculture, yet in 2005, nearly 55 per cent of it was being used for some kind of agricultural production (Mas et al.

Box 4.1 Desertification

Desertification is an extreme form of damage to soil as a result of climatic variation and human activity. Desert or arid lands, which account for about a quarter of the area of Latin America and the Caribbean, are sensitive to inappropriate soil use and over-exploitation. Reports to the UN Convention to Combat Desertification (UNCCD) suggest that Latin American and Caribbean countries are affected by significant levels of desertification, coastal erosion, drought and natural disasters. According to the UN's Food and Agriculture Organization, desertification threatens about 30 per cent of the region (FAO 2008). About 10 per cent of Brazil's semi-arid areas (98,000 km^2) have been very seriously affected, in Mexico degradation had affected about 560,000 km^2 by 2006, and in Bolivia 41 per cent of national territory is threatened by desertification (MMA Brasil 2000; SEMARNAT 2006; MDSP Bolivia 2000). In 2003, it was estimated that losses to 11 Latin American and Caribbean countries from desertification amounted to $27 m (ECLAC 2007a).

2004, FAO 2008). Social and legal factors, such as shifts in land rights, can drive changing land use patterns (see Sunderlain, Hatcher and Liddle 2008; UNEP 2010).

Extractive activities: mining and hydrocarbons. Mining for metals, minerals and coal has always been a significant economic sector in Chile, Argentina, Peru, Colombia, Brazil and Mexico, and is growing rapidly in Bolivia. In 2010, mining and quarrying accounted for 2.6 per cent of GDP in the region, but in some countries it accounts for a much greater proportion (see ECLAC 2011c; Highfield 2011). Mining is important not only because of the revenues it generates in world commodities markets, but because it is a major source of foreign investment. Other activities such as machine production "cluster" around it. Foreign investment in the Latin American and Caribbean mining sector has increased 400 per cent since 2000, now stands at about $10 bn per year, and in Peru grew by more than 1,000 per cent in the 10 years to 2009 (Bebbington 2009; Bebbington and Bury 2009). Yet, since colonial times, mining has been one of Latin America's most polluting activities. It has a significant impact on other natural resources such as water, forests and soils, and generates polluting waste. Modern mining requires huge volumes of water for separating minerals from rock, a process that also often involves the use of toxic substances like cyanide. Breaking up rock also releases toxic substances that can be carried downstream. Mining can cause deforestation, loss of plant cover and soil erosion; alters how water basins function; and can disturb organic soils (Jiménez, Huante and Rincón 2006). In Latin America and the Caribbean, small-scale and often illegal mining is also a major source of pollution. The use of mercury to extract gold and minerals has damaged the Amazon since the 1990s (see Sponsel 2011). Rising mineral prices since 2007 have resulted in huge levels of investment in the mining sector in Latin America, and new projects are generating environmental conflicts (see Box 4.2). Some NGOs monitor mining activities, such as the Observatorio de Conflictos Mineros de América Latina (OCMAL, Observatory of Mining Conflicts in Latin America). Some governments in the region are now even prepared to turn down mining projects because of environmental concerns. In June 2013, for example, the government of the Dominican Republic rejected a request by Glencore Xstrata to explore nickel in a mountainous area after accepting advice from the United Nations Development Programme (UNDP) that voiced concerns about its environmental impact.

Oil and gas extraction play an essential role in development, forming key productive sectors in Mexico, Venezuela, Ecuador, Brazil, Bolivia and increasingly Cuba and Argentina. Latin America and the Caribbean has over 10 per cent of the world's oil reserves and carries out about 14 per cent of production, yet accounts for just 8.3 per cent of consumption (UNEP 2010) The economies of countries such as Mexico and Venezuela – the region's main oil exporters – are highly dependent on the extraction of fossil fuels. The region also contains more than 4 per cent of the world's natural gas reserves and is responsible for 6 per cent of gas production, mainly in Argentina and Bolivia, while accounting for 6 per cent of consumption (IEA 2008, 2009; Omar Farouk 2007). Oil drilling can incur high environmental costs ranging from the transformation of land-based and marine ecosystems to the damage caused by spills and leakage, discharges by tankers, broken pipes, waste from oil platforms and discharges from inland activities as wastes are transported to the sea by river. An example of the potential scale of this damage came in late 2011 when

Box 4.2 Mining disputes in Peru

In Peru, in late 2011, José de Echave, the deputy environment minister, resigned amid violent protests against the country's largest ever mining project – the $4.8 bn (£3.1 bn) Minas Conga open-cast gold and copper mine in the northern Cajamarca region. He condemned environmental impact studies on the project as weak, outdated and lacking in credibility. Shortly afterwards, the US-based Newmont Mining Corporation – the majority partner in the Minera Yanacocha joint venture – said it was halting construction of the project in an effort to ease tensions. The move exposed divisions within the administration of President Ollanta Humala and highlighted how weak institutions unable to ensure that decisions are made on the basis of robust information can undermine green policymaking. Plans by Yanacocha to divert water from four mountain lakes into new reservoirs generated protests by local farmers. Yanacocha said steps proposed in the project's environmental impact assessment (EIA) – that was approved by Peru's water authority and energy and mines ministry – would protect water supplies but a review of the project by the environment ministry stated that the plans would destroy ecosystems. Peru has been the scene of recurrent protests over mining. In 1999, representatives of more than 1,200 communities in nine regions formed the Confederación de Comunidades del Perú Afectadas por la Minería (CONACAMI, National Confederation of Communities Affected by Mining) to counter the negative environmental impact of mining and large gaps in regulation (see Poole 2010a). Zeltsman (2007) has examined cases of serious environmental pollution caused by mining in Peru. In 2000, for example, a truck travelling to the Yanacocha gold mine at Cajamaraca spilled 332 pounds of mercury along 25 miles of highway, including Choropampa, a small market town on the mine's outskirts. Zeltsman argues that after the incident 2,000 adults and children at Choropampa endured the effects of mercury poisoning (see also Boyd and Cabellos 2002).

Brazilian prosecutors said they would be demanding $10.6 bn from the US oil company Chevron for environmental damage caused by oil spill in the Frade oil project, 370 km off the coast of Rio de Janeiro (bbc.co.uk 2011).

Pollution. Intensive farming that uses chemical inputs, waste products and machinery all pollute agricultural land and water systems. In

Latin America and the Caribbean the use of fertilizers and pesticides is associated with a number of environmental and health problems. Pollution has a significant impact in developing economies by generating healthcare costs and reducing labour productivity. Intensive agriculture is also thought to cause about 25 per cent of the world's CO_2 emissions, 60 per cent of its methane gas emissions and 80 per cent of nitrous oxide emissions. Regional statistics on the use of pesticides are hard to come by, but in Central America, for example, fertilizers are used heavily (UN 2010a, 2010b; UNEP 2010). Large US chemical manufacturers dominate the export of biocides to Central America. Companies in the developed world have also at times exported waste to parts of Latin America and some sub-regions (such as Central America) have been the target of dumping (see Faber 1993). In 2012, for example, a UK company admitted illegally exporting non-recyclable household waste to Brazil against OECD regulations. However, pollution has also resulted from political decisions. In Colombia's Andean region huge areas that include natural reserves have been deliberately defoliated by Plan Colombia targeting drug crops.

Land use is highly sensitive to market conditions and policymaking, and degradation can result from changes caused by the geopolitics of trade or price fluctuations on commodity markets, which influence agricultural practices (see Chapter 5). The main foreign market for Latin American and Caribbean agricultural exports is China (soya), followed by the US (fruit, sugar and flowers) and the EU (fruits and oilseeds) (ECLAC 2007b). Policymaking responding to market conditions can create incentives that change land use. Rising prices of soya, for example, have increased its importance at the expense of food crops, resulting in policies in countries such as Argentina, Brazil, Paraguay and Bolivia that encourage the expansion of large monocultures in order to meet foreign demand (see Box 4.3). This "agriculturalization" whereby areas once used for livestock are converted to agricultural use and monoculture displaces other crops, results in deforestation and increases migration to urban areas. Food security concerns are also changing land use, leading some Caribbean countries to convert marginal-soil areas to farming using agrochemicals. Cattle ranching has also grown in significance and between 1990 and 2007 the head of livestock in Latin America and the Caribbean increased from 326 million to 392.3 million (UNEP 2010). Ranching and grazing degrades natural vegetation, deforestation rates tend to match increases in

Box 4.3 Soya farming transforms Paraguay

Abramson (2009) has examined the growth and impact of soya farming in Paraguay, where industrial soya production has expanded rapidly, generating social conflicts. Paraguay is the world's fastest-growing producer of soya beans and the fourth-largest soya exporter in the world, and in 2007 soya covered 6.2 million acres of the country. This expansion is the result of rising demand for meat, and hence cattle feed, in China, and the growing biofuel industry in Europe. The soya boom has displaced small farmers occupying government-allotted public forest land which Abramson argues the Paraguayan government has given away or illegally sold to political allies in the soya bean industry and foreign corporations, including Brazilian producers. The result is increasing concentration of land: today, about 77 per cent of Paraguayan land is owned by 1 per cent of the population. Since 1990, about 100,000 small-scale farmers have migrated to cities, and about 9,000 rural families are evicted by soya production each year. Moreover, 85 per cent of the soya produced in Paraguay is genetically modified and produced using large volumes of chemical inputs. Paraguay's soya boom has generated significant peasant resistance to agro-industry. Land reform has become the most important political issue and was a priority of President Fernando Lugo (2008–12). It was as a result of a violent clash between landless farmers and police trying to evict them that Paraguay's legislature voted to impeach Lugo in June 2012, a move denounced across the region as a de facto coup.

livestock, and cattle ranching can also threaten food security (see ECLAC 2007a; Bekoff 2003).

Deforestation

Forests are crucial natural resources providing materials for building, tools, products such as paper, fuel, food, medicinal plants, and shading for crops such as coffee and cocoa. Forests are also essential for regulating climate and limiting the impact of extreme weather phenomena. They are a crucial filter in watersheds to ensure clean water and are also the most important providers of terrestrial carbon storage and hence vital in the battle against climate change. Tropical forests are particularly important, representing about 40 per cent of the world's forested area but containing about 60 per cent of forest biomass. Forests also contain 90 per cent of the world's terrestrial biodiversity (see GFN 2010; Pollard 2010; Canziani and Diaz 2000).

The loss of forest cover has been identified as one of the most significant environmental issues in Latin America and the Caribbean. There are 9 million km^2 of forest cover in the region representing about 45 per cent of its area, and its tropical forests account for about 22 per cent of global forest coverage (see FAO 2005; UNEP 2010). Tropical and sub-tropical forests shape the Latin American and Caribbean climate, play a huge role in global carbon storage, contain a major share of the world's plant and animal species and are economically essential for millions of people.

Forest cover in Latin America and the Caribbean has declined over the long term as a result of economic development, causing considerable ecological problems (Silva 1997). Between 1990 and 2005, the Latin American and Caribbean share of the world's forests fell from 24.1 per cent to 23.2 per cent (UN 2010a; UNEP 2010). The region has the second highest rate of net loss of forest among regions in the world, with annual losses between 2000 and 2005 averaging 0.5 per cent – nearly three times the global average (UN 2010a; UN-DESA 2009; UNEP 2010).

There is no single universal cause of forest loss and deforestation is the result of a combination of complex factors and disruptions to historical patterns of land use. In Latin America and the Caribbean, the expansion of agricultural and livestock activities and logging have, historically, been the main threats to forests while the expansion of infrastructure for urban development and tourism are also causes. Given this range of potential explanations, it is important to acknowledge the economic, political and social factors that make deforestation likely, from changes in peasant livelihood strategies to the incentives of political elites and corruption (see McCarthy and Tacconi 2011). A number of socio-economic causes of deforestation have been identified by scholars:

- ***Economic development***. State-led industrialization and national development strategies, often involving large multinationals, caused much of the deforestation that occurred prior to the 1980s. Economic reforms in the 1980s created private-sector incentives to expand extractive activities and land-use, escalating deforestation. Rising world prices for commodities such as tropical timber have fuelled deforestation (see McCarthy and Tacconi 2011).

- ***Population pressures***. Population growth and urbanization increase demand for food and income, encouraging people to convert forests to agricultural use or grazing for livestock. Deforestation is aggravated by peasants' need of wood for fuel, and urbanization and the growth of shanty towns on the outskirts of cities can also degrade fuelwood sources.
- ***Political factors and policy***. McCarthy and Tacconi (2011) have assessed studies that have investigated the relationship between types of political regimes and rates of deforestation based on a presumption that in more democratic states deforestation is less likely (see also Scrieciu 2007). In Latin America, democratization has been accompanied both by rapid economic development and also the growth of the private sector, both of which are implicated in forest loss. Deforestation often highlights underlying issues of policy failure, a lack of enforcement of regulations, corruption, and the influence that large corporations may have over policymaking, "regulatory capture" (see Simms and Reid 2006).

Another significant cause of deforestation in Latin America and the Caribbean is fire, including arson. Forest plantations in countries such as Chile face a considerable fire risk in periods of drought, and it is common for peasants to clear forest by burning it. Nearly 3.3 million hectares were lost to fire in Latin America and the Caribbean between 2000 and 2004, for example (FAO 2007a; UNEP 2010). Forest fires can have political repercussions: in Chile, wildfires in 2012 caused tensions after authorities blamed the indigenous Mapuche of causing a blaze in Araucania, a region beset by land conflict.

Deforestation damages biodiversity and ecosystem services such as the supply of water in aquifers, and changes in the ecology of forests can result in soil erosion, silted streams and dried river beds, and the extension of coastal dunes and sandbanks at the mouths of rivers. Alongside its impact on biodiversity, there is evidence that deforestation in Brazil is also influencing plant traits themselves, by causing trees to produce smaller, weaker seeds that are less likely to regenerate. Deforestation in Latin America and the Caribbean also contributes to global warming and is estimated to be responsible for 48.3 per cent of the global CO_2 emissions associated with changing land use, nearly half of which originate in Brazil (UNEP 2007). The Amazon rainforest has become the global symbol of the relationship between deforestation and climate change (see Box 4.4; see also Kozloff 2010).

Box 4.4 Deforestation in the Amazon

The Brazilian Amazon has been identified by Lambin, Geist and Lepers (2003) as the largest tropical arc of deforestation in the world, with average deforestation of about 17,000 km²/year in 1988–2000, 22,000 km²/year in 2001–05, approximately 12,500 km²/year in 2006–08, and an estimated 7,000 km²/year in 2009 (see also Malhi et al. 2008; INPE 2009). Deforestation rates have varied significantly since 2009 (see Table 4.1).

In 2010–11 rates of deforestation began to rise again rapidly, an increase associated by many experts with the passage of a controversial new forestry law that imposed a deadline on an amnesty for past deforestation, encouraging landowners to clear land quickly before this began. Cumulative deforestation of the Brazilian Amazon accounts for about 17 per cent of the original forest area. Even the achievement of government targets for an 80 per cent reduction in annual deforestation by 2020 would bring cumulative loss to nearly 20 per cent (CBD 2010). The effects of climate change are also likely to modify the structure of the Amazon basin and the way it functions. Rising CO_2 levels will warm Amazonia leading to "dieback" in some areas (Vergara and Scholz 2011). There is rising uncertainty about changing weather patterns in the Amazon; severe drought in 2005 was followed by record flooding in 2009 and drought in 2010.

Table 4.1 Deforestation in the Legal Amazon, 2000–11 (km²/year)*

State/year	1988 (1)	1995	2000	2005	2007	2009	2010	2011	Accumulated, 1988–2011
Amazonas	1,510	2,114	612	775	610	405	595	502	20,045
Maranhão	2,450	1,745	1,065	922	631	828	712	396	23,266
Mato Grosso	5,140	10,391	6,369	7,145	2,678	1,049	871	1,120	135,345
Pará	6,990	7,845	6,671	5,899	5,526	4,281	3,770	3,008	132,007
Rondônia	2,340	4,730	2,465	3,244	1,611	482	435	865	53,066
Total Legal Amazonia	21,050	29,059	18,226	19,014	11,651	7,464	7,000	6,418	392,201

* Selected states and overall total

Notes
1. Average 1977–88

Source: Instituto Nacional de Pesquisas Espaciais (INPE), Brazil, 2011 (www.obt.inpe.br/prodes/prodes_1988_2011.htm).

Although concern about deforestation and species extinction in the Brazilian Amazon is often seen as contemporary to growing global environmentalism in the 1980s and 1990s, for more than a century competing groups have fought over the area (see Figure 4.1). Violent conflicts over land are considered an indicator of deforestation in the Amazon, and these have increased as Brazil has grown into an agricultural superpower. The battle lines over Brazil's new forest code reveal the contemporary face of these disputes – between farmers anxious about the cost of compliance with environmental laws alongside advocates of land reform; and a loose coalition of environmentalists and carbon investors seeking to monetize conservation of the forest (see Chapter 6). The Amazon's role in regulating global climate has strengthened the case for projects that reward sustainable management of forests. The Brazilian government's Amazon Fund was created in 2008 and by late 2012 was worth $361m.

Figure 4.1 Extent of accumulated deforestation in the Brazilian Amazon up to 2011

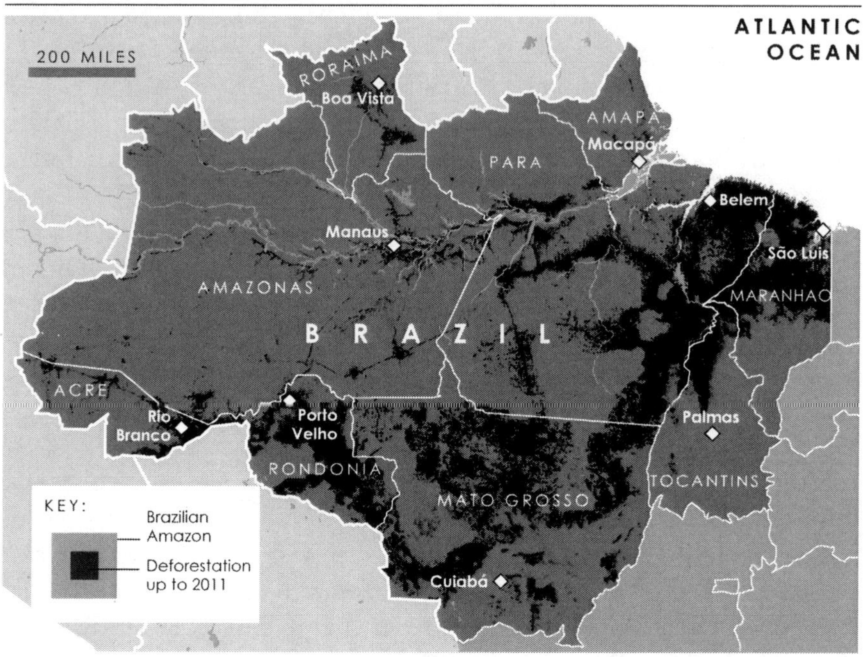

Source: IMAZON, Desmatamento na Amazônia Legal até 2011. (www.imazon.org.br/mapas/desmatamento-acumulado-2007-2010/desmatamento-acumulado-na-amazonia-legal-ate-2011/view).

If forestry policies are unfair or regulations are not enforced, this can generate social conflict. In Honduras, activists have long claimed that timber concessions granted to a powerful logging industry take priority over water conservation and the livelihoods of farmers in areas such as the Río Telica Valley east of Tegucigalpa (see Simms and Reid 2006).

Biodiversity

Biodiversity, the variability among living organisms, is key to the functioning of ecosystems and underpins the services they provide that enable human survival. Latin America and the Caribbean is home to an immense variety of ecosystems and is considered one of the planet's most significant repositories of biodiversity. Although the region constitutes only 15 per cent of the Earth's surface, it is home to 20 per cent of the terrestrial, marine and fresh water ecoregions identified by the World Wildlife Fund (WWF) as priority areas for global conservation (UNEP 2010). The Amazon River is the world's largest single source of fresh water runoff and the Amazon's hydrological cycle is a key driver of global climate. The Pantanal (Brazil, Bolivia and Paraguay) is the largest wetland area in the world. Latin America and the Caribbean is one of the world's richest regions in terms of forest diversity, has a huge variety of grasslands, shrub lands and deserts and is the second most diverse region in the world for vascular plant species (FAO 2009; Canziani and Diaz 2000; Mittermeier et al. 1997; Hillstrom and Collier-Hillstrom 2004; UNEP 2010). Animal life in the region is highly diverse and six countries (Brazil, Colombia, Ecuador, Mexico, Peru and Venezuela) have been included among the world's 17 megadiverse countries that are home to 70 per cent of the world's species of mammals, birds, reptiles, amphibians, plants and insects, and most of its moist tropical rainforests, coral reefs and high-priority ecosystems. (UNEP 2010; see Table 4.2). The greatest density of amphibian species in the world are found in Mesoamerica.

So diverse is the region that new species are still being discovered: in 2010, 10 new species of frogs were found in the forests of Darién, Colombia, and 30 new species of frogs and salamanders in Ecuador (UNEP 2010). The Amazon Basin alone contains 40,000 plant species, 427 mammals, 1,294 birds, 378 reptiles, 427 amphibians, 3,000 fish

Table 4.2 Number of known species in Latin America and the Caribbean as a percentage of the total number of known species in the world

	Total known species	Species in Latin America and the Caribbean	Percentage of world total
Birds	9,990	4,110	41
Mammals	5,847	1,791	30
Amphibians	6,347	3,148	50
Reptiles	8,734	3,060	35
Fish	30,700	9,597	31

Sources: UNEP 2010; IUCN (www.iucnredlist.org/mammals); Birdlife International (www.birdlife.org); Frost 2008. *Amphibian Species of the World: An Online Reference* (http://research.amnh.org/vz/herpetology/amphibia/index.php); Uetz 2008. *The Reptile Database* (www.reptile-database.org); Froese and Pauly 2008. *FishBase* online publication (www.fishbase.org).

and a million identified insect species (Simms and Reid 2006). A huge variety of fish and marine mammals can be found along the region's coasts.

The biodiversity of Latin America and the Caribbean has played a crucial role in human development because of the large number of food species and economically important varieties that originated and diversified there (see Casas et al. 2007; Brack 2003; MacNeish 1992). Its people have played a disproportionately important role in capturing value from nature. Pre-Columbian farmers domesticated or manipulated at least 118 economically important plant species, and, globally, a fifth of the 100 species that form the main basis of agricultural production – including maize, wheat, barley, rice, beans, soya and cotton – come from Mesoamerica, and a quarter from the Andean region of Peru (UNEP 2010). Biodiversity is also crucial for controlling diseases by providing the sources of medicines, and also plays a significant role in controlling climate.

However, research suggests that the population size and geographic range of the majority of species is declining (CBD 2006). The Living Planet Index (LPI) developed by World Wide Fund for Nature (WWF) and UNEP's World Conservation Monitoring Centre (UNEP-WCMC) monitors the state of biodiversity by tracking trends in animal populations, and this shows a 28 per cent global decline in biodiversity health since 1970 (WWF 2012). The tropical Living Planet Index declined by more than 60 per cent from 1970 to 2008, reflecting widespread land-use changes and industrialization across Latin America since 1970 and, in the case of amphibians, the spread of fungal disease (see Pollard 2010). Similarly dramatic declines have also been identified in the Marine Living Planet Index and the Freshwater Living Planet Index.

The biodiversity of Latin America and the Caribbean is at particular risk from human activity, with the region home to five of the 20 countries with the greatest number of endangered species of fauna and seven of the 20 countries with the greatest number of endangered plant species (IUCN 2008a, 2008b, 2008c; UNEP 2010). In 2012, for example, the last giant tortoise of Pinta Island in Ecuador's Galápagos islands died, confirming the extinction of this sub-species. In 2008, the Red List Categories and Criteria of the International Union for Conservation of Nature (IUCN), which assesses extinction risks, showed that in Latin America and the Caribbean a total of 8,931 species of mammals, birds, reptiles, fishes, molluscs, other invertebrates and plants were either critically endangered, endangered or vulnerable, and amphibians are particularly at risk (Vié, Hilton-Taylor and Stuart 2009). Latin America and the Caribbean is also among regions with the greatest number of endangered, threatened or vulnerable tree species (see FAO 2005; FAO 2007a; UNEP 2010).

Human activities strain biodiversity, which decreases as demographic pressures and consumption levels rise (see CBD 2006; Firor and Jacobsen 2002). In Latin America, the most important cause of habitat loss has been the expansion of large-scale commercial agriculture for export products such as soya, biofuels, beef cattle, fruits, vegetables and cut flowers (World Bank 2007; UNEP 2010). According to the Intergovernmental Panel on Climate Change (IPCC), the greatest threat to biodiversity in South America is deforestation and forest degradation (see above; Magrin et al. 2007; UNEP 2010). Growing demand for fresh water by rising populations is placing an unsustainable burden on habitats. Loker (2004) examined landscape transformations in El Cajón, Honduras, caused by construction of a large dam and drew attention to a dramatic decline in forest cover and growing dependence of agricultural systems on agrochemicals.

Water: fresh water

Providing good water supplies is a challenge facing much of the developing world. Access to clean water is uneven and in the developed world its use is wasteful. In developing countries, population growth and rising consumption levels mean demand for fresh water is growing. The Stockholm Environment Institute (2005) predicted a large increase by 2025 in the proportion of the world's population living in countries of significant water stress – the lack of a sufficient supply of fresh water for domestic use, agriculture and industry. However, in many places river basins and wetlands are being damaged making them less able to provide supplies and maintain ecosystems.

Latin America is rich in fresh water systems and large river basins, which are essential to aquatic and terrestrial ecosystems, biodiversity and human livelihoods from fisheries, aquaculture and tourism. The Latin American and Caribbean region has about 31 per cent of the planet's 35 million cubic kilometres of fresh water resources while being home to only 10 per cent of the population (UNEP 2010). After Europe, Latin America and the Caribbean has the largest number of basins with rivers that cross national borders (61), and the Amazon river basin channels water from eight countries and the La Plata River Basin from five. The Andean countries and Brazil include the world's largest watershed, with the Amazon discharging nearly 20 per cent of the fresh water that the earth's rivers empty into the sea. Groundwater is an important source of fresh water, and the region has 64 aquifers. High average annual rainfall give Latin America nearly 40 per cent of the planet's total renewable water resources. Waterways have become crucial to regional development by offering a valuable transportation network and a key source of energy. The region also possesses nearly a quarter of the world's hydroelectric potential.

Yet, despite abundant resources, Latin America and the Caribbean still faces important challenges to guarantee everyone access to clean and safe water. A lack of infrastructure, investment and weak institutional and regulatory frameworks affect how water is used. Needs are growing: available data shows that per capita consumption of water in countries such as Mexico has risen considerably since 1980 (see OECD 2008). Areas such as northern Mexico, north-eastern Brazil, coastal Peru and northern Chile have major difficulties meeting their water needs, and about two-thirds of Latin America is arid or semi-arid (Canziani and Díaz 2000). Rainfall – and hence the availability of fresh water – varies considerably across the region. Inadequate and inefficient water infrastructure inhibits growth and a lack of dams and reservoirs to cope with floods and droughts can result in high losses in human life and a wasteful use of water resources. Central America, for example, is prone to hurricanes, floods and droughts which have a considerable impact on water infrastructure and economic development, and of the region's 40 million people, 70 per cent live on the Pacific coast where just 30 per cent of the water resources are available. This means that access to drinking water and sanitation is uneven, with rural populations often highly disadvantaged. Severe shortages have also at times affected many densely populated areas such as Chile's Central Valley, the Cuyo region in southern Argentina, and coastal areas.

Potable water through household connections is available for 80 per cent of the region's population, but about 50 million people still lack access to it (UNEP 2010). About 125 million of the region's inhabitants also lack access to adequate sanitation facilities (WSP 2007). The quality of provision also varies enormously, and water supplied to urban shanty towns and many rural areas is often not suitable for drinking. Variation in levels of access to safe drinking water and adequate sanitation can often be a reflection of an urban–rural divide or social class. Economic crises and earthquakes and floods also affect infrastructure, further limiting maintenance and water quality in cities such as Managua and Havana. In Latin American and the Caribbean, urban wastewater is usually discharged into rivers or lakes without having been treated and this often affects neighbouring non-urban areas. The provision of wastewater treatment varies considerably and some countries have very low treatment rates such as El Salvador (3 per cent) and Haiti (5 per cent), whereas others have high rates such as Santiago in Chile (80 per cent) (WSP 2007; UNEP 2010).

Much of the available water supply in Latin America and the Caribbean is used for agriculture and raising livestock, industry, power generation and mining (see UNESCO-WWAP 2006). Irrigation is growing, particularly in Mexico, but its efficiency varies considerably. Rapid population growth in rural areas combined with uneven land ownership can exacerbate these problems.

Pollution of fresh water resources poses major risks to human and environmental health, especially in cities. Industrial effluent is often untreated and contains heavy metals such as mercury and lead which can be carried along rivers into the sea, affecting both riverine and marine ecosystems. In July 2013, in Jalisco, Mexico, for example, tens of thousands of dead fish washed up on the banks of a reservoir at Acatlán de Juárez, which hundreds of local fishermen are dependent upon for their livelihoods, after a local firm dumped huge volumes of molasses into a canal that flows into it. Throughout Latin America effluent treatment is frequently inadequate in the mining, petrochemical, fishmeal and cannery industries. In the Caribbean, cruise line operators often dump waste at sea to avoid paying for waste treatment. Sometimes different pollutants all come together. On the Patos/Mirim Lagoon system on the border between Brazil and Uruguay, estuarine habitats that once provided Brazil with fish are threatened by rice cultivation that uses water from the lagoon. Biocides and fertilizers are used in the rice paddies and contaminated runoff pollutes water supplies and increases treatment costs.

Water: marine resources

Coastal and marine resources in Latin America and the Caribbean provide important ecosystem services and biodiversity but are being profoundly affected by human development.

Coastal areas. Much of Latin America and the Caribbean's growing population is migrating to large cities and coastal areas in search of work. Pressure on coastal ecosystems is leading to the loss of biodiversity and increased sedimentation from erosion, and this in turn places fisheries and tourism sectors under pressure. Coastal lagoons and estuaries, tidal mudflats, and sandy and rocky shores are all being affected by pollution. The degradation of coastal and marine ecosystems has reduced the coverage of kelp forests, sea grasses and corals which provide nursery areas for juvenile fish and crustaceans act as filters and stabilize sediments. In the Caribbean, land reclamation and coastal and port construction associated with tourism have caused major damage to sea grass beds and reduced water clarity. Construction in fragile coastal areas can destroy biodiversity: in July 2012, for example, conservationists reported that bulldozers called in to redirect a river that was eroding Grande Riviere beach on Trinidad's northern coast in front of a hotel used by tourists to watch leatherback turtles had crushed thousands of turtle eggs and hatchlings. The impact of urbanization on coastal areas of South America resulted in the Declaration of Santa Clara in Argentina in 2005 in which fishermen, NGOs, scientists and indigenous groups expressed concern about unregulated development in coastal areas.

Wetlands. Latin America and the Caribbean has 227 "Ramsar" sites – designated as significant under the 1971 Convention on Wetlands of International Importance – covering an area of about 36 million hectares, with the largest in Mexico, Peru and Bolivia (UNEP 2010). Wetlands include mangroves and saltwater coastal lagoons, highly productive ecosystems along sheltered tropical coastlines. Rising demand for timber and unsustainable harvesting of wood from them, construction and aquaculture are putting mangrove forests under strain, and about 20 per cent of mangroves in Latin America and the Caribbean have disappeared since 1980 (Valiela Bowen and York 2001). Commercial shrimp farming in countries such as Mexico also threatens mangroves (see Box 4.5). In the Brazil Current region and Caribbean, tourism and marinas, golf courses and airports are destroying mangroves. The high productivity of coastal wetlands and sea grass beds mean they are important for carbon sequestration in sediment, biomass and plants and animals. Their loss can potentially lead to the release of large amounts of stored carbon.

Coral reefs. The Caribbean contains two important barrier reefs: the MesoAmerican reef (MAR) system which extends about 1,000 km along the coasts of Mexico, Belize, Guatemala and Honduras, and a smaller reef north of Providencia Island (Colombia) in the south-west. Extensive fringing reefs also parallel much of the coast of Cuba and encircle smaller Caribbean islands. The wider Caribbean region contains about 7 per cent of the world's coral reefs and over 1,000 species of coral. Humans use these as sources of food, construction materials and medicines and they attract tourism. Reefs are threatened by overfishing, pollution, dynamiting, disease, bleaching by warmer sea temperatures as a result of climate change and ocean acidification linked to higher concentrations of dissolved CO_2 (CBD 2010). More than a third of the Caribbean's coral reefs are within 2 km of the coast, putting them at risk from development, sedimentation, overfishing

Box 4.5 Commercial shrimp farms threaten mangroves

Call (2003) has examined the struggles of environmentalists and coastal communities in Union Hidalgo in Oaxaca, Mexico, and Champerico in Guatemala against commercial shrimp farmers which have often resulted in violence. Commercial shrimp farms grew rapidly everywhere in the 1980s and 1990s to meet rising demand in the US and Japan for shrimp. The aquaculture industry looked to Latin America for coastal sites, including Ecuador and Mexico. According to Call, in 1998, the production of shrimp farms surpassed that of artisan fishermen for the first time in Mexico. At Union Hidalgo and other indigenous villages many local people make their living catching fish and shrimp in coastal lagoons or harvesting palm products, firewood or salt from wetlands. Coastal communities that depend on local ecosystems fear the impact on the environment of intensive shrimp farming, which has often destroyed tropical mangrove forests. Shrimp farms require artificial nutrients, pesticides, antibiotics and fresh and salt water and emit large quantities of these along with shrimp excrement. In the 1990s, shrimp farming was promoted by the Mexican government as part of a World Bank-funded plan and by 2002 there were 51,800 acres of artificial shrimp ponds in the country. Disputes over these projects have increased, often sparked by disagreements over land tenure.

and pollution. The coverage of coral in the Caribbean Basin has declined by as much as 10 per cent in the last three decades (Gardner et al. 2003; UNEP 2010). As with land-use, the main cause of damage to the marine environment is economic development:

- ***Tourism and urban development***. Tourism is vital for the economies of many Latin American and Caribbean countries and in the Wider Caribbean Region accounts for about a quarter of GDP. It leads to the construction of marinas, dykes and ports and Latin America's attractive beaches have seen tourism complexes proliferate. Resorts worsen pollution levels by increasing the quantity of wastewater and runoff emptied into coastal waters (UNEP 2010).
- ***Overfishing and aquaculture***. The Latin American and Caribbean seas contain some of the most important saltwater fisheries in the world and are of great economic importance (see FAO 2007b; Valbo-Jorgensen Soto and Gumy 2008). However, increasing demand in

international markets has led to over-fishing, and fisheries are also under pressure from destructive catching methods – often responding to government policies – and pollution. In the Caribbean Sea, rising production has meant one-third of fish species are thought to be overexploited (UNEP 2010). In Chile, in mid-2012, hundreds of small-scale fishermen clashed with police during demonstrations in Valparaiso against a new law setting out quotas that they said favour industrial fleets. Aquaculture has also grown rapidly in Latin America and the Caribbean, where production rose from 722,000 tons in 2002 to 1 billion tons in 2006 (FAO 2008; see also FAO 2007b). Both marine and land-based aquaculture farm non-native species using intensive production techniques that can spread diseases to wild stocks.

- ***Pollution***. Sea pollution has become a serious concern in sub-regions such as the Caribbean and is caused by human activity in coastal areas: oil discharges and spills, the transport of agrochemicals, waste from industry and hydroelectric plants discharged into rivers, untreated urban wastewater and waste and bilge water from boats (see Burke and Maidens 2004).
- ***Invasive species and diseases***. Globalization has spurred a massive movement of species between regions of the world in ballast water and sediments, and the introduction of invasive species can have a serious impact. In Venezuela, for example, predatory trout, tilapia and some larger mojarras have been introduced as food but compete strongly with native species. In Mexico, the suckermouth armoured catfish from the Amazon, popular for use in aquariums, has changed some aquatic ecosystems (UNEP 2010).

Cities

Latin America is the most urbanized part of the developing world, and about 79 per cent of the region's population is concentrated in urban areas and cities account for 90 per cent of economic activity (Simms and Reid 2006; UN-HABITAT 2007; UNFPA 2008). The region is unusual for having the highest proportion of its population living in "mega-cities" of 10 million or more inhabitants, and the largest of these are: Mexico City (18.1 million), São Paulo (17.9 million) and Buenos Aires (12 million) (UN-HABITAT 2011a, 2011b; see also Sá 2007). More than 60 per cent of the population of Latin America and the Caribbean lives in smaller cities of less than one million inhabitants, which often grow fastest (UN-Habitat, 2008; UNEP 2010). Migration from rural areas has driven urban growth and is the result of factors such poverty and the demand for public services. Given the importance of cities in Latin America and the Caribbean, the quality of life for citizens living in them has become a key theme in politics (see Lora et al. 2010). Visible characteristics of many cities in the region are poverty and inequality and a high proportion of its urban population suffers from deprivation (UNEP 2010). Migrants from the countryside usually settle in marginal or informal urban areas that are unplanned and lack basic services and infrastructure (see Lloyd-Sherlock 1997). By 2005, informal settlements were home to about 27 per cent of the region's population, more than 117 million people; in 2001, in Brazil alone, about 42 million people lived in shantytowns (UN-HABITAT 2008; Simms and Reid 2006). Poverty, rapid growth, weak institutions and poor policymaking mean Latin American and Caribbean cities face serious environmental problems.

Water and sanitation. Supplying clean drinking water for residents is one of the key challenges facing rapidly growing cities, which often over-exploit limited resources (see above). Economic crises and events such as earthquakes and floods can damage infrastructure and limit the supply and quality of water in cities such as Managua and Havana. Shanty towns face recurrent problems of poor sanitation. Lack of access to water threatens the health and livelihoods of families and penalizes marginal residents who may have to pay higher prices for water of poorer quality. These problems are exacerbated by policy weaknesses, and the development of water and sanitation infrastructure is directly related to the investment capacity of local and central governments as well as their rating policies and ability to collect charges. Outdated infrastructure can be a matter of life and death: in 2007 and 2010, for example, two enormous "sinkholes" appeared suddenly in different parts of Guatemala City and swallowed up buildings, killing at least three people.

Air quality. Air pollution has a high-profile in Latin America and the Caribbean and imposes significant health and economic costs on society. About 100 million people in the region are exposed to air pollution close to World Health Organization safe levels. A "Green City Index" compiled by *The Economist* (2010) that looked at indicators on environmental performance in 17 major Latin American

Box 4.6 Air and water in Mexico City

The size and location of Mexico City confronts authorities with significant policy challenges in managing air quality and providing water and sanitation. The Mexico City Metropolitan Area (MCMA) has experienced a huge increase in population during the twentieth century and today is home to about 20 million inhabitants and 40,000 industries. About four million vehicles on the city's streets consume more than 40 million litres of fuel a day and produce thousands of tons of pollutants. The MCMA sits on the bed of the former Lake Texcoco in the Valley of Mexico surrounded on three sides by mountains. Its mild climate and altitude expose residents to high levels of ozone and secondary particulate matter. Transportation constitutes 37 per cent of emissions within Mexico City itself and emissions from nearby urban areas also contribute to the MCMA's problems. Alongside the risk to residents of the city itself, Mexico City generates about 20 per cent of the entire country's greenhouse gas emissions, and 2.1 per cent of the emissions of Latin America as a whole (Simms and Reid 2006). Barkin (2004) examined the problem of water shortages in Mexico City and how these have been exacerbated by poor policies, but domination of the country's political system by one party, the Partido Revolucionario Institucional (PRI), was a key factor explaining the problems of air pollution and water shortages. The policies of the PRI over generations bolstered the growth of urban areas, which represented a valuable source of political support. After the PRI lost control of the mayoralty of Mexico City in 2000 to the opposition Partido de la Revolución Democrática (PRD, Party of the Democratic Revolution), significant progress was made on improving environmental conditions. In 2007, under Mayor Marcelo Luis Ebrard Casaubón (2006–12), Mexico City drew up and published a 15-year cross-disciplinary Green Plan (Plan Verde) with the backing of the World Bank and UN that developed integrated policies on public spaces, waste handling, land use, transport and sanitation.

cities suggested that only five (Belo Horizonte, Brasilia, Medellín, Quito and Curitiba) meet WHO guidelines on levels of sulphur dioxide, nitrogen dioxide and particulates in the air. Pollution levels are influenced by topography, weather, demography, transportation networks, fuel quality and usage, industrialization, and development

Table 4.3 Latin America and the Caribbean: total motor-vehicle fleet, 2002–08, selected countries*

	2002	2003	2004	2006	2007	2008
Brazil	–	35,932,607	38,270,718	–	48,899,365	–
Chile	2,147,796	2,180,759	1,742,161	2,617,564	2,783,792	2,979,454
Guatemala	–	979,425	1,053,098	1,302,272	1,558,145	–
Mexico	19,966,132	21,238,641	20,878,438	24,830,598	26,747,197	29,114,072
Panama	315,122	342,527	357,215	372,427	390,350	406,788
Venezuela	2,092,000	2,173,000	2,466,000	–	4,044,012	–

* Includes passenger vehicles, buses, trucks, vans and motorcycles.

Source: *ECLAC, Anuario estadístico de América Latina y el Caribe 2011*, Microsoft Excel file "3.8 Transporte/Transport; 3.8.1.2 Parque automotora/Motor-Vehicle Fleet a/" (www.eclac.cl/publicaciones/xml/7/45607/LCG2513b.pdf).

levels. In Mexico air pollution and other environmental issues such as water provision is exacerbated by both geography and politics (see Box 4.6).

Air pollution also affects smaller cities and about 85 million people live in other urban areas such as Arequipa, Bogotá, Fortaleza, Lima, Medellín, Santiago and San Salvador that have at times not met WHO guidelines (PAHO 2005). Economic development has resulted in a large increase in the number of vehicles in use, especially in cities, often far exceeding population growth (see ECLAC 2007a; see Table 4.3). Between 1970 and 1980, the total motor vehicle fleet in Latin America and the Caribbean increased by 137 per cent (an annual average of 9 per cent) compared with growth of the global motor fleet of only 67 per cent (an annual average of 5.3 per cent); between 1980 and 1990, the number of vehicles in Latin America and the Caribbean increased by 47 per cent (an annual average of 4 per cent) while the global figure was 42 per cent (an annual average increase of 3.6 per cent) (Onursal and Gautam 1997). Transportation emissions are made worse by the use of old, badly maintained vehicles.

The generation of electricity, industrial processes, water treatment and the use of consumer products also contribute to air pollution. Industry, mining activities and oil drilling can be major sources of emissions, and according to the Organización Latinoamericana de Energía (OLADE, Latin American Energy Organization), 19 per cent of CO_2 emissions are released by the industrial sector (UNEP 2010).

Exposure to air pollutants has been linked to an increased risk of mortality and morbidity, including respiratory and cardiovascular diseases, especially in children and the elderly.

Waste disposal. As populations have grown and industry and commerce have expanded, cities have generated ever larger amounts of waste, although comparative data suggests that Latin American countries are not among the worst offenders globally when it comes to generating municipal (mainly domestic) waste (see OECD 2010). Bad waste management can have a significant impact on human health and the environment. In Mexico City, for example, a central artery of the drainage system is a 29-mile ditch, mostly above ground, called the Grand Canal, which carries sewage and rainwater out of the city. Rapid population growth long ago overwhelmed its capacity and management of the canal and the 13,000 gallons of sewage generated in the city every second has become a major public health concern. Solid waste management is a critical issue throughout Latin America and the effectiveness of waste collection and final disposal systems varies considerably and is tied to a country's financial constraints. In Haiti, the region's poorest country, just a third of household waste is collected and the rest is thrown into ravines, drainage canals or on to the streets. Nonetheless, Latin American and Caribbean cities have made strides in improving waste management and while informal recycling is still common, whereby poor people pick through dumps for things of value, there has been progress in regulating recycling (see Godoy 2012). In Mexico City, for example, a "barter market" was launched in 2012 whereby residents give recyclable rubbish to government employees in return for vouchers they can exchange for vegetables grown by farmers on the outskirts of the city.

Climate change

Global warming is the most pressing issue facing humanity and assessments of the Intergovernmental Panel on Climate Change (IPCC) have concluded that global warming is unequivocal and temperature increase is widespread across the planet (see IPCC 2007; Spray and McGlothlin 2002). The IPCC has pointed to rising sea levels and observed decreases in snow and ice, significant changes in rainfall patterns and increases in the area affected by drought and intense tropical cyclone activity, and has argued that many natural systems are being affected by regional climate changes, particularly rising temperatures. Most scenarios project that greenhouse gas (GHG) concentrations will increase between now and 2100, thereby raising average global temperatures, but by how much and how quickly remains a matter of debate. In 2011, the International Energy Agency (IEA) warned that the world was likely to build so many new fossil-fuelled power stations, factories and inefficient buildings over the next five years that it would become impossible to hold global warming to safe levels (see Harvey 2011). In the same year, the US Department of Energy warned that the global output of heat-trapping CO_2 jumped by a record amount in 2010 to the extent that levels of GHGs are higher than the worst case scenario outlined by climate experts just four years previously (see Associated Press 2011). In 2012, the Organization for Economic Cooperation and Development (OECD) said GHG emissions could rise 50 per cent by 2050 without more ambitious climate policies (see Chestney 2012). Studies suggest that warming will not be evenly distributed around the world: land areas will warm more than oceans; high latitudes will warm more than low latitudes; most of North, Central and South America are likely to warm more than the global average; and in most areas winter will warm more than summer. These changes will have a huge impact on human society, and their political repercussions could include the creation of up to 1 billion "environmental refugees" by 2050.

Climate change can provide a lens through which all other environmental issues can be understood because it favours an approach to understanding issues as part of a system in which contributing factors cannot be understood in isolation. This has been an underlying premise in the development of the concept of environmental governance that requires the adoption of coherent multilateral management in a range of key areas by a large number of stakeholders (see Box 3.1).

In Latin American and the Caribbean, climate change is already having a significant effect on ecosystem goods and services and has risen up the agenda of public policies. Academic scrutiny of this issue has gathered momentum throughout the region in recent years (see, for example, Honty 2011). Latin America is not considered to be a main contributor of the GHGs that are causing climate change, so far

Table 4.4 Latin America's contribution to greenhouse gas emissions compared to the developed world

	Population (millions)	GDP ($US billions – 2005)	Electricity consumption (kWh/capita)	CO_2 emissions (Mt of CO_2)*	CO_2 emissions per capita (t CO_2/capita)
World	6,825	50,942	2,892	30,326	4.44
OECD	1,232	37,494	8,315	12,440	10.10
Non-OECD Americas**	455	2,197	1,992	1,065	2.34

* From fuel combustion only. Figures for world include emissions from international aviation and international marine.
** Mexico joined the OECD in 1994; Chile joined in 2010.

Source: *Key World Energy Statistics 2012* © OECD/IEA 2012, pp. 48–49 (www.iea.org/publications/freepublications/publication/kwes-1.pdf).

Table 4.5 CO_2 emissions from fuel consumption, 1971–2009 (million tons), selected OECD economies

	1971	1990	2000	2005	2007	2009
Brazil	91	194	303	322	342	338
Chile	21	31	53	58	67	65
Mexico	97	265	349	386	410	400
US	4,291	4,869	5,698	5,772	5,763	5,195

Source: OECD Factbook 2011-12 (online data): Economic, Environmental and Social Statistics, Emissions of carbon dioxide (http://dx.doi.org/10.1787/factbook-2011-en).

having contributed only about 4 per cent of global emissions, yet it is likely to be a disproportionately affected by it (Simms and Reid 2006; see Table 4.4).

However, since the 1970s, CO_2 emissions of some of the more developed economies such as Mexico, Chile and Brazil have grown rapidly with greater levels of development (see Table 4.5). This makes Latin American and Caribbean nations examples of the principle recognized by the UN Framework Convention on Climate Change

(UNFCCC) agreed in 1992 in Rio that recognizes how countries have common, but differentiated, responsibilities when it comes to the causes of climate change and their capacities to address it. Yet, despite the level of global concern about this issue, evidence of climate change and changes in biological systems in Latin America remains under-documented, and one reason for this is the region's complexity: it is highly diverse in terms of its climate, ecosystems, population distribution and cultural traditions, which, combined with rapidly changing forms of land use, makes it difficult to identify patterns of vulnerability (IPCC Working Group II 1997). Nonetheless, certain key features make the region susceptible to climate change:

- Climate variability, particularly the El Niño/La Niña-Southern Oscillation (ENSO) phenomenon, which already causes adverse impacts on many countries – especially those of Central America, Ecuador, Brazil, Peru, Bolivia, Chile and Argentina.
- A significant amount of production in Latin America and the Caribbean derives from its ecosystems and development is biased towards extractive and export sectors.
- The region is highly unequal, and inequality and poverty drive environmental change which will only be exacerbated by climate change.

Given these vulnerabilities, climate change is likely to have multiple effects in Latin America and the Caribbean (see Figure 4.2).

Extreme weather events

Extreme weather and other natural events (earthquakes, tropical storms, hurricanes and floods) have always been a feature of life in the region. Climate change will exacerbate the effects of the El Niño phenomenon that typically reverses weather patterns, bringing more rainfall to the coast and drought inland at higher altitudes, and is often followed by La Niña, where patterns behave in the opposite way (Simms and Reid 2006). Extreme events can often be linked to El Niño and global warming may make these more frequent and severe. More frequent heavy rains will have major implications for cities by making flooding and landslides more common, and the frequency and severity of flooding has generally increased in the last decade (UN-HABITAT 2011a). Variable rainfall can alter water supply and quality and changing precipitation and snow patterns are

Figure 4.2 Latin America and the Caribbean: summary of climate change patterns projected for 2100*

* The confidence levels are based on the statistically significant levels of coincidence determined for the sign of change by a certain number of models (at least 80 per cent for high confidence, 50 per cent to 80 per cent for medium confidence and less than 50 per cent for low confidence).

Source: ECLAC 2010, on the basis of information from Instituto Nacional de Pesquisas Espaciais (INPE) of Brazil (www.eclac.cl/dmaah/publicaciones/xml/9/41909/2010-914-Climate_change-COMPLETO_WEB.pdf).

already putting pressure on the availability of fresh water in Peru, Bolivia, Colombia, Chile and western Argentina. Climate change is likely to result in more rain in eastern South America but less in central and southern Chile (Simms and Reid 2006). Droughts have become more common in the tropics and sub-tropics since 1970 and extreme heat events are predicted to become more frequent, intense and longer lasting everywhere (UN-HABITAT 2011a). If El Niño effects contribute to dieback in the Amazon rainforest, this threatens to release into the atmosphere huge amounts of carbon from forest decomposition that could trigger irreversible global warming (Simms and Reid 2006). Warming in mountainous regions melts snow, ice and glaciers – already disappearing rapidly in the Andes – affecting water availability. Greater frequency and severity of extreme weather will cause more humanitarian emergencies, and extremes of heat and cold will increase deaths among vulnerable groups. Drought and changing rainfall patterns will damage agriculture and worsen hunger. Higher temperatures and long periods of drought damage infrastructure such as roadways, necessitating costly repairs (UN-HABITAT 2011a).

Land use

Although certain areas of Latin America could benefit from climate change through the effects of elevated CO_2 on crop growth, the impact on agricultural production will vary. Decreases in production are likely for several major crops in Mexico, Central America, Brazil, Chile, Argentina and Uruguay, extreme weather could hit banana production in Central America, and studies in Brazil, Chile, Argentina and Uruguay suggest decreased yields of barley, grapes, maize, potatoes, soya beans and wheat (IPCC Working Group II 1997; Canziani and Diaz 2000). Agriculture that relies upon irrigation will increase, placing greater demands on water supplies. Intensive agriculture using chemical inputs is also likely to increase. Global warming could exacerbate problems caused by animal and plant diseases, which threaten marginal groups disproportionately (Canziani and Diaz 2000). These phenomena and health problems are likely to foster significant migrations of rural and coastal populations, potentially generating national and international tensions. Climate change is likely to worsen the impact of land degradation in Latin America and the Caribbean, and the impact will again be highly uneven (see Table 4.6).

Table 4.6 Latin America (selected countries): projections of degraded territory, 2050 and 2100*

	2050	2100
Chile	20.8	41.2
Ecuador	28.9	57.2
Bolivia	11.2	22.2
Paraguay	33.5	66.3
Peru	31.3	62.0

* Percentages of each country's territory.

Source: ECLAC 2010a (www.eclac.cl/dmaah/publicaciones/xml/9/41909/2010-914-Climate_change-COMPLETO_WEB.pdf).

Forests

Climate change is likely to have a significant impact on forests in Latin America and the Caribbean. Negotiations have increasingly put forests at the centre of mitigation efforts through initiatives such as the UN's REDD programme (UN Collaborative Programme on Reducing Emissions from Deforestation and Forest Degradation in Developing Countries). Global warming is likely to have its greatest impact on the Austral forests of southern Chile and Argentina, and in Mexico temperate forest, particularly in the north, will be affected by warmer conditions. Tropical forests will be more affected by changes in water availability than by temperature, and deforestation, fire and climate change could result in widespread "dieback" in the Amazon, with forest areas becoming savanna, reducing rainfall, hitting agriculture and increasing carbon emissions (CBD 2010). Research suggests the potential extinction of 24 per cent of tree species in central Brazil by 2050 if temperatures rise by 2°C (Magrin et al. 2007).

Ecosystem change and biodiversity loss

Climate change represents a significant threat to global biodiversity and tropical plant and animal species are highly sensitive to small variations. Loss of habitats such as the tropical rainforest will, in turn, contribute to global warming and hence further loss of biodiversity (UNEP 2010). The Amazon is likely to suffer species losses, increased insect infestation and the spread of infectious diseases. Mesoamerica and the Caribbean are considered biodiversity "hotspots" where climate change will have a significant impact. When ecosystems are changed or fragment this can alter food chains and disrupt forms of interdependence. The distribution of species and vegetation types is likely to shift radically. Ecosystem "migration" could result in the loss of many tropical species (UNEP 2010; see also Phillips et al. 2002; Arriaga and Gómez 2004; Wright and Calderón 2005). Migration of marine species to cooler waters could make tropical oceans less diverse (CBD 2010). Changes in ecosystems will have an impact on their value to human beings, and evidence suggests climate change could lower the productivity of low-lying tropical forests along Mexico's Pacific coast, Costa Rica, Venezuela and Brazil (Sánchez-Azofeifa et al. 2009). Biodiversity loss hits the poor hardest and has implications for food security and healthcare. Ecosystems and sectors most likely to be affected are those related to agriculture, livestock raising and fisheries.

Fresh water systems

Considerable attention has been given to the likely impact of climate change on hydrology and water availability (see Strzepek and McCluskey 2010). It will result in both droughts and floods by changing rainfall patterns, river flows, the levels of lakes and systems that recharge groundwater. Changing weather is already having unpredictable consequences on how Latin American and Caribbean water resources are managed. Changes in land use, waste disposal and rates of water extraction will affect fresh water systems. This is likely to exacerbate existing inequalities in the supply of water across Latin America, with severe shortages affecting eastern Central America, for example. Climate change will also affect the quality of water resources for human and animal use and demand in certain seasons (World Water Assessment Programme 2009). The Fourth Assessment Report of the Intergovernmental Panel on Climate Change indicated that by 2020 up to 81 million people in Latin America and the Caribbean could be affected by water shortages, rising to up to 178 million in 2050 (Magrin et al. 2007; Arnell, 2004). Climate change will affect systems and resources in two main ways: altering the intensity and distribution of rainfall, surface runoff and groundwater recharge; and exacerbating glacial retreat. The loss of glaciers poses a serious threat to water supplies and there is already evidence of drastic shrinkage in the Andes and Argentine Patagonia. In the short term, glacial melting could burst reservoirs and cause mudslides, and in the longer term it could reduce water supplies and push up global sea levels. Catastrophic

Box 4.7 Glacial melting and land use

In Ecuador, glacial melting has been linked to soil loss, desertification, extinctions and loss of agricultural land. This threatens the country's food security and has a disproportionate impact on Andean indigenous communities. Higher temperatures force people to farm at higher altitudes, adding to deforestation, which, in turn, undermines water sources and leads to soil erosion. Climate change also has a cultural impact, with the move to higher lands meaning the loss of places where a culture is rooted. The native communities of the Imbakucha Basin in Otavalo are already feeling the impact: elders say they no longer know when to sow because the rains do not come as expected. In Colombia, the rocks of the El Cocuy region store underground water resources, making its glaciers crucial for the hydrological cycles and a vital source of water for the indigenous U'wa people, who regard the snow as sacred. As the glaciers disappear, local communities will have to cope with lower net flows of water and higher risks of flooding, mudslides and soil erosion. In the Ibans lagoon area of Honduras, climate change is increasing pressures on coastal land and the area is frequently affected by tropical storms such as Hurricane Mitch in 1998, which, combined with the high rate of erosion, increases the risk of flooding in villages. In 2005, hurricanes led to heavy rain in the hills that caused the rivers to rise rapidly, washing away houses, crops and livestock in river communities.

glacier floods and mudflows such as have occurred in the Cordillera Blanca in Peru and at the Copiapó River and the Villarrica Volcano in Chile have claimed thousands of lives. The threat posed by glacial shrinkage to water availability has become a major policy issue in Andean countries (see Box 4.7).

Marine environment

Pressures on marine systems from industrial and artisanal fishing, fleet transport and tourism, pollution and waste are likely to increase due to the warming of coastal waters, the death of coral and the impact of climate change on fish stocks. The main effects on the marine environment will be rising sea levels due to thermal expansion – the increase in volume of ocean water as it warms. In Latin America and the Caribbean, coastal areas and the small Caribbean island states are particularly vulnerable to rising seas, which will exacerbate floods, storm surges, erosion and other coastal hazards (World Water Assessment Programme 2009; IPCC 2007). Millions of people in densely populated low-lying coastal areas may be at risk of flooding by storm surges. Of the world's cities considered most vulnerable to rising sea levels, 904 (27 per cent) are in Latin America and the Caribbean (UNEP 2010). As about 50 per cent of the region's population lives within 100 km of the coast, this could make 290 million people vulnerable. Seawater intrusion also threatens coastal aquifers such as those that supply fresh water along the Río de la Plata to highly populated areas such as Buenos Aires (Canziani and Díaz 2000). In Central America, rising sea levels, severe storms and the salination of aquifers could have major implications for infrastructure and agriculture. Climate change combined with other stresses on the marine environment may also reduce fish quality and stocks in coastal waters, encouraging over-fishing.

Cities

Climate change presents unique challenges for urban areas and will affect water and energy supplies and industry. It has the potential to disrupt economies and destroy homes and livelihoods, fuelling migration. These phenomena will reinforce existing inequalities and poverty, especially in regions such as Latin America that are heavily urbanized. Groups particularly vulnerable to the impact of climate change include those living in coastal areas and shanty towns around large cities, especially in flood-prone areas or on unstable hillsides. The impact on urban infrastructure could be severe, pushing up the need for investment and public spending, especially in coastal zones (see Table 4.7; De la Torre, Fajnzylber and Nash 2009; UNEP 2010). Coastal erosion and saltwater intrusion can ruin buildings and damage highways, ports, bridges and runways (UN-HABITAT 2011a). Cities retain heat more than surrounding rural areas, exacerbating the impact of extreme heat events.

Cities are likely to bear the main burden of increased migration as people leave areas affected by drought, flooding and storms. Projections suggest about 200 million people globally may be displaced by 2050 due to climate change-related factors (UN-HABITAT 2011a; IOM 2009). Research from Mexico links migratory flows with droughts and areas of desertification (see Leighton and Frank 1997). Research

Table 4.7 Projected impacts on urban areas everywhere of changes in extreme weather and climate events

Climate phenomena	Likelihood	Major projected impacts
Fewer cold days and nights	Virtually certain	Reduced energy demand for heating
Warmer and more frequent hot days and nights over most land areas	Virtually certain	Increased demand for cooling
Warmer temperatures	Virtually certain	Reduced disruption to transport due to snow; ice effects on winter tourism. Changes in permafrost, damage to buildings and infrastructures
Warm spells/heat waves: frequency increases over most land areas	Very likely	Reduction in quality of life for people in warm areas without air conditioning; impacts on elderly, very young and poor, including significant loss of human life. Increases in energy usage for air conditioning
Heavy precipitation events: frequency increases over most areas	Very likely	Disruption of settlements, commerce, transport and societies due to flooding. Significant loss of human life, injuries; loss of, and damage to, property and infrastructure. Potential for use of rainwater in hydropower generation increased in many areas
Areas affected by drought increase	Likely	Water shortages for households, industries and services. Reduced hydropower generation potentials. Potential for population migration
Intense tropical cyclone activity increases	Likely	Disruption of settlements by flood and high winds. Disruption of public water supply. Withdrawal of risk coverage in vulnerable areas by private insurers (at least in developed countries). Significant loss of human life, injuries; loss of, and damage to, property. Potential for population migration
Increased incidence of extreme high sea level (excludes tsunamis)	Likely	Costs of coastal protection and costs of land-use relocation increase. Decreased freshwater availability due to saltwater intrusion. Significant loss of human life, injuries; loss of, and damage to, property and infrastructure. Potential for movement of population

Source: UN-HABITAT 2011. *Global Report on Human Settlements 2011. Cities and Climate Change: Policy Directions.*

in Ecuador showed that climatic vulnerability influenced rural–urban migration from the altiplano, and that migration towards border areas intensified during droughts (see UNEP 2010). Climate change will increase water stress by raising the demand for water and its availability, by affecting its quality and even how it is treated in cities if extreme weather damages infrastructure. Changes in weather conditions such as extreme heat affect public health, especially in cities, and these problems are compounded by poverty. Deaths from heat are already significantly underreported and as cities grow higher temperatures and an aging society increase the threat (UN-HABITAT 2011a; Haines Epstein and McMichael 1993; Kalkstein 1993; IPCC 1996). The greenhouse gases generated in urban areas have contributed significantly to global warming. Air quality is sensitive to temperature and weather conditions, meaning that climate change has important implications for cities (see IAI 2011; SEMARNAT/INE 2006).

Social repercussions of climate change

Climate change is likely to have a significant impact on the economies and politics of Latin American and Caribbean countries.

Economic impact

Evidence suggests that there is a relationship between levels of economic development and vulnerability to extreme weather events, because losses caused by disasters undermine growth and hamper poverty reduction (see World Water Assessment Programme 2009). Floods and droughts disrupt economic activities and subsequent disaster relief and reconstruction deplete government resources. Disasters destroy infrastructure and impose high health costs on societies. The increasing vulnerability of Latin America and the Caribbean to extreme weather such as tropical storms, hurricanes and floods will be costly. In 2012, for example, the UN in Haiti warned that 1.5 million people were at risk of not having proper access to food in 2013 due to the destruction caused by Hurricane Sandy and other disasters.

Climate change will have a significant impact on ecosystems and sectors related to primary production such as agriculture, livestock raising and fisheries. While it may have beneficial effects on agricultural production in mid- to high latitudes, in low latitudes, where most developing countries are located, it will hit yields for major cereal crops (World Bank 2008; WTO 2009). If water availability for temperate grasslands decreases, livestock production could also decline. Agriculture that requires irrigation could expand, increasing pressure on water supplies. Agriculture is likely to use more chemical

Box 4.8 Bolivia and climate change

A World Bank study (2010e) into the potential costs of climate change in Bolivia and adaptation to it identified huge challenges facing the country. Andean glaciers that supply drinking water and energy for cities like La Paz and El Alto are already melting, average temperatures are rising, rainfall patterns have changed and the rainy season is growing shorter and more stormy. In the Altiplano, inter-Andean valleys and Chaco that are home to most of the country's population this is causing desertification. Bolivia is also vulnerable to drought but only 15 per cent of agricultural land is irrigated, meaning that cultivated areas rely on rainfall. Researchers found that the poorest groups who live in dry zones such as the Altiplano, valleys and plains and along riverbeds in lowland areas are most vulnerable to climate change because of their dependency on rain-fed agriculture, small-scale livestock farming, forest harvesting, hunting and fishing and seasonal labour. Indigenous groups are particularly vulnerable because of existing social exclusion. In rural areas, better-off households are more resilient to climate change because of their livelihood strategies: irrigated agriculture; semi-enclosed livestock production or large-scale livestock farming; dairy farming; and service sector employment.

inputs, threatening groundwater quality. The unpredictable impact of climate change in Latin America and the Caribbean on water management (see above) is already having a knock-on effect on some sectors. The World Bank examined the potential impact of climate change in Bolivia, concentrating on how it could affect water resources (see Box 4.8).

Fish production will also suffer if coastal wetlands and other habitats that serve as nurseries are lost through rising sea levels. Increasing storm activity could hit offshore extraction, shipping, recreation and tourism. Changes in river flows may affect navigation and reduce the reliability of power supplies, hitting economic development. Reduced rainfall has already disrupted hydropower production in Central America. Brazil's dependence on hydropower makes the country especially vulnerable to power shortages in drought years.

The increasing frequency and intensity of extreme weather events makes economic assets more vulnerable and increases the cost of doing business, especially by damaging buildings and infrastructure. Climate change will affect trade, manufacturing, tourism and the insurance industry as well as energy generation, distribution, demand and supply, and storms and flooding can damage electricity transmission infrastructure (UN-HABITAT 2011a; see also Bulkeley and Betsill 2003). Bad weather suppresses growth indirectly through factors such as delays and cancellations to transportation, problems with communications and power networks, and fluctuating consumption patterns. Disruptions to supply chains and transportation hit retail and commercial services sectors, and the tourism industry is highly dependent upon reliable transport networks. The insurance and financial services industries are also vulnerable to climate change, which could push up premiums while reducing insurability. Macroeconomic factors can exacerbate these sectoral effects of climate change and restrict policymakers' ability to respond to environmental problems. For example, because ecosystem services lack effective markets or prices, this can mean the costs of environmental problems are not accounted for, delaying official responses (UNEP 2010; see Chapters 5, 6).

Political impact

Climate change poses significant challenges for policymakers and will affect political competition. First and foremost, it is likely to exacerbate poverty and inequality. Poverty intensifies pressure on the environment in many different ways, although the relationship between income level and environmental degradation is complex (see Box 4.9). In 2011 ECLAC reported that the poverty level in Latin America and the Caribbean is at its lowest for 20 years, falling from 48.4 per cent to 31.4 per cent between 1990 and 2010. The rate of extreme poverty or indigence also fell from 22.6 per cent to 12.3 per cent. These figures are encouraging but despite rising incomes poverty remains extensive and statistical declines conceal the fact that there are still 177 million poor people in the region (ECLAC 2012b).

Climate change is a distributional phenomenon because of how its impact on individuals and groups is influenced by wealth and access to resources (see UN- HABITAT 2011a). Climate change will affect some areas and social groups more than others, affecting poorer people in the marginal areas of cities disproportionately. The urban poor are most at risk because they lack assets, their livelihoods are already

Box 4.9 Income levels and environmental degradation

A good deal of scholarship has been devoted to identifying which actors cause environmental degradation in developing countries and frequently these are identified according to income distribution. In 1987, the Brundtland Commission drew attention to the relationship between income distribution and environmental degradation (Brundtland et al. 1987). It argued that the poor cause considerable damage to the environment in developing countries because poverty forces people to disregard the long-term consequences of their activities in their struggle to survive (see also UN 1990; World Bank 1992; Kirdar 1992). The argument provided a response to environmentalists concerned that economic development would lead to ever greater environmental degradation. However, critics argued that the poor were not the major producers of environmental degradation because

- the poor have good knowledge of their environment and are experts at preserving it (see, for example, Durning 1992; Clay 1988; Moody 1988);
- the poor know that their livelihoods depend on conserving the environment (see, for example, Broad 1994);
- very poor (indigent) people may degrade the environment but poor people in general conserve it (see, for example, Annis 1992);
- the rising middle class are those with most responsibility for damaging the environment because of their consumption habits (see, for example, Timberlake 1986);
- a small wealthy elite are mostly responsible for environmental damage through pollution and consumption (see, for example, Broad and Cavanagh 1993).

This position chimes with dependency theories (see Chapter 5) that blame environmental degradation in developing countries on agro-exports and consumers in the industrialized countries, multinational corporations and domestic elites. Yet it is likely that all of the above groups share some blame for ecological damage. Political ecology has focused on the interconnections between class and the environment, usually without taking an approach that seeks to identify a single culprit, and seeks the social, historical and economic roots of environmental degradation (see Hecht and Cockburn 1990; Durham 1979; Goodman and Redclift 1991; Moore 1996). Such literature goes beyond identifying the groups that damage or save the environment and instead seeks to explore the *interactions* between classes (Lele 1991). It accepts that the poor may be the agents of environmental degradation, but the responsibility for this lies with the elites whose behaviour maintains poverty (see, for example, Durham 1994; Sawers 2000).

unreliable and they tend to live in areas at risk of disasters. Hundreds of thousands of poor people live precariously on hillsides vulnerable to erosion and flooding. Landslides in Rio de Janeiro, Guatemala City, Medellín, Mendoza, Mexico City, Santos and São Paulo have killed many people and left many more homeless. Poverty also means these communities are less able to adapt to changing conditions, tend to benefit from lower levels of state assistance when there is a disaster and lack legal and financial protection such as insurance. Changes could generate a vicious cycle whereby the poor bear the burden of warming, preventing them from escaping poverty and exposing them to yet more negative change. Given this, the disproportionate impact of climate change is likely to worsen inequality. Climate change may also deepen gender and racial inequalities, affecting minorities and women disproportionately.

As climate change will have a direct impact on the infrastructure of cities, urban policymakers will also face a growing need to ensure the continuity of basic services, such as water and energy supplies. Variability in water supplies could exceed the institutional capacities of some cities to manage their systems. Extreme weather can destroy crucial infrastructure such as bridges and flyovers, and subsidence caused by drying subsoil threatens homes, shops and factories. The problems faced by cities may exacerbate an existing urban bias and centralization in politics.

Conclusion

If Mother Nature were an artist, there is no doubt that Latin America and the Caribbean would be one of her great masterpieces, home to an immense variety of landscapes, ecosystems and species and one of the most significant repositories of biodiversity anywhere. But the region has been under pressure from human activity for millennia, and the challenges it faces have grown in proportion with the population and its ever greater aspirations in a globalized world that is increasing both opportunities and competition. This chapter has tried to sketch a picture of the multiple challenges posed by how the land is exploited for agriculture, forestry and extractive activities, and the damage caused by pollution and unsustainable levels of production. It has explored an issue with a high global profile – deforestation – and how this is driven by economic development and population pressures. It has considered the impact of human development – from intensive farming to tourism and urban development – on terrestrial biodiversity and on the rich aquatic and marine panoramas that exist throughout the region. Human society has increasingly evolved in an urban context, but the pressures caused by the rapid growth of great cities has entrenched great inequalities and created serious hurdles to the provision of water and sanitation services, waste disposal and air of acceptable quality. Overshadowing all these issues is a test that Latin American and Caribbean citizens share with the rest of humanity – climate change – which can provide a lens through which all environmental issues can be understood because it favours an approach to understanding them as part of a system. The changing climate is likely to have multiple effects in Latin America and the Caribbean in all the thematic areas normally associated with environmental studies discussed above – but is also likely to have major economic, social and, ultimately, political implications. This chapter has introduced some of the ways climate change is already affecting the region and is rising up the policy agenda.

Recommended reading

Boyd, Stephanie and Ernesto Cabellos. 2002. *Choropampa: The Price of Gold* (documentary film). Lima: Guarango Association. Available to view online at www.youtube.com/watch?v=dW7zn0SbrV4 [accessed September 2012].

Canziani, Osvaldo F and Sandra Diaz (eds). 2000. *The Regional Impacts of Climate Change*, Chapter 6, "Latin America". World Meteorological Organization/United Nations Environment Programme. www.grida.no/publications/other/ipcc_sr/?src=/climate/ipcc/regional/173.htm [accessed January 2014].

Díez, Jordi and OP Dwivedi (eds). 2008. *Global Environmental Challenges: Perspectives from the South*. Peterborough, ON: Broadview Press.

Sponsel, Leslie. 2011. "The Master Thief: Gold Mining and Mercury Contamination in the Amazon", in Barbara Rose Johnston (ed.), *Life and Death Matters: Human Rights, Environment, and Social Justice*. Walnut Creek, CA: Left Coast Press.

UNEP. 2010. *Latin America and the Caribbean: Environment Outlook GEO LAC 3*. Panama City: United Nations Environment Programme. Available online at www.unep.org/publications/contents/pub_details_search.asp?ID=4149 [accessed July 2011].

Useful websites

Centro Latinoamericano de Ecología Social (CLAES, Latin American Centre for Social Ecology): www.ambiental.net

Confederación de Comunidades del Perú Afectadas por la Minería (CONACAMI, Confederation of Communities in Peru Affected by Mining): www.movimientos.org/enlacei/conacami/

Convention on Biological Diversity (CBD): www.cbd.int/

Global Environment Facility: www.thegef.org/gef/home

Global Water Partnership: www.gwp.org/

Intergovernmental Panel on Climate Change: www.ipcc.ch

International Institute for Sustainable Development (IISD), Biodiversity Policy and Practice: http://biodiversity-l.iisd.org/

International Organization for Migration (IOM), Migration, Climate Change and the Environment initiative: www.iom.int/jahia/Jahia/activities/by-theme/migration-climate-change-and-environment/cache/offonce/

Millennium Ecosystem Assessment: www.maweb.org/en/index.aspx.

Observatorio de Conflictos Mineros de América Latina (OCMAL, Observatory of Mining Conflicts in Latin America): www.conflictos-mineros.net/home

Observatorio Latinoamericano de Conflictos Ambientales (Observatory of Environmental Conflicts in Latin America), Chile: www.olca.cl/oca/index.htm

Organization of American States (OAS), Department of Sustainable Development, Integrated Water Resources Management Section (IWRM): www.oas.org/dsd/WaterResources/

South American Emissions Megacities and Climate (SAEMC) project sponsored by the Inter-American Institute for Global Change Research (IAI) (CRN 2017): http://saemc.cmm.uchile.cl/

Summit of the Americas, Joint Summit Working Group, "Promoting Environmental Sustainability": www.summit-americas.org/pubs/pub_0610/ingles/pdf/promoting_environmental_sustainability.pdf

UN Framework Convention on Climate Change http://unfccc.int/2860.php

UN-REDD, UN Collaborative Programme on Reducing Emissions from Deforestation and Forest Degradation in Developing Countries: www.un-redd.org/

World Resources Institute (WRI): www.wri.org/

Worldwatch Institute: www.worldwatch.org/

CHAPTER FIVE

The environment and economic policy

THE ECONOMIES of Latin America and the Caribbean have distinctive features shaped by the region's unique pattern of development since Independence. Development has been determined by its position since then as a supplier of raw materials within an emerging global economy dominated by other states controlling surplus capital. Growth has traditionally been heavily dependent on the export of commodities, extracting a heavy toll on the natural environment. But in the twentieth century there were also significant levels of industrialization in some countries that aimed to reduce their dependence on exports, generating new environmental problems. In turn, the impact of industry and the growth of the state's role in the economy led during the 1980s and 1990s to radical "neoliberal" structural adjustment policies, the liberalization of trade and privatization as a new phase of economic globalization unfolded. Industrialization and neoliberal policies – and the contemporary consumer societies they have consolidated – have merely deepened the impact of centuries of development on the Latin American and Caribbean environment. This chapter examines the relationship between environmental change and the model of capitalist economic growth based on the exploitation of natural resources for global commerce. It introduces notions in environmental economics and examines a key theme in debate – the relationship between development and environmental quality. A tension persists in the region between the urge to extract resources in order to raise living standards and the need to protect them for the future.

Models of development

The economies of Latin American and Caribbean countries during the post-Independence period developed on the basis of agro-exports controlled by a small number of oligarchic landowners. This model of development limited the emergence of industry and tied the fate of these countries closely to the external markets for their agricultural commodities and raw materials (together known as primary products). It was supported by the doctrine of comparative advantage in international trade, which implies an international division of labour in which some countries stick to producing commodities for sale to others that produce industrial goods. In Argentina, for example, Latin America's most prosperous economy by the early twentieth century, comparative advantage suggested the country was best served by concentrating on the production and sale of beef produced intensively and cheaply from huge herds of cattle grazing on the vast pampas plains.

Export-led growth shaped political development by nurturing states dominated by oligarchies who maintained close relations with the foreign interests with whom their export markets were linked, copied their consumption patterns, and excluded the vast majority of people from politics. At the same time, economic modernization and the growth of cities generated new, mainly urban classes that would begin to exercise political pressure on the state, eventually undermining the oligarchs.

The Great Depression that followed the Wall Street crash of 1929 forced Latin American and Caribbean countries to reconsider their relationship with the international economic system, and countries began to nurture their own industries through protectionism by substituting imports with products made locally – "import-substitution industrialization" (ISI). Interest in Keynesianism advocated a greater role in development for the state – which grew stronger as a set of institutions – and a nationalist climate justified hostility to foreign interests. Countries once shaped by agriculture and mining now made industrialization a priority as a new "structuralist" perspective in economics emerged that suggested the world comprised a "centre" of developed industrialized countries and a "periphery" of those that only produced agricultural goods and raw materials that were at a natural disadvantage in any trading relationship (see Gómez-Galvarriato and Williamson 2009). Structuralist ideas were influential in multilateral bodies such as the United Nations' Comisión Económica para América Latina (CEPAL, Economic Commission for Latin America, later incorporating the Caribbean). Moreover, from within this tradition came more radical perspectives about development in the 1960s and 1970s emphasizing the limitations imposed by Latin America's dependent status within the international economy – the dependency or *dependencia* school (see Box 5.1).

By the 1950s, most governments in Latin America and the Caribbean had embarked on unprecedented state intervention in the economy ("statism") to direct ISI, which became a cornerstone of development strategies until the 1980s. By the end of the 1950s, ISI shifted towards more complex industrial products and this coincided with global expansion by large US and later European corporations. Many Latin American and Caribbean governments welcomed multinational corporations (MNCs) into their countries and most achieved the capacity to produce basic goods, with a few creating heavy industries. The oil crisis of the 1970s accelerated the exhaustion of ISI but also created conditions in which governments grew over-exposed to foreign debt, resulting, from 1982, in a debt crisis followed by stagnation. The deep policy reforms that ensued have been the subject of extensive debate in Latin America and the Caribbean, and a critique of them was key to the rise of left-of-centre governments in the region since 1998 (see Panizza 2009). Policies in the aftermath of the debt crisis aimed at long-term "structural adjustment" to reduce the role of the state in the economy. Neoliberals advocated privatization and deregulation, and reorienting the focus of economic growth back to exports in a globalizing economy by dismantling trade barriers. Some environmentalists suggested that the international development establishment embraced environmentalism to legitimize this agenda. In recent years, the neoliberal orthodoxy and the export-led, market model have been reassessed (see, for example, Kingstone 2010). Yet despite the ascendance of left-of-centre governments, neoliberal policies remain largely intact.

Structural adjustment, trade liberalization and privatization had a significant impact on the environment in Latin America and the Caribbean. During the 1980s and 1990s, exports of natural

Box 5.1 Relations with China – a new dependency?

The notion of dependency became influential in the 1960s and suggested that the crucial decisions affecting international trade were taken by countries in the centre, meaning peripheral countries were dependent on these for growth. An important analysis of dependency was developed by the Chilean Oswaldo Sunkel (1969). These ideas grew in popularity amid the ideological competition of the Cold War period because they coincided with theories of imperialism. Dependency theory was particularly critical of foreign investment and also appealed to nationalist sentiments that blamed foreign capital for underdevelopment at a time when multinational corporations were investing heavily in Latin America. The dependency perspective has had important implications for debates about the environment in Latin America and the Caribbean. It has reinforced a sense that the region has not succeeded in converting environmental change into welfare and economic growth despite the expansion of the extractive frontier (see Lederman and Maloney 2007). By contrast, the extraction of natural resources has led: to a concentration of benefits; to a failure to ensure transparent governance of the natural resource economy and the income it generates; and to the transformation of ecosystems at the expense of human well-being and environmental health (see, for example, Santiago 2006; Loker 2004; Van den Hombergh 2004). Some environmentalists in Latin America subscribe to notions of eco-dependency by which surplus extraction by the global capitalist system takes the form of ecological pillage (Dore 1996a). They argue that multinational corporations earn a higher rate of profit in the region than in the industrialized world by taking advantage of regulatory weaknesses that results in disproportionate damage to Latin America's environment, which in turn damages its resource base and reduces its own long-term potential for growth – keeping it dependent. The notion of dependency has been employed to draw attention to the close economic relationship between more traditional centre-periphery relationships, such as that between Mexico and the US under the North American Free Trade Agreement (NAFTA, see below), as well as the more recent appetite for Latin America's natural resources among rapidly developing countries such as China. The rapid growth of industry in China has generated an appetite for Latin American raw materials and energy, and is creating economic relationships that could have important geopolitical implications for the region (see Gallagher 2008; Lederman, Olarreaga and Perry 2006; Lall, Weiss and Oikawa 2005). The response of Latin American states to growing trade with China has often been to invest in new infrastructure developments that have serious environmental implications (see Lyons 2009).

resources rose throughout the region. To comply with the policy conditions of international financing institutions such as the IMF and World Bank, governments sought private investment to expand exports and competed to provide the most favourable conditions for investors, including lax environmental restrictions. Weak regulations encouraged the use of production methods that ensured short-term profits but with no regard for sustainability. Industries may have been attracted to the region because they could dispose of toxic wastes and extract resources with limited state interference. Mexico, for example, lured many low-wage, polluting industries to the border zone because of its proximity to the US. A report by ECLAC in 1999 concluded that emissions from the manufacturing sectors in Argentina, Bolivia, Brazil, Chile, Colombia, Costa Rica, Mexico and Peru rose significantly after the reforms of the 1980s and 1990s (see Schatan 1999; see Box 5.2).

The take-up of neoliberal policies in Latin America occurred according to different phases, making an overall assessment of its impact complex, but neoliberal reforms may have contributed to environmental degradation in several ways:

Regulation. The impact of privatization has been the theme of much debate, although most liberal economists believe it has, overall, been positive. However, simply privatizing corporations does not in itself resolve the inefficiencies associated with state ownership: privatization has to be accompanied by regulations to protect consumers from monopolistic behaviour. Critics of privatization say Latin American governments desperate for funds failed to introduce strong regulatory frameworks. They subtly competed for foreign capital by weakening environmental rules or, where regulations were introduced, by not monitoring them. Foreign capital was a significant source of privatization revenues, accounting for 39.7 per cent in Latin America between 1990 and 1995 and jumping to 76.7 per cent in 1995 (Franko 1999). However, privatization in some cases resulted in popular resistance, often because governments failed to regulate concessions in sectors such as water. The depth of Latin America's problems and the new orthodoxy imposed by neoliberalism also often meant that environmentalists raised issues of sustainability only in terms acceptable to multilateral development agencies for whom export promotion, free markets and a small state were dominant

Box 5.2 Neoliberal reforms and pollution

Exports determined the environmental impact of the economic reforms of the 1980s and 1990s. Emissions from the manufacturing sectors in Argentina, Bolivia, Brazil, Chile, Colombia, Costa Rica, Mexico and Peru rose significantly after the reforms, and this was because of the growth of the export sector, particularly resource-intensive exports. According to Schatan (1999) industrial pollution stemming from export-related activity grew much more than that from manufacturing production following reforms. Trade liberalization drove up manufacturing exports reforms while reducing the relative weight of industrial output in the GDP of nearly all Latin American countries. According to Schatan, it was this boom in exports that caused an increase in toxic emissions, not the redirection of production towards polluting sectors. Industrial pollution caused by expanding exports grew 213 per cent from the 1970s, before the reforms were implemented, to the 1990s, after they had been implemented, while pollution arising from manufacturing increased just 32 per cent in the same period. Schatan distinguishes between larger economies such as Argentina, Brazil and Mexico and smaller ones. Mexico and Argentina tended to evolve towards more advanced manufacturing, which is generally less polluting, while Brazil intensified exports of pollution-generating raw materials as advanced technology exports grew weaker. Smaller countries specialized in simple manufacturing and greater use of raw materials, indicating an erosion of protections for natural resources. Schatan argues that commodity production of this kind is not a reflection of weaker environmental regulations in Latin American countries as compared with industrialized nations, but of a combination of abundant natural resources and cheap labour. It would therefore be wrong to describe these as "pollution havens" (see below) and more accurate to refer to them as "natural resource havens" that are attractive to investors because of the availability of natural resources whose prices do not include the environmental costs of their unsustainable use or non-renewable nature (see also Jenkins 2003).

tenets. In some cases, privatization was even presented as a way of addressing environmental problems based on the argument that private sector cost–benefit calculations will result in environmental improvements because the costs of ecological deterioration and natural resource depletion will compel firms to reduce pollution and conserve ecosystems (see Dore 1996a). In Chile, a new water market created through policies promoted by international organizations offers an example of how the neoliberal model developed a free market approach to public goods and natural resource management in ways that harmed underprivileged people (see Galaz, 2004; see Box 5.3). International agencies such as the World Bank promoted the Chilean water regime as a model for developing countries and it became the basis of reforms in Bolivia, Peru and Central America (see Bauer 1998; Dourojeanni and Jouravlev 1999; Silva 1995; Haughton 2002; Briscoe et al. 1998). In Bolivia, a 40-year concession to supply water and sanitation services to Cochabamba was awarded in 1999, but five months later the population rioted against higher water charges and it was cancelled.

Poverty. Poverty is an important cause of ecological degradation because it intensifies pressure on the environment in many different ways. Neoliberal policies in Latin America did not produce the investment or growth rates required to have an impact on underdevelopment and did not create a sufficient number of jobs to bring down unemployment or have a major impact on poverty and inequality, which remain a cause of environmental degradation (see ILO 2009). Between 2002 and 2008, the percentage living in poverty fell by 11 points, and indigence fell by 7 points (ECLAC 2009). Poverty reduction in recent years has also failed to eradicate high levels of inequality in Latin America compared to other regions of the world (see World Bank 2009b). According to Stallings and Peres (2000), during the 1990s, only in Chile was a sustained pattern of declining inequality achieved. The *quality* of employment in Latin America and the Caribbean has also declined since the 1990s with a large growth in the "informal" sector in which workers lack employment rights.

Trade reform. The value of Latin American exports did not keep pace with an expansion in world trade in the 1990s, although neoliberal reform left the region better placed to take advantage of a commodity boom that began in 2003, fuelled by growing trade and demand in the US and China for oil, metals and minerals. However, vigorous growth between 2003 and 2008 demonstrates the region's *continuing* dependency on the export of natural resources. Although the share of manufacturing exports as a proportion of GDP has also grown in Latin

Box 5.3 Water as private property

The introduction of a market that treats water as private property has been portrayed by some economists as a solution in developing countries to scarcity caused by bad management (see Bjornlund and McKay 2002; Bakker 2002). This perspective suggests that the creation of a free market in water gives users incentives to increase environmental efficiency by allocating resources to their most valuable uses – a notion sometimes called free market environmentalism (FME) (see Anderson and Leal 1991; Smith 1995; Winpenny 1994). However, in developing countries a free market approach to natural resource management has implications for the poorest water users. Galaz (2004) has argued that the introduction of a water market in Chile created an incentive for powerful users to violate the rights of underprivileged users. Galaz argues that proponents of the market model failed to address weak institutions and the ways in which natural resource markets function in societies where there are asymmetries of wealth and power. In 1981, Chile's military government established a new water code, laying the groundwork for privatization whereby water rights can be freely transferred, sold and bought as private property. This gave the state a minimal role in resolving conflicts, which would be done through private negotiations between users and the judicial system. However, argues Galaz, an assumption in FME is that if natural resource users are rational and pursue their self-interest a change in the institutional environment is likely to change behaviour, thereby affecting the incentives of different water users. Evidence from Chile indicated that underprivileged users are in a weaker position to challenge water rights violations. For example, despite court rulings in their favour, peasant farmers in a water conflict with a real estate investor had been unable to stop continued violations of water rights and small farmers were unable to stop a company extracting water they needed for irrigation despite rulings in their favour by the DGA (General Directorate of Water) – the governmental agency in charge of granting new water rights. Galaz employs game theory to understanding these competing incentives of natural resource users and argues that such an approach acknowledges what proponents of FME ignore: that natural resource users, especially in developing countries, differ in terms of their power. These asymmetries can mean that there are many disincentives for peasants to report violations to water conflict resolution institutions in Chile.

America, diversification and recent growth in demand have done little to change this reliance on commodities. Critics of trade liberalization point to the high social cost of export diversification, which they argue exacerbates inequality and damages the environment, especially in smaller economies where trade reform heightens dependence on the export of primary products. The development of non-traditional exports has been seen on both left and right as a way of ending a dependence on commodity exports. Ecuador's success in exporting flowers provides an example of this: the share of the flower industry from 1987 to 2002 of the country's non-petroleum export earnings rose from less than 0.2 per cent to 9 per cent (see Sawers 2005a). Yet the development of non-traditional exports can have serious environmental consequences: all new exports are, by definition, non-traditional, meaning they add to existing forms of production rather than substitute them. In Ecuador the flower industry has brought with it health and environmental problems because of the pesticides used in flower cultivation (see Box 6.2; Sawers 2005a).

The relationship between neoliberalism and environmental policy-making in Latin America has been the subject of debate (see, for example, Liverman and Vilas 2006). Chile again offers an example of a country in which neoliberal policies have shaped environmental regulation. Tecklin Bauer and Prieto (2011) suggest that its environmental regime expresses a strongly market-enabling quality instead of the market-regulating character commonly ascribed to environmental law and policy (see Box 5.4). They argue that this makes Chile an example of why the analysis of environmental policy in developing countries must resist a tendency to focus on superficial legislative developments and pay closer attention to the way in which the institutional context determines regulatory performance.

Policies removing barriers to foreign investment and liberalizing trade built on the notions of "globalization" a term embraced by neoliberals because it limits the ability of a national state to resist the dominant norms of the international economy. Globalization reflects the increasingly transnational nature of capitalist development. National borders become less relevant as large MNCs grow in strength relative to national governments. A good example of this was an agreement by Mexico and the US in 2012 to work together to develop deepwater oil and gas fields that straddle their maritime border in the Gulf of Mexico. Traditionally, Mexico has been highly sensitive

Box 5.4 Chile, the environment and the market

Tecklin, Bauer and Prieto (2011) argue that in Chile environmental policymaking has been tightly constrained by institutional and political arrangements fixed according to neoliberal principles. As a result, the underlying environmental regime remains strongly market-enabling. They argue that environmental policymaking has been driven primarily by external forces linked to globalization rather than by the domestic societal and political changes that commonly drive environmental policy. The legislation this has given rise to tends to diverge from the conventional regulatory flavour, demonstrating how law can be used to promote natural resource markets. The researchers highlight how Chile's internal politics and policymaking institutions over the last two decades have connected with the incentives and norms of globalization. With Chile's 1990 return to democracy, there were reasons to expect that environmental protection would become institutionalized. However, this only happened when internal demands for environmental legislation coincided with the concerns of trade and commercial policy. Policy was shaped by an externally determined timetable, international norms and the priorities of trade alongside an institutionalized neoliberalism. The resulting environmental law, the 1994 Ley de Bases Generales del Medio Ambiente (National Environmental Framework Law), reflected neoliberal priorities. It avoided issues such as environmental zoning, imposed weak regulatory and enforcement measures and emphasized an environmental impact assessment (EIA) process that limited the state's role to evaluating and approving private initiatives, providing security for investment, and reducing the transaction costs for investment. This framework was successful in helping Chile to attract considerable levels of foreign direct investment.

about protecting its boundaries, but the deal ended a moratorium on oil development near the maritime boundary in the western Gulf and created a legal framework for companies to develop cross-border fields jointly, allowing US oil giants to work in partnership with the Mexican state oil company Pemex for the first time. Globalization has created poles of growth in the world economy based on regional integration, with multinationals identifying regions in which to base their labour-intensive operations and develop markets. Within Latin America and the Caribbean, Mexico and Brazil have been the two most important targets of FDI (see below). Supporters of globalization say it will intensify economic growth in ways that ultimately benefit everyone. Critics argue that globalization aggravates existing problems in Latin American and Caribbean societies and creates new ones that can still be discussed using terms such as imperialism and neocolonialism (see Harris 2002; Petras 2002). Latin America and the Caribbean offers a valuable laboratory for the analysis of globalization and scholars have often adopted the "transformationalist" position asserting that this process is giving rise to complex transformations in economics, politics and culture that have an uneven and sometimes contradictory impact on nations, regions and sectors. Focusing on Central America, Robinson (2007, 2008) has developed an influential model of globalization that bears some similarity to that of dependency theory. Gwynne and Kay (2004) argue that the new mobility of international capital since the 1970s has made Latin America's economies more dependent, reducing their policy autonomy.

Development and the environment

At the heart of environmental change in Latin America and the Caribbean today is this model of capitalist economic growth based on the exploitation of natural resources producing for global markets and responding to an increasingly consumerist culture (see Chapters 1, 2). There is a close relationship between many of the environmental problems that have developed in the region and how natural resources have been managed for growth (see Dore 1996a). Enduring extractive sectors such as mining and logging that export to economies hungry for raw materials to fuel their own industrial revolutions are having a significant impact on the environment. Moreover, neoliberal prescriptions in Latin America and the Caribbean promoted a "one-size-fits-all" model of development, an approach that is only now being tested in debates on sustainable development and climate change. Effective responses to climate change will have to differ according to local circumstances, requiring a flexible, plural notion of development that is neither rigidly statist nor based solely on a free market.

Several key themes can be examined in order to understand the impact on the environment of the economic development that has taken place in Latin America and the Caribbean.

State versus free market. At the heart of economic debates in Latin America and the Caribbean has been the tension between state-led and free-market development that ideas such as neoliberalism, and more recently neostructuralism, have sought to resolve. There is ample historical evidence that both states and markets bring benefits and disadvantages to the process of growth and, in practice, economies that are mostly mixed and recognize roles for both state and market prevail throughout the region. Moreover, the nature of the market in Latin America and the Caribbean has meant that the state's economic role is closely related to its other roles, and if it does not regulate economic activities well these can have ecological and social impacts. Illegal logging, for example, destroys biodiversity but can also generate informal, unprotected labour relations in the forestry sector thereby reducing the income of forestry workers working in the legal sector (see World Bank 2012b). What this means is that institutional weaknesses can often result in environmentally damaging behaviour. A study in 2008 of the economy of the urban market of the Colombian city of Leticia, for example, drew attention to how institutional factors fuel illegal logging (Trujillo Cabrera 2010).

Most economists argue that markets are the most efficient way of organizing economic activity by allocating resources in the most rational way. A key principle underlying environmental economics – shared by many economists in Latin America and the Caribbean – is that markets often *fail*. In environmental terms, different forms of market failure can occur (see Hanley, Shogren and White 2001):

- ***Externalities***: whereby individuals do not shoulder all the costs, or gain all the benefits, of their actions; negative externalities are social or environmental costs (such as pollution) resulting from production in one sector that harms productivity (or quality of life) in another;
- ***Public goods***: these are goods which when one person consumes remain available to others, although some people can be excluded from benefits such as biodiversity;
- ***Common property* (“the commons”)**: we all have access to these but one person's use of them may deplete them, encouraging people to capture their benefits as quickly as possible;
- ***Lack of information:*** when people may not be able to see what those who damage the environment are doing.

There are structural reasons to explain market failures in Latin America, not least the fact that many people subsist *outside* formal market structures either as indigenous communities practising collective forms of agriculture, subsistence farmers or urban informal workers. Crucial to a successful market system are well-defined property rights that outline an owner's relationship with a resource or asset. One form of market failure occurs when property rights are ambiguous or cannot be defined clearly, meaning that they cannot be transferred or protected. In Latin America, ambiguous or contested titles to land resulting from collective forms of property ownership often not recognized by states, or even from civil wars, are commonly at the centre of disputes over natural resources.

Although market failures create environmental problems, societies through states have the power to control or create new markets in order to manage resources more sustainably. Governments can, for example, assign property rights then allow people to negotiate over their price, or they can set a price allowing individuals to bargain over allocation (Hanley, Shogren and White 2001). Green taxes and tradable permits are examples of market mechanisms than aim to achieve environmental outcomes (see Volume 2). However, some green economists have grown sceptical about the extent to which these can compel people who harm the environment to internalize the costs of their actions, concluding that only either anti-capitalism or significant levels of state intervention will be able fully to protect the environment. Changing forestry policy in Costa Rica offers the opportunity to compare the impact of free market and statist approaches to policy on the environment, and to gain insights into the limitations of a hybrid policy seeking to reconcile these approaches. Brockett and Gottfried (2002) analysed three periods in the country's economic development: "laissez-faire", when deforestation was largely unrestrained and left to the devices of the market; an "interventionist" period, when the state began to protect some wild areas, but regulatory policies produced mixed results; and the present "hybrid" period", mixing market-oriented and interventionist approaches, albeit not always coherently. They found that despite significant successes "hybrid" policies would not provide sufficient incentives to maintain the desired amount of forest cover unless the international community compensated Costa Ricans for the benefits that their forests provide the world.

At the heart of the state versus market debate is the potential impact of continual economic growth on natural endowments. Capitalism is reliant on growth for its stability and states use this to measure performance, with debate concentrating on which indicator best reflects progress. Growth as measured by GNP, for example, is not synonymous with "development", which can be interpreted in a broader way through indices such as the UN's Human Development Index that include social and environmental indicators of well-being. Although GNP and HDI omit direct references to the impact of growth on the environment, they can still tell us about sustainable development. Evidence supports the notion, for example, that poverty and inequality are bad for sustainability because the rich benefit more from activities that degrade the environment (see below; Hanley, Shogren and White 2001). Early economic thought was particularly exercised about the idea of diminishing resources and scarcity, although for generations economists ignored environmental and resource issues. In the 1970s, the *Limits to Growth Report* – which predicted economic collapse through a shortage of natural resources combined with population growth and increasing pollution – spurred the development of environmental economics (see Meadows et al. 1972). The implication of this model was that the environment imposed clear limits on development, and so a balance had to be achieved between economic growth and human survival. Today, the discipline of environmental economics is based mainly on rational choice theory and our understanding of market success and failure, suggesting that environmental problems can be addressed with conventional economic policy tools. Many people believe that economies can *grow* their way out of environmental problems, a view supported by multilateral bodies and developed countries often referred to as the Environmental Kuznets Curve theory (see Box 5.5).

By contrast with mainstream positions on the relationship between growth and the environment, ecological economics – which emphasizes the interdependence of economies and ecosystems – stresses constraints such as finite fossil fuel stocks. Some environmental economists argue that growth should aim to achieve a "steady state" in which a stable population and level of consumption remain at or below the planet's "carrying capacity" – its maximal load (see Hanley, Shogren and White 2001). The Global Footprint Network has developed a way of illustrating this – the Ecological Footprint accounting framework – which tracks humanity's demands on the

Box 5.5 The Environmental Kuznets Curve

The Kuznets Curve hypothesis envisages a relationship between income levels and environmental quality in the form of an inverted U-shape (see Hanley, Shogren and White 2001). It states that as per capita incomes grow so does damage to the environment because of increasing use of land and resources and rising levels of waste. The transformation from agriculture to industry increases emissions as manufacturing becomes the dominant activity. However, rising incomes then reach a turning point where demand among citizens for greater environmental quality results in policy measures to protect the environment and in green consumerism. Technological improvements make production cleaner and the evolution from manufacturing to service sector activity or high-tech industry results in less pollution. Theoretical literature has advanced many ideas to explain this "non-linear" relationship, but is the Kuznets Curve actually present? Although empirical evidence supports this theory for some pollutants, the relationship between income growth and pollution varies according to the type of pollution and other factors such as levels of trade or even political criteria, and studies in relation to greenhouse gas emissions have also produced contradictory results. The hypothesis has been applied to cases where trade liberalization leading to economic growth may have had implications for environmental quality such as that of NAFTA (see below). Proponents of NAFTA argued that free trade would improve environmental conditions in Mexico while opponents said these would worsen because Mexico's lower standards would make it a pollution haven for US industry (see Gallagher 2004). Early studies indicated the point at which economies begin to become less pollution-intensive was a per capita income of about $5,000, but Mexico had reached this level in 1985 – a decade before NAFTA. Gallagher (2004) found no evidence that pollution began to decrease after Mexico passed this turning point nor that other environmental indicators showed improvement. In short, the Kuznets Curve is not a reliable indication of what economic growth will do to the environment or how the market resolves its failures. It may be even less applicable to global pollution, where the environmental costs of greenhouse gas emissions may be borne by people in other countries.

biosphere and compares these with the planet's capacity to regenerate (see Pollard 2010). GFN argues that humanity's Ecological Footprint has doubled since 1966 and that by 2007 it had exceeded the Earth's biocapacity – the area available to produce renewable resources and absorb CO_2 – by 50 per cent. New anti-consumerism discourses are emerging that challenge the notion that perpetual growth is possible (see, for example, Jackson 2011). Other ideas emphasize mechanisms to reduce the profit motive and overconsumption, such as local markets, participatory economics (sometimes called "parecon") or local economic transaction schemes (LETS) as an alternative to conventional currencies (Albert 2006; North 2006; Hines 2000). LETS schemes have been attempted with significant local benefits in both Mexico (with currency called "Tlalocs") and in Argentina, where the Global Exchange Network (GEN, using "creditos" that had parity with pesos) represented a grassroots response to the deep financial crisis of the late 1990s.

Export dependence. Exports remain the motor of Latin American and Caribbean growth and the region is reliant on the sale of commodities produced by extractive sectors such as hydrocarbon exploration, mining and forestry. This reliance on exports has shaped the structure of society and politics. Oligarchic rule and dictatorships often reflected the relationship between landholding export elites and the US where the main markets for their products developed; in countries such as Venezuela, the exploitation of oil for export was intimately related to state-building and fostered centralization and corruption. However, the notion that there is a relationship between natural resource abundance on the one hand and corruption and slow growth on the other has been challenged (see Di John 2009). While state control enabled the development of extractive sectors and deepened dependence on the export of key commodities such as oil, this may have stifled the development of other economic sectors. The "resource curse" thesis, for example, has been applied to the Venezuelan state, whose evolution was influenced by the income generated by a relatively small workforce in the oil sector after the 1920s. This thesis refers to the apparent paradox of countries with an abundance of natural resources tending to have lower growth and development than countries with fewer natural resources (see Karl 1997). The rise of market economics in the 1980s intensified Latin America's export drive, with negative consequences for the environment (see Stewart 1996; Thrupp 1996; Kimerling 1996; Alexander 1996). A commodity boom between 2003 and 2008 only served to illustrate the difficulties faced by governments in the region trying to wean themselves off primary goods. Under President Evo Morales, for example, Bolivia has become even more dependent on hydrocarbon and mining exports, according to a recent report by the Center of Studies for Labor and Agrarian Development (CEDLA) (see Ruiz-Marrero 2011). Latin America and the Caribbean is also being marketed as a tourist destination because of this sector's ability to generate foreign currency, with the advent of mass tourism also taking an environmental toll (see Pattulo 1996; McDonald Beckles 1996). This emphasis on primary commodities and tourism raises questions about long-term sustainability: structuralist arguments suggest that the price of manufactured goods tends to be stable or rise over time while the prices of raw materials such as oil fluctuate (see Roberts and Thanos 2003). Latin America itself has little consumption capacity for commodities produced by its own capitalist export sector – for example, as beef exports from Central America rose in the 1990s, domestic beef consumption remained low (see Faber 1993). The overwhelming importance of commodity exports to Latin American and Caribbean economic development is a response to rapidly growing external demand based on continuous global growth driven mainly by the increase in human population (see UNFPA 2011). The region's population of 591.4 million is projected to rise more slowly than some other developing regions, however, with implications for food supplies: a move away from food self-sufficiency toward agro exports has created an incentive for some governments to promote transgenic crops, often with little consideration for the environment (see Box 5.6 and Volume 2).

Another reason for the dependence on extraction is Latin America's abundant stock of natural resources. For example, hydrocarbon "blocks" in which companies buy the right to explore for and exploit oil and gas, cover more than 70 per cent of the Peruvian Amazon; two-thirds of the Ecuadorean Amazon is zoned for hydrocarbon expansion; and 55 per cent of Bolivian national territory is considered to be of potential hydrocarbon interest; in Central America, hydrocarbon concessions dot the entire Mosquitia and Pacific coast (see Bebbington 2009).

Box 5.6 Transgenic crops in Latin America

In Latin America and the Caribbean, the introduction of transgenic crops coincided with neoliberal restructuring which created an incentive for governments to promote them as a means of boosting exports. Developing countries have generally lacked the capacity fully to assess – and hence appropriately to regulate – the environmental consequences of these GMOs. Otero (2008) addresses the environmental impact of GMOs in Latin America by concentrating on the experiences of Mexico, Argentina and Brazil. His collection suggests that the adoption of new biotechnologies has widened disparities in rural incomes and landholdings while reducing food self-sufficiency in Latin America. In developed countries, environmental and consumer groups have generally had a significant voice in regulations governing the adoption of transgenic crops, but this has not universally been the case in Latin America. In Argentina a dramatic growth in agricultural exports has excluded small-scale farmers unable to buy transgenic seeds, and production for domestic markets has fallen, generating food insecurity. In Brazil there has been greater debate of transgenics and several states have banned them. Biotechnology may pose additional threats to biodiversity: the smuggling of seeds from Argentina, for example, has turned most of Brazil's soya bean crop transgenic and in Mexico hybridization risks threaten a crucial reservoir of maize genes. Otero (2009) has also examined the impact of transgenic products in the NAFTA countries and has argued that although transgenics are not suitable to be used as food, rising global food prices are strengthening industry pressure on policymakers to back them as a solution to food insecurity. Otero's analysis of the impact of transgenics in Mexico suggests that this has increased strains in the countryside generated by NAFTA. He examined the growth of transgenics in the context of Mexican food consumption patterns relative to Canada and the US in the period 1985 to 2003 and concluded that they offer little prospect of solving food insecurity.

Export dependence can have a dramatic impact on the environment, encouraging exporters forced to compete globally to reduce costs by compromising on worker safety and environmental protection. Low wages often paid seasonally to migrant labour have been essential for ensuring the profitability of Central American agro-exports, for example, and this in turn perpetuates peasant subsistence on tiny plots or lands that are not ecologically sustainable. Poor rural producers tend to overexploit limited natural resources, resulting in deforestation, soil erosion, loss of watershed and shortages of fish, wildlife and wood fuel. Environmental and social issues are often played down in large-scale economic projects geared towards mining and oil drilling or infrastructure projects (see Baud, de Castro and Hogenboom 2011; van Dijck 2013). The rapid growth in production of transgenic crops in Latin America is closely related to the impact of trade liberalization. Export dependence is driving new, highly productive multinational agro-industrial sectors growing transgenic crops that critics say are promoted with no consideration for the environment.

Making extractivism the centrepiece of development strategy poses questions about long-term sustainability as resources deplete. Orihuela (2008) considered whether extractivism is sustainable in Peru – where more than 50 per cent of exports comprise raw materials – by examining the country's mining sector using an approach called "genuine investment". This states that development is sustainable if the change in wealth (measured as capital valued at constant accounting prices) over a short period of time is non-decreasing. He argued that the Peruvian mining sector was not sustainable in the 10-year period prior to 2005 because: mining rent (royalty) was not optimal; the sector's "natural capital", that is, *proven* reserves, fluctuated significantly, making the genuine investment value vary; and the sector had not contributed significantly to the creation of other kinds of capital.

Some Latin American environmental economists such as Alberto Acosta, a former mining and energy minister in Ecuador, have talked of the need to make a transition to a "post-extractive economy" by limiting the exploitation of resources and moving away from petroleum use. This idea was the basis of the Yasuni-ITT Initiative by which Ecuador was to have refrained from exploiting the oil reserves of the Ishpingo-Tambococha-Tiputini (ITT) oilfield within the Yasuni National Park in exchange for receiving 50 per cent of the value of the reserves ($3.6 bn) over 13 years from the international community. "Set-aside" policies such as the Yasuni-ITT Initiative could protect large areas but highlight the real difficulties faced by governments trying to find alternatives to extraction. Under the Yasuni-ITT plan, leaving the oil underground would have avoided the emission of a quantity of CO_2 roughly equal to the amount produced annually by Brazil with the cash raised used to develop renewable energy initiatives. However, contributions to the fund fell significantly short and in 2013 Ecuador's government abandoned the scheme and reverted to an extractive approach. In El Salvador, a fierce debate is underway about whether to ban metals mining entirely (see Chapter 6).

Globalization. Annual "globalization indexes" based on trade and investment indicators are now produced that include Latin America and Caribbean economies. In 2008, Latin Business Chronicle's index suggested that the region was becoming far more globalized, and identified Panama and Costa Rica as its most globalized economies (see Latin Business Chronicle 2008). The globalization of markets in food commodities and agricultural technology has had a profound impact on development in rural areas (see Rothstein 2007). Some radical critics even argue that the impact of food globalization will result in a form of "genocide" against small farmers (see Shiva and Bedi 2002). Globalization is not producing a uniform social and environmental landscape, creating poles of growth in the world based on regional integration and exacerbating inequalities within countries. Since the 1990s, there has been a significant increase in bilateral and sub-regional free trade initiatives both within Latin America and the Caribbean and between countries in the region and trading partners such as the US and EU. The latest deals between the US and other countries – involving Panama and Colombia – were approved by the US congress in 2011. Free trade initiatives are likely to increase pressure on the environment by generating more economic activity, transportation and hence waste. Free trade works against sustainable practices by forcing small producers and farmers out of business and encouraging urbanization (see below). Globalization is also driving infrastructure development and is behind the Latin American regional construction programme known as the Iniciativa para la Integración de la Infraestructura Regional Suramericana (IIRSA, Initiative for the Integration of the Regional Infrastructure of South America), which highlights the ambitions of the region's governments in global commodities markets (see Baud, de Castro and Hogenboom 2011; van Dijck 2013). By the end of 2012, IIRSA encompassed 531 transport, energy and communications projects across South America representing a total investment of $116 bn.

Conservation International is among environmental organizations that have expressed serious concerns about the impact of IIRSA projects on the environment (see Killeen 2007). In Mexico, a project to expanded highways across the Isthmus of Tehuantepec forms the centrepiece of the multi-billion dollar Plan Puebla-Panama (PPP, also known as Project Mesoamerica), which was launched in 2004. Critics say it will lead to the control of the region by foreign interests, destroy fragile rainforest ecosystems and displace indigenous peoples (see Call 2002).

Globalization is also changing cultural attitudes, and the European Union "global trends" report has argued that, by 2030, the demands and concerns of citizens in different countries across the world are likely to converge, with a major impact on international relations. This will be the result mainly of greater awareness among the world's citizenry of shared aspirations and grievances, creating a global citizens' agenda that emphasizes fundamental freedoms, economic and social rights and, increasingly, environmental issues (see Vasconcelos 2012). In particular, globalization is changing attitudes towards the natural environment and how traditional knowledge is used, particularly through the commodification, popularization and politicization of local ecological knowledge and genetic resources (see Moret 2008). In Cuba, for example, Afro-Cuban ritual activities have proliferated, pushing up demand for medicinal plants employed in hybridized religions such as santería and palo monte. Resistance to globalization can also change the terms of environmental debate. In Ecuador, for example, Sawyer (2004) has shown how the struggle of the Organization of Indigenous Peoples of Pastaza (OPIP) in the Amazon against the incursions of transnational petroleum corporations selectively uses environmentalist language to generate international support and new concepts such as "territory" that go beyond established cultural norms.

Foreign investment and debt. Since the early 1990s, attracting FDI has been a central plank of development strategy in Latin America and the Caribbean and despite variations in the average amount of capital that has flowed into the region every year overall levels have grown considerably. Today, foreign investment is seen by bodies such as ECLAC as essential to creating the conditions for sustained development. The rise in FDI to Latin America and the Caribbean has also been driven by high prices for key commodities such as hydrocarbons and metals. Latin America is an increasingly important destination for FDI in extractive industries: at the start of the 1990s, for example, the region received about 12 per cent of global investment in mining, but today its share is about 33 per cent (see Bebbington 2009). However, the vigorous flow of foreign finance disguises profoundly uneven patterns of investment between countries and different economic sectors in the region. Environmentalists have also frequently tied FDI to chemically intensive agriculture, ecologically harmful oil extraction, mining, logging and ranching projects, and highly polluting industries. Foreign investment and debt have also enhanced the economic and political influence of external forces in Latin America and the Caribbean able to link the capital they offer to their policy preferences. The US, for example, has played an important role promoting a development model that has expanded, modernized and diversified capitalist export-agriculture and industry, with major social and ecological consequences. Central American countries have long been highly dependent for their prosperity on US markets for commodities such as coffee and bananas. The US has also exerted influence over the political development of these countries with policies that supported the interests of US-based multinational corporations and banks and to ensure the continued predominance of an export sector elite (see Faber 1993). The growth of FDI in the region from countries such as China has geopolitical implications: a consequence of the growth of the extractive frontier is the declining geopolitical weight of the US in relation to other sources of FDI.

Political conditions play a role in determining the levels of FDI that countries receive, with investors shying away from political instability and hostility to the presence of foreign corporations making them nervous. Globalization strengthens the influence of multinational corporations in national policymaking within Latin America and the Caribbean by limiting states' room for manoeuvre through the fear of a withdrawal of capital. Modern states spend much time and energy trying to ensure a "favourable investment climate" by pursuing economic policies that offer stability to investors by obeying international norms. Critics of FDI sometimes argue that it can foster environmentally damaging "enclave economies" when foreign companies contract out to other multinationals and import inputs from overseas, not locally (see Gallagher and Zarsky 2007).

Against these criticisms, multinational corporations are also often seen by governments as beneficial for bringing positive "spillovers" – knowledge, skills and technology that local firms can benefit from as well as environmental practices from other parts of the world that help to improve local standards (Ocampo 2009). MNCs can also transfer clean technology, particularly environmental management systems, and can diffuse good practices along business supply chains, for example through labelling schemes for exports to regions such as Europe. Nonetheless, there is little evidence that foreign companies operating in Latin America and the Caribbean are more likely than domestic ones to comply with environmental laws (see Ocampo 2009). According to a report by the Working Group on Development and Environment in the Americas, an academic initiative at Tufts University, FDI in Latin America has fallen far short of stimulating broad-based economic growth and environmental protection (Gallagher et al. 2008). Its findings included the observations that FDI was attracted by traditional determinants, such as a country's labour costs, and not necessarily whether it represents a pollution haven for foreign firms; and that the environmental performance of foreign firms was mixed, in some instances leading to higher standards, such as the forestry sector in Chile, but in others performing the same or worse than domestic counterparts (Gallagher et al. 2008). One outcome of the tensions generated by foreign investment has been "resource nationalism", the desire to restrict ownership of natural resources to the state in the interests of sovereignty. Resource nationalism has had implications for the environment in Latin America and the Caribbean, weakening the coalitions that brought leftwing leaders to power after 1999 (see Box 5.7).

Box 5.7 Resource-nationalist environmentalism

In October 2007, Peru's then president, Alan García, wrote a newspaper article entitled "El síndrome del perro del hortelano" ("The Dog in the Manger Syndrome"), the first in a series in which he described what he understood to be the main problems facing the country and how to cure them (Bebbington 2009). He argued that Peru's main problem was that its immense natural resource endowments are not legally titled and therefore cannot be traded, do not attract investment, and do not create jobs, thereby perpetuating poverty. He maintained that this situation persists because of a stance once taken by old-style communists who he said had evolved into the environmentalists of the twenty-first century. With the Peruvian Amazonia mainly in mind, García argued that the solution would be to formalize property rights, sell large areas of land and attract investment and modem technology. He proceeded to pass a series of executive decrees to break up community land and resources and make them easier to concentrate in private hands. Disputes between Peru's indigenous communities and its government over concessions granted to extractive industries such as mining and oil drilling have been fuelled by García's perspective and these steps. Nonetheless, the Peruvian president was in fact only articulating a continent-wide push to open up frontiers for extracting hydrocarbons, mining, harvesting timber and expanding agroindustry with huge potential gains to the country. His attitude – like that of his peers in countries such as Bolivia and Ecuador – was that environmental damage was a small price to pay given the billions of dollars that extractive industries generate (see Poole 2010b). That attitude has been much in evidence when accidents have occurred. In 2010, a barge belonging to the Argentine transnational Pluspetrol spilled 400 barrels of oil into the Marañón River in Peru's north-eastern Loreto department, which the Cocama and Achuar peoples depend upon. Extensive contamination was reported by government scientists but the then minister Pedro Sánchez dismissed the spill as small. It was just the latest in a series of environmental accidents that have characterized expansion in Peru of the mining, logging and oil sectors (Poole 2010b). Similarly, in Bolivia, hydrocarbon concessions overlap with protected areas and indigenous territories, and there have been conflicts over the extractive policies pursued by the government of President Evo Morales, whose rationale for this expansion is that these resources are needed to finance social policy. Morales has criticized those opposing hydrocarbon expansion in terms remarkably similar to those of García in Peru, as has President Rafael Correa in Ecuador (Bebbington 2009). Bebbington (2009) argues that the positions of García, Morales and Correa are akin to a current of environmentalism concerned primarily with increased state access to and control over natural resources – resource-nationalist environmentalism. This criticizes foreign and private control of natural resources rather than extraction per se, and can accept the infringement of certain rights if the nation benefits.

Alongside foreign investment, debt remains a key issue in Latin America and the Caribbean, and multilateral lending institutions have considerable policy influence in the region. Debt and aid have in the past often been in the form of loans from organizations such as the IMF, World Bank or US government, conditional on economic reforms. In Central America during the 1990s, for example, structural adjustment policies required recipient nations to boost the production of traditional and non-traditional exports, intensifying the exploitation of natural resources and worsening ecological degradation (Faber 1993; see also Hamilton and Fischer 2003). Some green thinkers such as Rowbotham (2000) have argued that globalization is a product of the debt crisis and a deliberate policy to make all countries compete to pay debt, thereby ensuring that international trade must constantly expand (see also Roberts and Thanos 2003). Some environmental organizations have also developed innovative new understandings of the concept of debt. Friends of the Earth and Acción Ecológica launched a campaign for repayment of the "ecological debt" that rich countries owe from the period of colonialism for accruing wealth at the cost of poverty and ecological devastation in the countries they colonized or controlled (see Carruthers 2008b). Agencies such as the World Bank have responded to criticisms by becoming far more sensitive about the environmental dimension of projects they fund, but many critics remain unconvinced. Nielson and Stern (1997) examined the impact of changes in World Bank lending policies to funnel more resources into its environment portfolio, and found that while it had increased its lending for environmental projects in response to critics, spending heavily favoured infrastructure and tightly focused anti-pollution projects with diffuse benefits.

Poverty and inequality. A product of export dependence in Latin America and the Caribbean has been a high level of poverty and inequality, which are linked to a political economy favouring the interests of a small elite and have exacerbated degradation of the environment (Roberts and Thanos 2003). An important challenge facing governments is to ensure more equitable development without degrading the environment, but, despite calls for more sustainable approaches to resource use, recent debates and proposed reforms continue to reflect a tension between the goals of economic development, social inclusion and ecosystem protection (see above). Latin American governments often refer to the Millennium Development Goals as an agenda simultaneously to improve social circumstances (e.g. poverty and food security) and environmental services (e.g. biodiversity and climate regulation), yet social and environmental issues continue to be sidelined in large-scale projects geared towards extraction or infrastructure. There is significant variation in the ways in which poverty is measured, which can often reflect a state's political and economic priorities. There has been growing recognition that income is a limited indicator of poverty: families with low incomes but who live in safe environments and have access to basic goods and services can be less poor than those with higher incomes who live in harsh conditions where basic needs cost more. In Colombia, a broad new method of measuring poverty was introduced by the government in 2010, the multidimensional poverty index (MPI), which goes beyond a focus on income in estimating poverty levels but also assesses education, health and the assets and housing that together reflect living standards. The MPI has been politically advantageous for the Colombian government, pushing down measured poverty levels (Glennie 2011). Inequality is usually measured by multilateral agencies through the Gini index, which indicates the extent to which the distribution of income or consumption expenditure among individuals or households deviates from a perfectly equal distribution: Colombia's Gini rating has worsened despite rapid economic growth and it is now among the most unequal countries in the region. Environmentalists in Latin America and the Caribbean have developed a notion of "environmental equality", by which citizens have the same rights to enjoy a safe and clean environment that is safeguarded for the future (Olivares Gallardo 2010).

The persistence of poverty and inequality in Latin America and the Caribbean and a political economy that continues to prioritize the export of commodities may point to "structural" explanations for the form of development that prevails in the region, and hence for the negative impact of poverty and inequality on the environment (see Faber 1993). High levels of poverty and inequality that result in ecological degradation can originate in factors beyond the control of governments. Record gold prices in 2009, for example, lured thousands of informal prospectors to the Madre de Dios region in Peru's Amazon region where their alluvial mining practices threaten precious biological diversity.

An important factor that has worked against the eradication of poverty in Latin America has been the absence or ambiguity of property titles, which has fuelled internal migration on to lands that may be seen as "common" over which legal rights are unclear. The commons is a potentially valuable concept in Latin American socio-environmental research that touches on the issue of property rights and the distribution of access and benefits to resources. The commons are resources owned by or shared within communities and traditionally comprised forests, rivers, fisheries or land used by everybody. They differ from private goods or public goods because they may contain public property and private property over which people have certain traditional rights. In theory, the commons have several important features: they cannot be commodified because if they are, they cease to be commons; unlike private property, the commons are inclusive rather than exclusive, because ownership is shared as widely rather than as narrowly as possible; and assets are meant to be preserved regardless of their capital value, and users have a duty to pass them on to future generations in the same condition as they received them (see Baud, de Castro and Hogenboom 2011). The distribution, management and value of the commons play an important role in determining competition over natural resources, and help to emphasize why well-designed policies that link environmental management to socio-economic trends are so important to achieving sustainable development. This is because the commons and groups such as the rural poor have borne a disproportionate share of the negative externalities of capitalist production in Latin America and the Caribbean (see Kaimowitz 1996). Studies by UNEP on the Economics of Ecosystems and Biodiversity (TEEB) have made the case that some of the world's largest and most successful companies would not be viable if they had to pay the full opportunity costs of using the natural resources that they require, highlighting the major challenge the "polluter pays" principle poses to the traditional extractive economy (see Stoddart 2011; TEEB 2010; Bishop et al. 2010). Moreover, groups such as the rural poor that shoulder disproportionate costs for protecting the environment are not always those that reap the benefits of initiatives to do so. Many investments in environmental solutions such as soil conservation or reforestation are long term, and may not benefit the current generation. This helps to explain why immediate poverty reduction strategies through social programmes can seem far more attractive to politicians seeking re-election than efforts to nurture longer-term sustainable development that address the structural causes of poverty.

Trade and the environment

Trade and environmental conditions are intrinsically related because all economic activity derives from the basic inputs (metals and minerals, soil, forests and fisheries) and the energy needed to process them that are provided by the natural environment – which is also where the waste generated by production and consumption is destined to end up. Trade has a profound effect on what and how countries produce, allowing them to specialize in certain goods and thereby enabling them to consume more than they would if they were restricted to using what they produced from their own resources. Economists have long argued that free trade benefits countries by providing an overall increase in welfare and, hence, that obstacles such as tariffs reduce welfare. These principles are the cornerstone of the policies that underpin global trading institutions such as World Trade Organization, and have led to ever-expanding rates of world commerce. It has been argued that this expansion can be beneficial for, or detrimental to, the environment. Greater output and the physical transportation of goods across the world will be more polluting; yet trade may also result in a reallocation of production to countries better able to deal with its environmental side-effects while increasing incomes to levels that encourage consumers to demand higher environmental standards (see Box 5.5).

Removing barriers to trade, liberalization, has been driven by a permanent negotiation to reduce tariffs and regulate competition between countries, and this in turn has led to the creation of multilateral institutions generating a body of international trade law. Chile was an earlier pioneer of trade reform and in the 1980s dismantled tariff barriers and became an export-oriented economy with a high rate of export growth in natural resource-based industries such as agriculture, fisheries, forestry and mining – all areas where it had a comparative advantage. Other governments in Latin America and the Caribbean followed suit and in the late 1980s dismantled protectionist measures and tried to diversify away from exporting a single commodity. Neoliberal policymakers tried to institutionalize trade reforms through free-trade agreements that co-ordinate the mutual reduction of tariff and other barriers to imports between countries. In 1994, Mexico joined with the US and Canada in NAFTA which represented a model for US aspirations to create a Free Trade Area of the Americas (FTAA), an initiative that eventually stalled and was replaced by bilateral agreements between the US and countries in the region. In the US, Democrats and labour officials argued that an FTAA would endanger jobs and the environment. Sub-regional and bilateral free trade agreements proliferated within Latin America and the Caribbean. In 1991, the Mercado Común del Sur/Mercado Comum do Sul (Mercosur/Mercosul, Common Market of the South) was formed and in 2008 the Unión de Naciones Suramericanas (Unasur, Union of South American Nations) was established in an effort to bring together Mercosur and the Comunidad Andina de Naciones (CAN, Andean Community of Nations), thereby extending the potential for a customs union across most of South America.

The trade–environment debate has often been characterized as one that contrasts those who promote trade liberalization as compatible with or even essential for protecting the environment, against environmentalists themselves who argue that these aims are incompatible (see Blair 2008; Heather Williams 2001). By this dualistic perspective, arguments in support of free trade suggest that, by propelling growth, it enables countries to spend more on environmental protection, raising standards (see UNEP/IISD 2005). Developing countries will have to adopt the higher standards of rich countries to enable their businesses to compete. Increased trade has other environmental benefits: it forces producers to be less wasteful and they are more likely to spend surplus on greener technologies rather than taking it as profit. Supporters of free trade point to a concrete result of liberalizing trade: the explicit incorporation of environmental themes into free trade negotiations. Research has duly focused on environmental concerns and actors in regional free trade areas such as NAFTA and the European Union in an effort to highlight means of preventing the negative environmental impacts that result from increased trade within the poorer partner countries of these areas. An institutional innovation was the North American Agreement on Environmental Co-operation (NAAEC), the environmental "side agreement" to NAFTA. There is evidence that US trade and investment deals that make reference to multilateral environmental agreements obliging signatory states not to weaken environmental laws to attract trade or investments have been accompanied by an increased interest in environmental issues (see Van Roozendaal 2009). In the other camp, critics of free trade say that more trade means more pollution because more goods are transported around the world. They argue that liberalization increases export opportunities and hence the burden on natural resources such as forests and fisheries. The critics say the free flow of goods and capital can weaken environmental rules when governments either seek to lure investment by softening regulations to the level of the lowest denominator or not enforcing them in a "race to the bottom", or refrain from strengthening them ("regulatory chill") (see Gallagher 2004). If competition resulting from liberalization generates efficiency gains, these are converted into price reductions and hence even greater consumption. Moreover, they say free trade arguments never acknowledge that the price of a good rarely includes the full value of the natural resource, transportation costs, the costs to society of pollution and increased CO_2. Furthermore, free trade may deepen inequalities and as a result exacerbate damage to the environment (see above; MacDonald and Stern 1997; Muñoz 1997; Carter 2007).

Trade economists have developed conceptual tools to examine how liberalization may affect the global environment through, for example, emissions (see Box 5.8).

Over time, trade and environment debates have broadened to include concerns that acknowledge the difficulties faced by developing countries in the world trading system and their priority of reducing poverty. Openness to trade and investment is essential to development, but rich countries have more power to protect their industries and dominate multilateral trading bodies such as the WTO. Banning or restricting trade on environmental grounds or demanding that poor countries comply with the standards of rich countries may be one way of perpetuating their advantages. The best way to ensure environmental protection, therefore, is to create fair rules to govern trade. Increasingly, multilateral trade agreements have included environmental criteria (see UNEP/IISD 2005; WTO 2001). This position was pioneered during the NAFTA debate in the US in the early 1990s, in which many ENGOs did not call for the rejection of all free trade agreements but for provisions within them to ensure that environmental laws and regulations would be safeguarded and even strengthened (see Blair 2008).

Box 5.8 How does trade affect GHGs?

Economists have developed a conceptual framework to examine how liberalization may affect the environment which breaks it down into three "effects":

- ***Scale***: how greenhouse gas emissions may increase due to increased economic activity;
- ***Composition***: the way trade liberalization affect the size of a country's production sectors;
- ***Technique***: the way in which cleaner technology reduces the emissions of production.

The scale effect presumes that trade opening will lead to economic growth, thereby magnifying the impact on emissions. The composition effect refers to how trade results in the expansion of some sectors and the contraction of others. A rise or fall in emissions will depend on whether the emission-intensive sectors expand or contract, but if trade reform means a country produces fewer emission-intensive goods, these may be bought elsewhere, generating emissions in other parts of the world. The technique effect refers to improvements in production methods that reduce emissions: open trade should make climate-friendly goods and services available and cheaper, and rising income levels generated by greater trade should increase public pressure for lower emissions (see Torras and Boyce 1998). Evidence about the effects of trade liberalization on emissions tends to suggest that open trade is likely to increase these, but some studies suggest that developed countries will improve while developing countries will deteriorate. Negotiations on trade agreements have usually included environmental assessments which highlight the concerns of negotiators and civil society groups about the environmental impacts of free trade. The EU conducted an environmental assessment of the EU–Chile Free Trade Agreement that examined its effect on the forestry sector and concluded that commercial plantations could slow down climate change by capturing carbon dioxide. The EU also examined the likely impact of an EU–Mercosur Association Agreement which identified mixed impacts of the proposed deal (University of Manchester 2009). Transportation is a key issue because of its role in generating greenhouse gas emissions and international trade greatly increases the shipment of goods. However trade opening may also contribute to climate change mitigation and adaptation efforts through the technique effect by opening doors to energy efficient goods and services and encouraging the spread of clean technology. (Main source: WTO/UNEP 2009).

Scholte (2005) has distinguished between neoliberal, reformist and radical policy approaches to globalization. Advocates of the reformist position accept the inevitability of trade liberalization and continued economic growth but emphasize the need for a substantial state role in environmental protection through regulation at both national and international levels. Reformist approaches to trade and the environment can take two different forms (see Blair 2008):

- strong reformism, endorsing extensive and stringent state regulation and international regimes with authority to enforce compliance (a position favoured by environmentalists);
- weak reformism using co-operative mechanisms such as promises to strengthen regulations, efforts to harmonise regulations, information sharing and capacity building (see also Esty 1994).

But does the liberalization of trade turn developing countries such as Mexico into pollution havens? The pollution haven hypothesis argues that free trade encourages polluting industries from developed countries to relocate to developing countries where environmental regulations are weaker and enforcement poor. Empirical studies have been inconclusive and evidence appears to suggest that dirty industries are *not* moving to developing countries to reduce environmental costs (see Marc Williams 2001; Hanley, Shogren and White 2001; Gallagher 2004; Muñoz 1997). Birdsall and Wheeler (1993) even argued, based on the case of Chile, that liberalizing trade had positive effects on the environment by increasing competitive pressures, thereby accelerating investment in non-polluting technologies. The Working Group on Development and Environment in the Americas, however, concluded in a report on the environmental impacts of trade liberalization and economic reforms in Latin America that, with some exceptions, free-trade policies have taken a heavy toll on the environment (see Schalatek 2004; Tosun 2009). It questioned the assumptions that trade and investment liberalization will automatically lead to growth and that this naturally leads to environmental improvements. Muñoz (1997) proposed a typology of the ways in which environmental protection policies are linked to trade liberalization: anticipatory or pragmatic policies aim either to facilitate a country's insertion into competitive markets which enforce strong ecological standards, or to facilitate negotiation of free trade deals with countries that have strict standards in order to neutralize political pressures regarding their level of environmental protection; while reactive policies respond to criticisms in the context of free trade talks with countries that have high environmental standards. Muñoz examined the cases of Chile, Mexico and Venezuela during the 1980s and concluded that in Chile free trade had both positive and negative effects, which varied according to the products and sectors involved and the period analysed; in Venezuela, liberalization did not have a positive or negative impact on the environment because oil, not trade, was the driver of the economy; and in Mexico NAFTA encouraged the enforcement of national environmental standards and a new environmental activism by the government (see Box 5.9). Muñoz suggested that the environmental impact of liberalization is not uniform, and by itself it is neither detrimental nor favourable to ecological well-being.

Other reports have taken a broader view of the relationship between economic reform and the environment by examining how agricultural trade liberalization affects the potential for sustainable development among small famers. Pérez, Schlesinger and Wise (2008) looked at the impact of export agriculture on smallholder agriculture and poverty reduction in Latin American countries. They argued that governments play a key role in overcoming market failures, and sustained agricultural development cannot be achieved under indiscriminate liberalization.

The prevailing consensus seems to be that trade policy may not be the best way for a country to achieve domestic environmental goals, restricting trade is not the way to deal with pollution, and devices such as emissions taxes or tradable permits may be more effective (see Chapter 6; Hanley, Shogren and White 2001). Nonetheless, although multilateral governance on the environment and on trade have developed two distinct spheres of international law, these have begun to interact and officials are now asking what institutions are needed to ensure that trade and environmental policies are mutually supportive (UNEP/IISD 2005). The incorporation of environmental themes in the trade agenda represents recognition that in many developing countries environmental policies continue to be weak or poorly enforced, strengthening the case for using elements of trade policy to support them. For this reason, many multilateral and bilateral trade agreements such as those between the US and Colombia and Panama in 2011 incorporate sections on the environment.

Box 5.9 NAFTA and the environment

NAFTA was the first international agreement seriously to address the environmental problems that may result from free trade (MacDonald and Nielson 1997; Muñoz 1997). The environmental institutions it established have been seen as a model for other Latin American countries negotiating bilateral trade agreements with the US (see also Deere and Esty 2002). Moreover, the North American Agreement on Environmental Co-operation (NAAEC), NAFTA's environmental "side agreement", has influenced proposals for global environmental governance mechanisms (see Blair 2008; Esty 1994; Runge et al. 1994). NAFTA became effective in 1994 and the NAAEC created a Commission for Environmental Co-operation (CEC) that can appoint arbitration panels to investigate complaints about a member state's non-compliance with its environmental laws. Analysis of the impact of these bodies and of the Mexican state's new commitment to environmental protection have generally supported the idea that liberalization was beneficial to Mexico's environment, but there have been misgivings:

- ***Pollution***. CEC studies have discussed the effects of NAFTA on greenhouse gas emissions arising from trucking and rail freight which are expected to rise substantially by 2020.
- ***Standards and enforcement***. While under NAFTA Mexican enforcement of regulations initially became stricter, subsequent enforcement has been erratic (see Vogel 2006). In 2008, for example, a number of claimants filed a submission with the CEC asserting that Mexico is failing effectively to enforce its environmental laws.
- ***Jurisdiction***. There have been disputes about jurisdiction and the rightful body for dealing with environmental issues. In 2007, for example, a NAFTA tribunal ruled that it lacked jurisdiction to hear a dispute brought by US-based water users against Mexico over water access.
- ***Civil society***. After success in the initial bargaining processes, the opportunities provided for ENGO participation in the environmental aspects of NAFTA have not been realized.

Scholars have mixed views on the NAFTA environmental institutions. Gallagher (2004) views the NAAEC as a potentially positive tool that could raise Mexican standards. Blair (2008) assessed NAFTA in terms of the contribution it has made to the predominance of neoliberal ideas that are ultimately harmful to the environment (see also Fougner 2006; Tosun 2009).

However, the liberalization of trade encouraged by organizations such as the WTO and the concerns of environmentalists have often been at odds. The WTO is still criticized for favouring unrestrained trade that environmentalists say benefits from an institutional structure that excludes global civil society (see Weber 2001; Chapter 6). Weber (2001) argues that the WTO's conception of the trade-environment link reflects a neoliberal bias in global governance prioritizing economic interests over the concerns of a "global public". ENGOs and environmental organizations have called for a "democratization" of the WTO to open global economic governance to ecological impacts.

Conclusion

Economic globalization has shaped the development of Latin America and the Caribbean since Independence and is the most important influence on policy today. The dependence on export markets, a close relationship with foreign capital and the impetus for regional integration have all been driven by economic forces external to the region or its responses to them. Today, Latin America and the Caribbean is globalizing fast and nowhere is that process more visible than in trade. The region is becoming ever more integrated into the titanic global flows of commodities and capital investment that are shaping our era. Global trade is having huge economic, social and political effects on the region's emerging economies – and has equally important implications for its environment. Trade and environmental conditions are intrinsically related, and the trade–environment debate has pitted those who promote "free trade" as compatible with environmental protection against those who argue that more trade merely means more pollution, a greater burden on natural resources – and weaker environmental rules as governments compete for investment by watering down regulations. Moreover, environmentalists often argue that the rich countries that promote free trade both have the power to protect their industries from competition from developing economies and dominate the multilateral bodies that set the rules of commerce. Latin America and the Caribbean offers a valuable laboratory in which to test the impact of economic liberalization and free trade on the environment.

Recommended reading

Gallagher, Kevin P. 2004. *Free Trade and the Environment: Mexico, NAFTA and Beyond*. Stanford, CA: Stanford University Press.

Hayden, Cori. 2003. *When Nature Goes Public: The Making and Unmaking of Bioprospecting in Mexico*. Princeton, NJ: Princeton University Press.

Otero, Gerardo (ed.). 2008. *Food for the Few: Neoliberal Globalism and Biotechnology in Latin America*. Austin: University of Texas Press.

Panizza, Francisco. 2009. *Contemporary Latin America: Development and Democracy Beyond the Washington Consensus*. London: Zed Books.

Tecklin, David, Carl Bauer and Manuel Prieto. 2011. "Making Environmental Law for the Market: The Emergence, Character, and Implications of Chile's Environmental Regime", *Environmental Politics*, Vol. 20, No. 6 (November), pp. 879–98.

Useful websites

Biofuelwatch: www.biofuelwatch.org.uk/

Economics Departments, Institutes and Research Centers in the World Resource and Environmental Economics, Energy Economics: http://edirc.repec.org/resource.html

Fairtrade International (FLO): www.fairtrade.net/

Global Footprint Network: www.footprintnetwork.org/en/index.php/GFN/

International Society for Ecological Economics (ISEE): www.isee2010.org/

Latin American and Caribbean Association of Environmental and Resource Economists www.alear.org/

Latin American and Caribbean Council on Renewable Energy (LAC-CORE): http://lac-core.org/

Latin American and Caribbean Environmental Economics Program (LACEEP): www.laceep.org/

Latin American and Caribbean Network of Environmental Funds (RedLAC): www.redlac.org/

Renewable Energy Finance Forum–Latin America and Caribbean (REFF-LAC): www.refflac.com/

The Principles for Responsible Investment (PRI) (convened by UNEP FI and the UN Global Compact): www.unpri.org

United Nations Environment Programme Finance Initiative (UNEP FI): www.unepfi.org

Working Group on Development and Environment in the Americas: http://ase.tufts.edu/gdae/wgoverview.htm

CHAPTER SIX

Sustainable development and climate change

SUSTAINABLE DEVELOPMENT refers to development that meets the needs of present generations without reducing the ability of future generations to meet their own needs, and although it offers something for those with environmental concerns across the political spectrum it does not imply a transformation of capitalism but proposes reforms to make it more environmentally friendly. In the business sectors of rapidly growing economies such as Brazil the concept of sustainability is often emphasized in terms of the ability to maintain and *expand* growth in finite agro-export sectors in areas such as Amazonia. Brazil sees itself as both an economic and a "biological" power, aiming to become the world's largest food exporter by 2025 – and sustainability is central to this economic ambition (see Rathbone 2011). But on what basis do policymakers make decisions that steer investment towards environmentally friendly forms of development? In order to advance sustainable forms of production and consumption, they need to be able to measure these, and this chapter introduces the notion of environmental accounting and examines how this can test established concepts of economic growth. International agencies and states are increasingly making efforts to determine the role played by ecosystem services within economic growth and how to place a value on these. In a region like Latin America and the Caribbean, where access to capital remains limited, governments pursuing sustainable development also have to find new ways to fund this. This chapter looks at innovative "green financing" mechanisms created at a multilateral level to help meet the cost of addressing climate change. It explores how Latin American and Caribbean states are also drawing upon an established repertoire of economic policy tools to use alongside traditional environmental regulation in their efforts to pursue sustainable development. Governments in the region are also identifying foreign corporations and the domestic private sector as promising sources of finance for green development. They are promoting the development of new green economic sectors themselves, such as organic farming and ecotourism. The pursuit of sustainable development has implications for how the benefits of a country's land and resources are distributed, and states are also turning their attention to the need for policies aimed at reducing poverty and inequality to interact with those aimed at achieving sustainability. Faced with the pressing need to address climate change, governments are also grappling with the economic implications of adapting to or mitigating the impact of changing weather patterns on their countries and searching for the best policies with which to respond to them.

Sustainability and growth

The notion of sustainable development begs important questions about whether continual economic growth is both possible and desirable, at the heart of which is the sense that countries face a trade-off between development and ecological degradation (see Hanley, Shogren and White 2001). Any consideration of sustainable development in Latin America and the Caribbean must also take into account how the forces of economic globalization influence its prospects for success (see Saha and Parker 2002; Markandya and Halsnaes 2002). Its relationship with international trade, for example, has been the focus of considerable study and many multilateral initiatives (see, for example, Gallagher and Werksman 2002; Deere and Esty 2002; Paehlke 2003). Whereas debates have generally considered how trade rules fit with environmental regulations and have been dominated by the positions of rich countries, discussions about trade and sustainable development have generally focused on ways of nurturing green growth in poor countries and have been dominated by voices from the developing world. Economists in developing countries often argue that the developed world's consideration of trade rules solely in economic terms may in fact hinder development by applying outside standards to countries that cannot afford them, and so also represent concealed protectionism. Similarly, sustainable development aims to balance growth across this and future generations by using resources appropriately, and debates often focus on the consumption patterns of the current generation (see Hanley, Shogren and White 2001; Assadourian 2010a). Advocates of sustainable development argue that, if resources are finite, continual economic growth and consumption cannot be sustainable.

These debates draw attention to the ways in which resources are exploited in an ideal free market and imply the need for targeted interventions by states to attain sustainability either, for example, by extending their control over key sectors in an effort to make a system less polluting and wasteful or by liberalizing markets to nurture cleaner forms of private enterprise (see below). The state versus market debate in Latin America and the Caribbean has hitherto tended to suggest that only either privatization or public expropriation can efficiently manage resources. At the same time, much scholarship has considered the impact of free markets upon isolated groups. In countries within Latin America and the Caribbean that fully embraced market growth, such as Chile, there is certainly evidence that the ambition to incorporate equity and sustainability goals within policymaking have caused developmental dilemmas in areas dominated by the private sector, such as agriculture (see Murray 2002). A common vision of sustainable development envisages a mixed economy in which states and markets work in harmony to sustainable ends. Saha and Parker (2002), for example, call for a partnership between states and markets as a way of realizing sustainable objectives, arguing that meeting the challenges of globalization requires regulated markets and a willingness by the state to provide a seedbed for enterprise and competitive advantage in areas that markets fail to reach.

In a similar way, development studies have often counterposed a tendency to declare as backward and in need of modernization any form of communal resource management – among indigenous communities, for example – against a view that vilifies the market per se. Small communities tend to organize economic life around diversification strategies, small-scale production and collective forms of work, land and resource tenure. By contrast, capitalist market norms tend to be based on mass production, mono-cropping and private

Box 6.1 Common property

Vaccaro, Zanotti and Sepez (2009) describe how common property – the "commons" – can in some circumstances be directed to a form of collectively controlled production able to integrate with the international market. The high profitability of a communally managed commodity may thereby subsidize development and allow other aspects of a local economy to remain viable. They examine cases in which communities have organized themselves to generate income from their commons while maintaining (or reinventing) collective identity and improving the possibilities for sustainability. The creation of Kayapó reserves in the Brazilian Amazon in the 1990s, for example, offered these communities new economic possibilities. External markets, resources and aid increased, and at the same time the Kayapó retained their own forms of governance. After experimenting with mining and logging, most Kayapó communities began to rethink their market activities, and with the help of NGOs and Brazil's Fundação Nacional do Índio (FUNAI, National Indian Foundation) sought alternative markets for common resources. Conservation programmes involving the Kayapó have begun to use Non-Timber Forest Products as the basis of forestry management strategies, and the market has opened up new niches for products such as Brazil nuts. For example, in the 1990s, two Kayapó communities entered into a relationship with the Body Shop which bought Brazil nut oil for cosmetics. Villages have also developed other sources of income: selling handicrafts, seasonal jobs, support from ENGOs and government jobs within the community. Similarly, in Mexico, there is a thriving community owned forestry sector in which hundreds of villages own and operate their own forestry businesses producing timber commercially. Klooster (2003a, 2003b) argues that this model of communal ownership generates environmental and social benefits. Barton Bray, Antinori and Torres-Rojo (2006) argue that the Mexican model has important implications for global forestry, demonstrating that government can itself create common property and social capital.

property norms that transform social and environmental relations. Many anthropological works have emphasized the historical viability of communal forms of resource management and how, in turn, these have been negatively affected by market incentives. Nonetheless, some research suggests that common property systems *can* engage with markets and through them global trade, arguing that it is possible and even desirable for indigenous communities to do this (see Vaccaro, Zanotti and Sepez 2009). In Brazil, for example, the creation of Kayapó indigenous reserves in the central Amazon in the 1990s gave small indigenous communities new access to resources and aid (see Box 6.1).

Environmental accounting and pricing ecosystem services

A crucial step on the road towards sustainable development, if investment is to be steered towards environmentally sound development, is the integration of the environment into economic policies. However, if policymakers and society are to prioritize sustainable forms of production and consumption, they need to be able to *measure* these. Governments need a detailed understanding of the contribution made by ecosystems to economies in order to determine environmental spending, making "environmental accounting" a key tool of sustainable development (see ECLAC 2002). An important requirement for assessing the use of economic policy tools to protect the environment, for example, is to place a value on the contribution the environment makes to development. Environmental accounts do just this by applying monetary values to "natural capital" – the resources that provide ecosystem goods or services – in order to inform policy decisions or to ensure that the environmental costs caused by some activities are "internalized" by producers.

There has been considerable debate about the best indicators with which to measure sustainable development and what is the best balance between growth and sustainability. Governments have, for example, sometimes focused on consumption patterns to account for future trends, or estimated the depreciation of both natural and man-made capital when considering reinvestment plans (see Hanley, Shogren and White 2001). Other indicators now being incorporated within national accounting include the notion of the "Ecological Footprint" or "carbon footprint" (see below).

The first challenge facing governments is calculating exactly how much is spent, and by whom, on managing and protecting the environment, and, since the early 1990s, many countries and multilateral agencies have been working on methodologies to measure environmental expenditure accurately. This can be used to evaluate: how environmental protection costs influence international competitiveness and employment; how to apply the "polluter pays" principle so those that damage the environment pay for doing so; and the level of demand for goods and services generated by the environmental management sector itself. A key difficulty in any assessment of what is and what should be spent on the environment is methodological, and there is no universally accepted way of measuring this. Since the early 1990s, a number of countries and international organizations have been developing systems for measuring environmental expenditure – the "Environmental Protection Expenditure Account" – in order to measure the cost of a society's responses to environmental problems. It is a complex task and most of these initiatives have been in developed countries based on the guidelines prepared by the OECD and the European Statistical Agency (EUROSTAT), which have worked closely with the UN Statistical Division (see EUROSTAT 2002)

When it comes to spending by the private sector, there are even greater challenges. In Latin America and the Caribbean, a key problem in measuring environmental spending by private corporations is a lack of information and of a suitable methodology, but some countries have tried to address this issue. Chile's Instituto Nacional de Estadísticas (INE, National Statistics Institute) has worked with business organizations to measure private environmental expenditure. INE surveys prior to 2001 revealed that fewer than 50 per cent of Chilean corporations had invested in the environment in the previous decade but about 45 per cent of them claimed to meet environmental standards (ECLAC 2002). Mexico, Colombia and Guatemala have introduced a model of valuation called the standardized System of Environmental and Economic Accounting (SEEA), UN-supervised accounting rules.

At the heart of efforts to measure sustainable development lies the concept of economic growth. Established measures of wealth such as GDP do not reflect the total economic value of ecosystems and treat common goods and services as free to use, usually indicating that countries that do not exploit their resources sustainably appear to be getting richer in the short term. However, if wealth is valued in other ways it could reveal that for many countries economic gains understood in this way are in fact illusory (CBD 2006). Even non-traditional export sectors developed by Latin American and

Box 6.2 Ecuador's sustainable floriculture industry

The boom in exports of flowers from Ecuador since the late 1980s has been seen as a classic example of diversification into non-traditional exports (see Chapters 1, 5). Growth was generated by trade liberalization in the agricultural sector generally and has been judged a success story (Sawers 2005a). From 1987 to 2002, the share of flowers in Ecuador's non-petroleum export earnings rose from less than 0.2 per cent to 9 per cent, with export earnings growing in real terms by 114 per cent in 1989 and then averaging 42 per cent annually until 1995. However, Sawers (2005b) has drawn attention to questions about the sustainability of floriculture in Ecuador and examined the impact of the flower boom in some regions. He argues that Ecuador is likely to maintain a strong economic position in the flower export market despite growing competition because of prime growing conditions in the country and its proximity to the US market. The growth of the labour-intensive floriculture industry has had positive economic effects on communities in which flowers are cultivated by raising incomes, providing jobs and slowing rural-to-urban migration. However, the gains in income have been offset by growing health and environmental problems posed by the pesticides used in the flower industry.

Caribbean countries to ensure economic growth while avoiding a dependency on traditional commodities can damage the environment and thus challenge the label "sustainable" that governments often apply to them (see Box 6.2).

One accounting method that has been devised to compare human demands on the biosphere with the regenerative capacity of the planet is the Ecological Footprint (see Chapter 5). This measures human demands on the environment – in terms of our need for resources such as crops and fish for food, the areas occupied by infrastructure, and the areas required for absorbing waste, including CO_2 – and compares these with the planet's capacity to regenerate ("biocapacity"). Both the footprint (representing the demand for resources) and biocapacity (representing the availability of resources) are expressed in global hectares (gha), with 1 gha representing the productive capacity of 1 ha of land at average productivity. The Ecological Footprint illustrates, predictably, that developed countries

Box 6.3 TEEB

In 2006, the *Stern Review on the Economics of Climate Change* pioneered new ways of thinking about the challenge of global warming and projected that extreme weather conditions could result in losses of $200 bn (Stern 2007). In 2007, the Economics of Ecosystems and Biodiversity (TEEB) initiative was launched at a meeting in Germany of environment ministers from the G8+5 countries who agreed to study the impact of biodiversity loss. TEEB represents a recognition that the loss of forests, soils, wetlands and coral reefs is related to the fact that these have so far been economically invisible. The initiative has published a series of reports aimed at showing how economic concepts and tools can give society a means of incorporating the value of nature within decision-making. TEEB's proponents argue that it can clarify two key issues: why prosperity and poverty reduction depend on maintaining the flow of benefits from ecosystems; and why successful environmental protection needs to be grounded in sound economics that recognize and distribute fairly the costs and benefits of conservation and the sustainable use of natural resources (see TEEB 2010).

with higher incomes make much greater demands on the Earth's ecosystems than poorer, less-developed countries. The most widely used indicator for development itself is UNDP's Human Development Index (HDI) which combines income, life expectancy and educational levels to compare countries. The relationship between Ecological Footprint and HDI is uneven but as development increases beyond a certain level so does per capita footprint. Ecological Footprint accounting has been championed by the Global Footprint Network (GFN) independent think tank and it is now being used throughout Latin America and the Caribbean (GFN 2010).

Environmental accounting is seen as a way of helping countries move towards "green" economies, a notion enshrined in 2008 by UNEP's Green Economy Initiative. An important element of this vision is a clear understanding of TEEB (the Economics of Ecosystems and Biodiversity), which places a value on ecosystem services (see Box 6.3).

The Millennium Ecosystem Assessment (2005) defined four categories of ecosystem services that contribute to human well-being:

- ***Provisioning services***: providing wild foods, crops, fresh water and plant-derived medicines;
- ***Regulating services***: providing filtration of pollutants by wetlands, climate regulation through carbon storage and water cycling, pollination and protection from disasters;
- ***Cultural services***: providing recreation, spiritual and aesthetic values, education;
- ***Supporting services***: providing soil formation, photosynthesis and nutrient cycling.

Nonetheless, the full economic value of these are rarely accounted for and this represents a blind spot in conventional economics because the amounts concerned are huge. In 2012, for example, a study by Conservation International, NatureServe, the US National Fish and Wildlife Foundation and the University of Wisconsin-Madison estimated that some of the world's poorest people would be $500 bn a year better off if the services they provide to the rest of the planet indirectly – by conserving natural habitats – were given an economic value (see Turner et al. 2012).

A key factor in turning environmental valuation into positive

Table 6.1 Willingness to pay 10 per cent more for gasoline to reduce air pollution*

	North America/Oceania	Australia	Canada	United States	Latin America	Argentina	Brazil	Chile	Colombia	Mexico	Venezuela	Northern Europe	France	Germany	Great Britain	Mediterranean	Greece	Italy
98		24	32	33		27	16	14	18	20	65		24	44	21		43	41
99		33	36	37		19	na	na	na	22	67		22	44	17		53	55
00		21	28	27		19	35	31	24	39	63		17	33	31		30	32
01		29	30	31		24	38	23	45	37	44		12	41	34		24	38

* "Strongly agree" 1998–2001. Question iem01_8est: "I would be willing to pay 10 per cent more for my gasoline or other fuel if the money was used to reduce air pollution."

Source: *The Environmental Monitor 2002, Environics International*, p. 190. Reproduced with permission of GlobeScan Incorporated: London, Toronto, San Francisco.

change is the willingness of the public to pay more for services that are less damaging. In the energy sector, renewable energy from wind or solar power tends to be more expensive than traditional energy, but if cost–benefit analysis considered the externalities associated with traditional methods of energy generation renewables could appear competitive (see Aravena Novielli 2009). There is evidence that people in developing countries, where criticism of prevailing models of economic development is more common, may be more willing to pay more for petrol in order to reduce air pollution (see Table 6.1; Gan 2002).

Renewable energy is growing more economically attractive in Latin America and the Caribbean for other reasons that include increasing demand for power due to population growth, greater prosperity and rising oil prices, causing concerns about energy security. In Chile, for example, where demand is rising rapidly, about 58 per cent of energy is generated using fossil fuels with the remaining 42 per cent by hydropower, which has sparked conflicts over the construction of dams in environmentally sensitive areas. Aravena Novielli (2009) investigated public attitudes and willingness-to-pay premiums for the development of renewable energy. She showed that

Table 6.1 *continued*

	Spain	Turkey	Eastern Europe/Central Asia	Czech Republic	Kazakhstan	Russia	Asia	China	India	Indonesia	Japan	Philippines	South Korea	Thailand	Africa	Nigeria	South Africa
98	23	21		na	48	29		40	61	13	18	na	15	na		21	17
99	23	24		na	29	27		45	58	10	13	na	na	na		25	na
00	18	21		na	40	32		45	65	19	13	30	27	18		18	18
01	16	15		10	33	29		36	55	23	11	29	27	31		23	13

the introduction of renewables is supported by Chilean households and there is a significant and positive willingness to pay premiums for their development, which increases with higher levels of education, knowledge about energy sources and income. She concluded that Chile's authorities should diversify the energy mix and consider implementing green "premiums", whereby households pay a green tariff for renewables.

Financing sustainable development

Governments face challenges financing the transition to sustainable development. The average annual cost of meeting Agenda 21 targets was estimated in 2002 at $600 bn, including $125 bn from the international community, with the remaining $475 bn to come from national and private resources (ECLAC 2002). Major differences persist between developed and developing countries over who should fund sustainable development. Developing countries generally say this should be in the form of aid from the developed world together with a more equitable distribution of FDI and equitable free trade (see Chapter 5). Developed countries, by contrast, say most funding should come from within developing nations themselves or be generated through policy reforms that make these countries more attractive to foreign investors. Nonetheless, the Monterrey Conference on Financing for Development in 2002 forged a consensus that substantial increases in overseas development aid (ODA) would be required for the poorest countries (ECLAC 2002). At the Johannesburg Conference on Sustainable Development in the same year, ECLAC and UNEP presented an analysis of financing flows for the environment in Latin America and the Caribbean which concluded that the region's environmental sector can, potentially, be seen as an economic opportunity if new innovative funding mechanisms are devised. However, ECLAC and UNEP also identified gaps in the region between the expectations for environmental sustainability enshrined in laws, the current trends of damage to the environment and the lack of resources to tackle this. Case studies conducted by ECLAC from 2001 to 2005 identified how policies frequently created incentives that ran *counter* to sustainability goals. Several factors have influenced financing for sustainable development in Latin America and the Caribbean:

Debt and aid. Foreign debt limits the ability of developing countries to devise viable sustainable development strategies. Latin America and the Caribbean has had considerable success in reducing its external liabilities yet the region is still hampered by debt which overall stood at $1,038 bn by the end of 2010 (see World Bank 2012a). Only some countries – Bolivia, Guyana, Honduras and Nicaragua – have benefited from initiatives for highly indebted poor countries (HIPC) launched by the World Bank and the International Monetary Fund (IMF). One approach to debt has been to make use of outstanding liabilities for environmental purposes through devices such as debt-for-nature swaps. Although debt-for-nature swaps were used extensively until the early 1990s, overall they have made only a limited contribution to debt relief. Nor are Latin American and Caribbean countries among the main recipients of flows of official development assistance which have been declining and represent significantly less than commitments made at the 1992 Earth Summit (see Chapter 5). In 2009, official development assistance to Latin America and the Caribbean amounted to just 7 per cent of global aid flows while Africa and Asia received 37 per cent and 30 per cent respectively (ECLAC 2011a, 2011c).

Private investment. International flows of financing, especially FDI, are the main channel through which globalization influences environmental management (see below). Globally, the amount of private finance for climate change initiatives in the form of direct equity and debt investments is almost three times greater than public finance. The vast majority of this goes towards spending on climate change mitigation measures, and very little towards adaptation. Private international financial flows to environmental projects have increased considerably since 1992, far exceeding official aid, but are volatile and heavily concentrated in a limited number of emerging economies, often bypassing poor countries. In 2011, $153 bn in FDI flowed into Latin America and the Caribbean – 31 per cent more than in 2010 – and the region recorded the highest percentage increase in FDI inflows of any region (ECLAC 2012a). However, foreign investment is flowing rapidly into resource extraction activities (mining and hydrocarbons) and services (especially finance, energy and telecommunications), and very little of it is targeted directly at environmental protection. Multilateral agencies are taking a much more proactive role in galvanizing green investment. In 2013, for example, the International Finance Corporation, the World Bank's private sector arm, issued its first ever benchmark-sized green bond, at $1 bn, and in 2012–13 invested $1.6 bn in climate-related investments.

Multilateral loans and grants. Lending by development agencies and multilateral development banks (MDBs) has been one of the most important sources of finance for environmental policy in Latin America and the Caribbean (see Chapter 6). Because of their past support for large projects and neoliberal reform, MDBs are viewed with distrust by many environmental groups and spending has tended to favour "brown" or urban infrastructure and anti-pollution projects – energy use and efficiency, urban industrial pollution control, urban environmental management and the provision of potable water (see Nielson and Stern 1997). There are sometimes also institutional incentives at development banks that prejudice lending towards brown rather than more complex resource-management projects. Lending patterns are also influenced by preferences in recipient countries, where political factors can favour brown borrowing, not least the electoral rewards for capital spending. Lending responds to the strength of environmental movements, and the larger and more institutionalized these are the greater the likelihood that policymakers will pursue environmental borrowing. Loans and grants by international agencies for environmental measures have increased substantially in Latin America and the Caribbean, which has the most extensive network of regional MDBs in the developing world (see Box 6.4).

Grants. Multilateral agreements such as the Montreal Protocol on Substances that Deplete the Ozone Layer (1989) paved the way for new financing mechanisms for environmentally sustainable processes in developing countries. Concessional funds – either grants that do not have to be paid back or loans that incorporate a large grant element – are among these. Under the Montreal Protocol, assistance is provided through a multilateral fund to developing countries for projects aimed at preventing or reducing emissions of ozone-depleting substances. The Global Environmental Facility (GEF), which implements both the Montreal Protocol and the Convention on Climate Change, is the main body financing environmental problems of global consequence (see below). It has been a significant source of new resources for environmental initiatives in Latin America and the Caribbean, with Brazil and

Box 6.4 Latin American Multilateral Development Banks and sustainable development

The Inter-American Development Bank (IDB) is the region's largest source of multilateral credits and has placed sustainability at the heart of its lending strategy. Its environmental focus has four priorities: competitiveness based on clean technologies and environmental products and services; improved quality of life, which links environmental policy with health and education; institutional and legal environmental frameworks; and regional integration to resolve environmental problems. Sub-regional development banks also finance sustainable development initiatives in the region. The Andean Development Corporation (ADC) operates a number of projects directly related to sustainable development, such as the Programa Latinoamericano del Carbono (PLAC, Latin America Carbon Programme), and was the first multilateral bank to sign the UNEP Finance Initiative (see below). An ADC/Andean Community/ UNCTAD initiative aimed to develop regional biotrade between 2001 and 2006 and the ADC's Fondo para el Desarrollo Humano (FONDESHU, Human Development Fund) has been a shareholder in the EcoEnterprises Fund that provides venture capital for biodiversity-related businesses (ECLAC 2002). The Central American Bank for Economic Integration (CABEI) has participated in the market for carbon certificates and has promoted clean production. CABEI projects incorporate significant proportions of protected areas in Central America where reforestation is under way, and have also pioneered renewable energy development. CABEI also administers the Fondo Centroamericano de Ambiente y Desarrollo (FOCADES, Central American Fund for Environment and Development) and the Alianza Centroamericana de Desarrollo Sostenible (ALIDES, Alliance for the Sustainable Development of Central America). (Main source: ECLAC 2002)

Mexico its main recipients in the region. For example, the GEF funds the Amazon Region Protected Area (ARPA) programme which has helped turn large areas into legally protected forestland. Under ARPA, between 2003 and 2007, it was estimated that established protected areas could prevent 272,000 km^2 of deforestation through to 2050, representing more than one-third of the world's annual CO_2 emissions (GEF 2012). Nonetheless, GEF allocations in Latin America and the Caribbean have been volatile, and concessional funds such as the GEF and the Montreal Protocol multilateral fund remain limited relative to the scale of global problems. The Kyoto Protocol also offers new approaches to financing for sustainable development such as the Clean Development Mechanism (CDM). This allows developed countries to meet emission-reduction targets at a lower cost than the equivalent investments required to bring about similar reductions on their own territory. The CDM enables the benefits of projects designed to combat climate change to be shared between developed and developing countries, helping the latter to leapfrog to cleaner forms of development (see Simms and Reid 2006). CDM projects are designed to include both non-state and non-profit actors, such as NGOs and local communities, and profit-seeking actors such as investors. Critics claim that this market mechanism relocates power from the state to corporate actors and thereby opens the door for a new form of "carbon colonialism" that will exacerbate environmental injustice (see Lohmann 2006; and Bachram 2004). A comparison of CDM projects that included those in Chile and Mexico concluded that the Chilean example highlights tensions between sustainable project practice and the profit-seeking ambition of private investors and host country governments, while the Mexican example indicated that the multilateral rules set up to secure additional emission reductions at lower cost can be at odds with the social and participatory aims of small projects (see Box 6.5). At the 2011 Climate Change Convention in Durban, governments agreed to launch the Green Climate Fund (GCF) in 2012. This is expected to become the main international climate fund and co-ordinate the allocation of $100 bn from developed to developing countries pledged by 2020 under climate change agreements.

Domestic funding. It has long been accepted that developing countries themselves will need to fund Agenda 21 with finance from both the public and private sectors. Funding comes mainly from public revenues through forms of environmental taxation, but private spending on the environment is growing (see below). Environmental budgets fluctuate widely and change in step with public finances in general. The economic reforms designed to curtail state spending in the 1980s and 1990s, for example, limited the budgets of environmental agencies and weakened the public sector's capacity to halt ecological degradation (see Chapter 1). ECLAC and the UNDP assessed trends in domestic financing for sustainable development in Argentina, Brazil,

Box 6.5 Clean development mechanism projects in Chile and Mexico

Lövbrand and Nordqvist (2009) examined the degree to which non-state actors affected by CDM hydroelectric and forestry projects in Chile and Mexico can influence how these are designed and implemented. In Chile they identified tensions between how sustainable projects are carried out in practice and the profit-seeking aims of investors and the government, and in Mexico they identified the challenges posed by multilateral rules for small-scale participatory CDM projects. In Chile, the La Higuera hydroelectric project in the Tinguiririca river basin, a joint venture between the Australian renewable energy company Pacific Hydro Limited (PHL) and the Norwegian hydropower company Statkraft Norfund Power Invest (SNPI), aimed to reduce annual CO_2 emissions by 477,586 tons. La Higuera was one of the first Chilean projects registered within the CDM framework which the country's government has seen less as a tool to achieve sustainable development and more as a way of attracting investment. Lövbrand and Nordqvist say that while Chile's speedy approval process was appreciated by the developers of the La Higuera project, its social aspects were given only scant attention by the Chilean environmental agency, CONAMA, raising questions about its sustainability. In Chiapas, Mexico, the Scolel Té project was one of the first land-use and forestry projects to be considered for trading in carbon credits. It promoted carbon sequestration and sustainable farming practices by providing farmers with financial incentives to shift from agriculture to agroforestry, convert pastures to plantations, restore degraded forest and improve forest management. The project had both a high potential for sustainability while improving the livelihood of the Mayan communities and preserving biodiversity, but although it grew over time, the number of farmers and land use activities involved eventually hampered its ability to meet its emission-reduction requirements.

Chile, Colombia, Costa Rica, Mexico and Trinidad and Tobago after 1992 (ECLAC 2002). They found large differences between countries: total private and public environmental spending between 1992 and 2002 generally did not exceed 1 per cent of GDP, and public-sector expenditure on the environment rarely rose above 3 per cent of total public spending. The study revealed that environmental budgets are not controlled exclusively by institutions that deal specifically with environmental affairs, and other ministries and agencies are also heavily involved in channelling environmental spending. OECD figures show that by 2004 in Mexico – at that time its only Latin American member state – public spending on pollution abatement and control represented 0.5 per cent of GDP, a figure that exceeded levels of some more developed countries such as the UK and Australia (see OECD 2007). National environment funds for financing environmental projects implemented by public institutions are found across Latin America and the Caribbean. The state may delegate management of these funds to civil society organizations. In Colombia, for example, the national environmental fund ECOFONDO is managed by civil society organizations that channel resources derived from debt negotiations with the US.

Economic policy tools for the environment

There has been a growing use of economic policy tools to supplement traditional environmental regulation in pursuit of sustainable development. A range of tools are employed to protect the environment, from traditional government spending to instruments which aim to harness market forces (market-based instruments, MBIs) that include eco-taxes, effluent charges, cap-and-trade systems, liability rules and tradable permits. MBIs apply the "polluter pays" principle that seeks to ensure that the price of a good or service incorporates the cost of environmental or "public" goods such as air and water that are affected by its production. MBIs or economic environmental policy instruments can complement and strengthen traditional regulations and have advantages over them: they provide flexibility by introducing price and cost incentives; they offer opportunities to secure financing for environmental management and investment; and potentially they prevent future damage by internalizing costs in private-sector production and consumption decisions (ECLAC 2002). However, compared with OECD countries, Latin America and the Caribbean has little experience in the use of such instruments, and the principles of environmental protection are still viewed by productive sectors and governments in the region as an extra cost hampering development. Some of the principal economic tools in a government's environmental toolbox are as follows:

Infrastructure spending and subsidies. A government may create infrastructure to improve the environment by investing in renewable energy or "green industries" such as the wave or wind power sectors. Latin American countries have taken steps towards employing clean technologies. Brazil, for example, sources half of its automotive fuel supply with biofuel from sugarcane and is generating electricity by burning sugarcane waste. Subsidies encourage producers and consumers to change their ways by buying cleaner technologies, shifting to less intensive forms of production or insulating their homes, but are an inefficient way of changing behaviour and can sometimes have a negative impact on the environment. For example, government subsidies to timber corporations in Chile to help them develop a resource that was considered to be a sustainable way of diversifying exports has resulted in a large extension of commercial plantations of non-native trees that have become prone to pest infestation, exacerbate forest fires and generate conflict with indigenous people. Existing but often concealed subsidies in other areas of public administration, such as fuel pricing, can also be reviewed to achieve environmental outcomes. Some multilateral agencies such as UNEP have argued that policy reforms should aim to reduce the "perverse subsidies" that have developed for fossil fuel use while encouraging green energy sources (UNEP 2010). Economic incentives have also been used in Colombia and Chile to address urban air pollution caused by vehicle fuel emissions (see Saldarriaga and Vergara 2008).

Eco-taxes. Green taxes on pollution or polluting forms of production have been employed longer than other market-based mechanisms but remain underused. They may take the form of direct charges for effluents or, if pollution is dispersed as with vehicle exhausts, a tax on the fuel source. Eco-taxes are straightforward because a government simply decides what level of pollution is acceptable and sets a tax to achieve it. A tax also gives the polluter flexibility over how to respond, with those making less progress paying higher taxes. Eco-taxes are considered more efficient than regulations because they achieve the same reduction in pollution at a lower cost to industry while providing an incentive for it to go even further. Because of the social benefits of tax incentives, multilateral agencies want developing countries to give these priority in plans for sustainable transport and renewable energy, measures to improve agricultural productivity, water management and sanitation. Green tax incentives operate in Costa Rica and Venezuela, and other financial instruments aimed at environmental protection take the form of credit systems (Mexico) or direct subsidies (Guatemala) (ECLAC 2002). Brazil uses environmental criteria in distributing receipts from a goods and services tax, the Ecological Value-Added Tax (ICMS Ecológico), to sub-regional authorities for environmentally sustainable development. Under the constitution, 75 per cent of the proceeds of this tax go to the states and 25 per cent to municipalities.

Service charging, fees and tradable permits. Charging fees for environmental services in order to fund government activities has become common throughout Latin America and the Caribbean. Colombia, for example, charges fees for waste disposal and emissions, water use, forest harvesting and fishery use, while Guatemala charges for municipal water services, energy and solid waste disposal and Venezuela charges fees for industrial wastes. In Brazil water charges were introduced under reforms of 2003 and evidence from the Paraíba do Sul River Basin suggests that this has been effective in inducing firms to minimize waste (see Féres 2007). In Colombia, a fee for water pollution generates revenues that fund environmental activities at a regional level and has increased the incentives for reducing pollution (ECLAC 2002). In Venezuela, the sustainable management of wild capybara populations, regulated by the government, allows commercial hunting on private lands. Government regulations assign a harvest quota and hunters pay taxes that, in effect, represent payments for each animal harvested. Tradable permits combine regulation with a financial incentive, and offer companies flexibility to reduce pollution cost-effectively. A government calculates an overall level of allowable emissions for an area and sets a target that is divided into individual permits that give an owner the right to release a specific volume of pollution. The government then sanctions the establishment of a market in which permits are sold or auctioned to polluters that gives firms an incentive to reduce pollution and sell any surplus permits for a profit (see Carter 2010).

Payments for Environmental/Ecosystem Services (PES). At the heart of policy innovation that aims to harness market forces to protect the environment are Payments for Ecosystem Services (PES) (see Arriagada 2008; Pagiola, Arcenas and Platais 2005; UNEP 2010). These are market incentives to resource owners who provide an ecological service with the underlying aim of promoting conservation. PES are dependent upon the monetary valuation of ecosystem services (see above). The UN-sponsored Millennium Ecosystem Assessment (2005) defined 24 specific ecosystem services from food production and the provision of genetic resources to the regulation of fresh water and pollination. Three in particular have emerged as most important in terms of the funds allocated to them: climate change mitigation, watershed services and biodiversity conservation. PES have become popular tools because they are simple and are seen as a way to generate conservation funds from new sources. They are commonly applied to protected areas in a compensation system for the UN's REDD scheme in which carbon buyers remunerate nation states or project developers for reducing deforestation. Recipient nations may pass on some of the REDD funds to landowners through PES schemes or use them to improve park management. In Latin America and the Caribbean, PES have emerged as important policy tools and there are many examples of their use in countries such as Costa Rica and Guatemala (see Arriagada 2008; Pagiola, Arcenas and Platais 2005; UNEP 2010).

Market-based instruments face considerable challenges and can sometimes be difficult to implement. For example, it is hard to determine the right levels for eco-taxes and governments often encounter resistance from business, trades unions or consumers, with the result that they are set at below optimal levels. In Latin America and the Caribbean, moreover, tax enforcement historically has been lax and large sections of the population survive outside the formal economy. Corruption can also complicate enforcement, and there have been cases in countries such as Honduras, for example, of the illegal sale of environmental licences. If subsidies are not properly managed they can extend private "rent-seeking" behaviour to public funds, whereby entrenched sectors accrue gains that were not intended. For example, Costa Rica's tree-planting incentive system operating in the 1980s was designed to achieve reforestation, and in exchange for planting specified species, planters would receive tradable tax credits. Poor regulations specified which species should be planted but not where, leading companies with little experience in forestry to exploit the system: some planted only the least expensive species in areas with inappropriate soil or climate; and in some cases natural forest was cleared to make way for new trees (see Ascher 1997).

Political factors also limit the application of MBIs and can reduce their effectiveness. Government-financed initiatives can be poorly targeted and badly monitored, and can sometimes be hijacked by political interests prioritizing regional development over environmental objectives. PES instruments are, similarly, not without problems. Where PES is used in protected areas or indigenous territories, it can face legal complications and needs to be carefully designed. The ambitions of PES can also be frustrated by non-compliance with conditions; poor targeting; and spillovers, whereby protecting a resource in one location places pressure on resources elsewhere. A significant threat to PES programmes can be "adverse self-selection", in which people who would have supplied the contracted service in the absence of a payment suddenly start to receive these to do what they had already been doing. There are many examples in Latin America of PES leading to perverse outcomes because of these factors. One study in Mexico, for example, found that PES payments to reduce the removal of forest cover had been concentrated on forests that were simply not at risk of deforestation (Muñoz-Piña et al. 2008).

The private sector in the green economy

Market-based environmental policymaking draws attention to the role of the private sector in the green economy. States and multilateral financial institutions alone do not have sufficient resources to engineer sustainable economies, and the private sector will play a key role. In Latin America and the Caribbean, companies and entrepreneurs committed to conservation have become important sources of funding and support for ENGOs and in countries such as Chile have played a prominent role. Ancient Forest International (AFI), a conservation organization, was behind the creation of the Cañi Forest Sanctuary, Chile's first private reserve, financed by three entrepreneurs (see Bradley 2006). The private sector has also shown growing interest in the environmental impact of production and consumption, with most private investment going to improving energy efficiency and promoting the use of technologies to cut production costs. Companies expect to obtain benefits that strengthen their competitive position: certification of quality or of better environmental practices, a boost to their brand image, or lower costs. Private green investment in Latin America and the Caribbean reflects the growth of new niches for emerging economies in the production of environmental goods and services. Key markets within the green economy now include the following:

Organic farming. Organic farming is a new opportunity area within the broader growth of non-traditional agro-exports and combines clean production with the sustainable use of natural resources. World sales of organic produce are increasing at a rate of about 20 per cent per year in northern markets, generating considerable South–North trade in organic tropical products, fruits and vegetables (Raynolds 2008). Latin America and the Caribbean has rapidly emerged as a world leader in this export market with almost all the countries in the region now exporting some certified organic foods. Leading players include Mexico, Brazil, Peru, Argentina and the Dominican Republic, which has become the world's foremost exporter of organic bananas and cocoa, a top exporter of organic coffee and an export pioneer in new commodities like organic mangos (see Box 6.6).

Organic production is often associated with fair trade initiatives in the developed world based on certification of soil integrity or production techniques, and these have grown rapidly in Latin America and the Caribbean. Fair trade is a market-based approach to helping producers in developing countries achieve better trading terms and promote sustainable development through the payment of a higher price to exporters and the promotion of higher social and environmental standards (see Bacon et al. 2008). An international association Fairtrade International (FLO) now exists to develop standards (see websites below) and such networks work to reduce the inequities and uncertainties that small-scale produce face in globalized markets. In Mexico and Central America, fair trade initiatives in the coffee sector have responded to a secular decline in coffee prices on world markets after 2005 that had a dramatic impact on producers, fuelling migration and damaging the environment as intensive farming took over (see, for example, Jaffee 2007.) However, fair trade and certification markets can still pose obstacles for small producers and high certification costs and low prices may not enable some to survive. The global market potential for some organic products such as coffee remains small and has become increasingly "saturated" with competition. In countries such as Costa Rica fair trade markets alone do not always meet the needs of small farming families (see Sick 2008).

Box 6.6 Organic farming in the Dominican Republic

Given its small size, the Dominican Republic has established a surprising global lead in the production of organic bananas, cocoa and coffee. Raynolds (2008) examined the organic agro-export boom in the Dominican Republic which she situated within broader forces fuelling the growth of non-traditional agro-exports globally. The growth of the Dominican Republic's organic sector has implications for agro-export policy throughout Latin America and the Caribbean, where peasants have long practised low-input forms of cultivation that resemble what is today called organic agriculture. Ecological and economic factors in the Dominican Republic have maintained peasant farming practices and limited the use of chemical inputs. In the 1980s, ENGOs began to recognize these factors as an advantage in promoting organic practices in the Dominican Republic and launched initiatives to train peasants in organic techniques for environmental aims and to improve food security (IFAD 2003). Neoliberal policies then began to reorient organic agriculture towards the export market as part of a wider state effort to promote non-traditional exports. As world markets for sugar, coffee and cocoa declined in the early 1990s, producers turned to niche specialty-goods markets and began to export Dominican organic cocoa and coffee. Organic exports expanded and financial and technical support for export production, certification and marketing came from business and government agencies, multilateral donors and foreign governments. In 1996, the Dominican Organic Agricultural Association was founded and today the country has about 14,000 organic growers that cultivate on 2 per cent of its agricultural land. However, the competitive advantage of small-scale producers is declining in the face of organic monocrop enterprises extending to hundreds of hectares, and supermarket quality regulations are beginning to exclude small farmers from organic markets.

In other Latin American countries the demand for organic crops has revived or created small-scale cultivation in poor areas. In Bolivia, the Asociación Nacional de Productores de Quínua (Anapqui, National Association of Quinoa Producers) has pioneered among Aymara and Quechua residents of the southern altiplano the production of organic quinoa which is exported to Brazil, Europe, the US and Japan (see Ballvé 2007). Mexico has also responded to growing demand in industrial countries by developing organic farming methods. Its Coyote Rojo (Red Coyote) is an organic bioregional label that began certifying producers in 2007 (see UNEP 2010).

Clean tech. The clean technology sector, often referred to as eco-industry, has grown dramatically and is seen as a source of significant trade potential. Growing demand for clean technologies, including those related to the objectives of the Kyoto Protocol aimed at reducing greenhouse gas emissions, has channelled private investment into research and development in fields such as renewable energy and recycling. Much of this research is carried out in the developed world by small and medium enterprises financed through venture capital. Growing demand in international markets for goods and services produced with clean technologies is generating pressures on corporations to take clean tech seriously. In 2008, UNEP launched a Green Economy Initiative aimed at mobilizing investment in clean technologies. Developing countries themselves are now competitive producers in sectors such as wind and solar power or efficient lighting, and some have achieved significant levels of exports in certain products. In 2007, for example, Brazil and Mexico were among the top five exporters of renewable energy products, and Mexico is the leading global exporter of solar water heaters (see WTO/UNEP 2009). New producer associations and financing initiatives are also springing up. In 2012, for example, the second Renewable Energy Finance Forum–Latin America and Caribbean (REFF-LAC) brought together producer associations such as the Latin American and Caribbean Council on Renewable Energy (LAC-CORE), financiers, policymakers and multilateral banks. Clean production and green enterprise are now buzzwords in countries such as Chile, where in 2001 the government created a Consejo Nacional de Producción Limpia de Chile (CPL, Committee for the Development of Clean Production). One mechanism Chile has used to link private and public initiatives has been voluntary Clean Production Agreements (CPAs) in areas such as agro-industry, mining and forestry. Chile's private sector has also organized clean production initiatives and small and medium enterprises have access to two environmental funds available through the Corporación de Fomento de la Producción de Chile (CORFO, Corporation for the Development of Production in Chile), a government investment promotion and innovation agency (see ECLAC 2002). Latin America and the Caribbean is also hosting transnational partnerships between researchers working in green technology areas. An innovative collaboration between researchers in Cuba and Scotland indicates the potential for applying scientific knowledge across borders to clean tech (see Box 6.7).

Box 6.7 Clean tech and collaboration

Marabu, a woody shrub, was brought to Cuba from Africa because of its attractive flowers and thrived, but the collapse of the Soviet bloc in 1989 led to the decline of the Cuban sugar industry and it spread rapidly over once productive land. Marabu wood was considered of little use because it does not float, cannot be used for building and emits too much smoke when burned to be used as domestic fuel. However, collaboration between the engineering faculty of Strathclyde University in Scotland and Cuban researchers discovered that the wood provides a raw material for high-grade filtration systems because it can yield high-quality carbon at low cost. The Scottish–Cuban research project began after a scientific mission to the island funded by Scottish Development International. Marabu carbon contains microscopic holes that increase its surface area and make it valuable as a filter for use in the production of rum, whisky and cleaning water. It could allow the Cuban rum industry to save millions of dollars currently spent on importing activated carbon. Moreover, marabu carbon can be mixed with a polymer then painted on to aluminium to create lightweight electrodes. The Strathclyde engineers and researchers at St Andrews University have also used the material to make non-toxic, rechargeable cells for lightweight lithium-oxygen batteries, making marabu carbon of great potential value in the production of electric cars. In a similar collaboration the British renewable energy company Havana Energy has signed a deal with the Cuban government to develop the technology for five biomass energy plants in the country which will generate power from sugar cane fibre and wild shrubs. Havana Energy believes that as much as 50 per cent of Cuba's energy needs could be provided by the burning of bagasse, the fibre left over after sugar cane is crushed at refineries. Marabu is also now being tested for its potential use in biomass burning (Main sources: Macdonald 2012; bbc.co.uk 2012).

Ecotourism. Tourism is an important economic sector worldwide and in 2011 international tourist arrivals globally increased by 4.6 per cent to 982 million, generating receipts that exceeded $1 trillion ($1,000 bn) (UNWTO 2012). The Americas recorded the largest increase in receipts in 2011 (5.7 per cent), although only one Latin American and Caribbean country, Mexico, was among the world's top 25 destinations, taking in $8.4 bn. Most of this tourism is not ecotourism, which refers to travel services grounded in values and rules governed by both environmental and social criteria: conservation and the well-being of local communities (see Chernela 2011). Ecotourism grew rapidly in the 1990s and the UN and the WTO designated 2002 the International Year of Ecotourism (see Hoad 2002). Today, multilateral banks and ENGOs themselves fund many projects with ecotourism components. Most countries in Latin America and the Caribbean promote some form of ecotourism and although there are no reliable statistics it is generally agreed that its growth in recent years has outpaced that of conventional tourism. Ecotourism has become an important sector in Central America and in particular Costa Rica (see Finley-Brook 2007; Honey 2003) (see Box 6.8).

Ecotourism has been depicted by some scholars as a potential saviour of some threatened areas such as Ecuador's cloud forests (see Fair 1996). Activities usually take place in official protected areas, such as national parks, but in recent years management by the private sector and by ENGOs has grown. In Costa Rica's Monteverde area, Chile's Pumalín Park and Argentina's Esteros del Iberá, for example, the protection of natural areas linked to ecotourism projects has been financed by private funds (ECLAC 2002). There is also growing interest in indigenous ecotourism, such as that pioneered by the Kuna people of the San Blas Islands in Panama (see Chernela 2011). However, like many nature-based economic activities, ecotourism can also result in market failures and needs to be managed by the state. In practice, many projects focus solely on meeting environmental criteria, with social criteria often secondary to conservation, which has meant local people sometimes being displaced from protected areas in the name of ecotourism (see Chernela 2011). There are also warnings about the potentially harmful impact of ecotourism on a large scale in fragile environments such as Caribbean marine ecosystems (see McDonald Beckles 1996; Pattullo 1996).

Bioprospecting. The term bioprospecting was coined in the late 1980s to refer to the interest of the pharmaceutical and biotechnology industries in using plants, microbes and traditional knowledge to develop new products (see Hayden 2006; see also Box 2.8). In 1993, an influential book, *Biodiversity Prospecting*, argued that life-saving drugs from genetic and biochemical resources obtained through bioprospecting from tropical rainforests could be a positive force

Box 6.8 Ecotourism in the Central American rainforest

Honey (2003) examines how Costa Rica has been a significant beneficiary of the boom in "green tourism" but also how this has not been without conflicts. Ecotourism was well established in the country as early as 1992 as tourism became Costa Rica's main source of foreign exchange, surpassing coffee and banana exports. As ecotourism has grown, entire rural communities such as Monteverde, Tortuguero and the Osa Peninsula have been converted into ecotourism centres and Costa Ricans have created auxiliary businesses such as tour agencies or restaurants associated with the sector. Ecotourism certification has been pioneered by the *New Key to Costa Rica* guidebook and Costa Rica's tourism ministry, which issues a Certification for Sustainable Tourism (CST). In 2002, tourism ministers throughout Central America officially embraced the CST model, and Brazil, Ecuador, Peru and Chile have based their own certification programmes on these standards. Costa Rica has been able to pioneer ecotourism on the basis of advantages not enjoyed by its neighbours, such as foreign perceptions of it as peaceful and stable. The country also has a valuable resource in its national park system, which today incorporates 25 per cent of its territory. National parks are complemented by hundreds of private nature reserves, and more than 110 of these contain "ecolodges" or provide tourism activities. Costa Rica also contains 5 per cent of the world's biodiversity, its environmental scientists and conservationists are regional leaders, and more than 100 ENGOs have branches in the country. Finally, ecotourism in Costa Rica has been able to build upon rapidly growing mainstream tourism and by 2000 the country was receiving more than one million visitors a year, many lured by its natural attractions. However, some studies suggest that ecotourism has only partially fulfilled its objectives of providing significant resources for national conservation efforts and benefits to local communities. Many projects and initiatives that claim the label "ecotourism" do so spuriously, and Honey says ecotourism in Costa Rica also includes "greenwashing" scams and ecotourism "lite".

for conservation (see Laird, Reid and Meyer 1993). There has been a long history of plant hunting and commercialization in Latin America and the Caribbean, which has been at the forefront of this development and pioneered new public–private initiatives and forms of collaboration. A number of formal bioprospecting arrangements have been agreed such as the US government's International Co-operative Biodiversity Groups (ICBG) initiative which funded research partnerships between scholars in the US and Latin America; and a 1991 agreement between the drug company Merck and Costa Rica's National Biodiversity Institute (INBio) (see Hayden 2006). Even small countries such as Honduras have either addressed the issues raised by the growth of biotechnology use in, for example, the cultivation of genetically modified crops, or have gone further by drawing up biosafety frameworks that seek to codify policymaking (see DiBio/SERNA 2007). Several countries and institutions are also implementing public–private agreements on bioprospecting based on new developments in biotechnology, molecular biology and bioinformatics. Under these, investors give them a share of future profits in exchange for access to their resources (ECLAC 2002). Linking biodiversity and biotechnology through bioprospecting requires developing countries to have a scientific and institutional base capable of allowing them to collaborate with the private sector and universities. Costa Rica's National Biodiversity Institute has collaborated in research on medical, pharmaceutical and agrochemical products with a broad range of private firms and institutes such as Merck and Givaudan-Roure. Hayden (2006) argues that the CBD promotes an explicitly market-mediated vision of biodiversity as a productive resource that can provide incentives for developing nations to save their forests. However, Dorsey (2006) has identified problems with bioprospecting, not least the fact that benefit-sharing arrangements can be complicated by the question of who should be identified as the main beneficiaries of bioprospecting (see also Hayden 2006). Diverse collection practices complicate issues of intellectual property and make corporate participants in these research relationships nervous about deals that lack clear beneficiaries. Although benefit-sharing provisions recognize community rights and traditional knowledge, they have led to struggles between competing claimants (see Box 6.9).

Green financing. A market for "green financing" – investment by private sector actors such as equity or venture capital funds in projects such as clean energy development – is growing rapidly in Latin America and the Caribbean. The business opportunities generated by new markets in environmental management and

Box 6.9 Biostruggles

Bioprospecting can generate significant opposition once communities learn of the potential value of the ecological resources in their territories. Indigenous and peasant movements and multilateral organizations have sometimes criticized what has been called "biopiracy" – resource appropriation by the corporations of northern states – and demanded new arrangements to share benefits. They have sought reciprocity, community consent and recognition of national sovereignty over these resources. As a result, under instruments such as the 1992 UN Convention on Biological Diversity and national laws, efforts to collect biological material for pharmaceutical research have been regulated and bioprospecting initiatives now incorporate contractual promises to share benefits with those who provide plants, microbes, insects and knowledge (see Hayden 2006). Disputes over bioprospecting combining social, political, economic and ecological factors have been called "biostruggles". In Mexico in 1998, for example, an international consortium of research institutions and a drug company announced a $2.5 m project called ICBG Maya to research local plants for possible commercial exploitation. Funded by the National Institutes of Health (NIH), the National Science Foundation and the US Department of Agriculture, the ICBG Maya project was to include researchers from Mexico's El Colegio del Frontera Sur (Ecosur), among others. However, unease among indigenous communities about who would benefit from the project resulted in an international campaign to shut it down (see Belejack 2002; see also Scheper-Hughes 2006). The project was bedevilled by misunderstandings and disagreements between some local indigenous groups and its advocates.

services are attracting capital from a variety of sources, including venture capital and private investors, and specialist providers have emerged. For example, Terra Capital is a fund that invests in Latin American enterprises that help to preserve biological resources and targets organic agriculture, ecotourism and certified sustainable forestry (ECLAC 2002). The Andean Development Corporation participates in a venture fund for biodiversity-related businesses. The Fondo Centroamericano de Ambiente y Desarrollo (FOCADES, Central American Fund for Environment and Development) supports biodiversity and climate change projects. A key effort to promote private green investment has been the UNEP Finance Initiative, which brings together banks and financial institutions such as Bradesco in Brazil and Financiera Rural in Mexico and addresses how financial services can tackle climate change by making access to green finance easier (see UNEP FI 2010). There is growing awareness among large institutional investment funds of their responsibility to factor environmental, social and governance issues into their decision-making. Increasingly, investors are seeing corporate policies on environmental and social issues as a guide to a company's quality of management, providing them with a basis on which to make investment decisions (see Cherneva 2012). The Principles for Responsible Investment (PRI) initiative is a partnership between investors with the UNEP Finance Initiative and the UN Global Compact to provide a framework for helping investors build environmental governance considerations into the investment process. PRI points out that the cost of environmental damage caused by the world's 3,000 largest publicly listed companies in 2008 was $2.15 trillion (UNEP FI/PRI 2010). It argues that it is in the commercial interests of large institutional investors to reduce externalities and minimize their exposure to these costs.

Other mechanisms have been devised to promote private funding in conservation and biodiversity initiatives, such as environmental trust funds and legal tools (see Castro 2003). Conservation trust funds, for example, have been effective ways of diversifying sources of funding for managing protected areas. One successful example of how these have become institutionalized is the Latin American and Caribbean Network of Environmental Funds (RedLAC) which has registered 1,113 grants with a value of $1.35 bn (Castro 2003). RedLAC promotes financial mechanisms for environmental management and conservation projects such as Colombia's Biohotels Programme, which links hotels, guests and the private sector in the conservation of protected areas.

Politics of sustainable development

According to the United Nations Environment Programme (2010), the pursuit of sustainable development has significant socio-political implications because a balance will have to be maintained between governments, civil society and the private sector as equal stakeholders in a green economy. This means that greater effort may be required to reduce inequality and poverty and distribute more equally the income gained from exploiting the natural resources on which current growth is based. In the long term, it may be more cost effective for societies to adopt an entirely new approach to equality. Berke and Beatley (1997) examined how prepared Caribbean countries were for natural disasters and the relationship of their preparedness with planning for sustainable development. They demonstrated that both the cost of disasters and the number of people affected have risen in recent decades and argue that if disaster relief programmes took a more long-term approach – by attempting to improve living conditions rather than merely replacing what is lost through disasters – the impact of disasters could be greatly reduced. Clean technology and sustainable development initiatives also offer considerable scope for job creation, but this may entail greater levels of state involvement in providing jobs. In 2009, during the world financial crisis, UNEP complemented its plans for a Green Economy by proposing a "green" fiscal stimulus package, the Global Green New Deal, to combine the shift towards greater sustainability with efforts to address economic downturn (UNEP 2008, 2009, 2010).

The Rio+20 conference in 2012 gave considerable attention to unemployment and the creation of green jobs, and its declaration recognized the limitations of GDP as a measure of well-being and sustainable development. A key debate at Rio+20 was over proposed sustainable development goals (SDGs) aiming to relieve poverty and improve health, education and jobs in developing countries along environmentally sustainable lines. Delegates were divided over whether the SDGs should commit rich countries to curbing their consumption of natural resources in order to leave more for poorer nations.

Sustainable development policies may also challenge how traditional political institutions operate, implying the need for reform. With a growing role for the private sector in sustainable development have come new forms of *private regulation* that circumvent state institutions. Private regulatory initiatives such as certification are often welcomed in developing nations where governments have a limited capacity to enforce environmental laws, although some critics see these initiatives as part of an effort by transnational corporations to limit regulation (see Clapp 1998; Haufler 2001; and Levy and Egan 1998). Industry groups and ENGOs have created their own schemes to improve industrial standards and practices around the world, often as a result of dissatisfaction with governmental efforts at regulation. Initiatives such as the Global Compact between the UN and business groups, the creation of the Dow Jones Sustainability Group Index and the UNEP Finance Initiative (see above) all aim to strengthen environmental quality through voluntary agreements. Business Councils for Sustainable Development exist across Latin America to stimulate public–private partnerships in fields such as eco-efficiency, recycling and corporate social responsibility (see ECLAC 2002). These voluntary initiatives allow private companies to improve their efficiency, thereby increasing profits. They may also strengthen consumer loyalty and reduce the risk of prosecution a company faces for non-compliance with environmental regulations. However, the impact of private regulatory initiatives can vary widely. The Forest Stewardship Council (FSC) has operated in Argentina and Brazil since the 1990s and the same environmental NGOs promoted the role of the FSC in both countries at about the same time. Yet, in Argentina, the FSC has struggled to establish itself and to grow, while in Brazil it has thrived (see Box 6.10).

Private sector regulatory programmes such as the FSC and the Marine Stewardship Council have informed debates about the extent to which they infringe upon or complement state environmental authority (see Mol 2010; Espach 2006; Chapter 5). The authority of states to regulate environmental issues derives from the way in which, conventionally, environmental goods have been understood as collective goods and environmental problems as market failures. At the same time, ideas about the state's role have changed according to the economic climate and the profile of environmental issues. In the 1970s and 1980s, scholars tended to accept state authority over environmental affairs (see Mol 2010). However, in the climate of deregulation and privatization of the 1990s, nurtured by neoliberal ideas that were more hostile to the state, challenges grew to its authority over environmental issues. In turn, growing environmental awareness placed the state back at the heart of environmental policymaking and its authority expanded through new environmental institutions. In recent years, however, as the multilateral framework of environmental governance has grown and globalization

Box 6.10 Private forestry regulation in Argentina and Brazil

There has been little research into the effectiveness of private regulatory initiatives within developing countries. Espach (2006) compared the performance of the Forest Stewardship Council (FSC) in Argentina and Brazil, both of which have forestry industries. The council is an international network of NGOs, producers and retailers of forest products and certification agencies founded in 1993 to promote standards for sustainable forest management. It is considered a pioneer of a market-based "eco-consumerist" approach to environmental change. Despite public demands for environmental management, both nations' regulatory regimes are institutionally and politically frail, underfunded and enforcement can be weak. Argentina's FSC chapter was established in December 2001 but by 2006 had still not completed writing local forestry standards and had failed to extend the programme's coverage to any significant sectors of the industry. In Brazil, since 1996, by contrast, FSC-Brazil has had three different sets of standards approved by the FSC-International and certification numbers are among the highest in the world. Espach found that this variation in the FSC programmes could not be explained either by market demand or advocacy by transnational corporations or ENGOs. Although transnational actors had been crucial to introducing the programmes in both countries, their effectiveness depended on the role of *local actors*. The success of Brazil's FSC programme was largely due to the network of local activists, firms, NGOs and certification agencies that had existed before the initiative but that had taken it up as a useful tool. In Argentina, on the other hand, the World Wildlife Fund sustained the initiative, but opposition to the FSC had come from transnational firms, led by Chileans, which collaborated with the agriculture ministry to fashion a more industry-friendly alternative.

gained ground, the state's authority over environmental management has again declined. As the monopoly of states over environmental functions erodes, other actors and institutional arrangements – such as the private sector and business associations – fill the vacuum (see Mol 2010).

The economics of climate change

Evaluating options for adapting to climate change can provide decision-makers with important information about the potential for alternative uses of scarce resources and how to invest in sustainable development. However, the economic analysis of adaptation projects – activities undertaken to ameliorate anticipated or actual losses in output and/or increases in production costs as a consequence of climate change – poses enormous methodological challenges (World Bank 2010a). A study funded by the governments of the Netherlands, the UK and Switzerland on the Economics of Adaptation to Climate Change (EACC) estimated that it will cost $75 bn to $100 bn each year for developing countries to adapt to a world warmer by 2°C from 2010 to 2050 (see World Bank 2010b). The EACC study was launched to help decision-makers assess risks and design better strategies to adapt to climate change (World Bank 2009a).

Estimating the costs and benefits of adaptation in conditions of uncertainty is complex and subject to many variables. The planning of an adaptation project usually involves two steps: evaluating the potential impacts that climate change could have on productivity; and evaluating costs and benefits of planned adaptations themselves. Adaptation can also form part of a broader development strategy aimed at providing benefits that go beyond managing climate risks, such as improving water-use efficiency – adaptations sometimes referred to as "no-regret" investments (Padgham 2009). In Mexico, for example, the $317 m Río Conchos Basin project to modernize existing irrigation infrastructure offers an example of a no-regret adaptation project (see World Bank 2010a). According to the World Bank (2010a), modernizing irrigation would create benefits from water savings while offering the opportunity to extend cultivation to higher-value crops.

Latin American and Caribbean policymakers have taken a prominent role in the effort to weigh up the costs of climate change and whether mitigation is likely to be more or less cost effective than adaptation (see, for example, Zedillo 2008). Mexico is among the countries that have tried to establish the likely costs of climate change and responses to it since the Stern report (2007). The largest contributors to Mexico's GHG emissions are the oil, gas and electricity sectors, which are state-run monopolies. This means that the Mexican government can achieve significant emission reductions through regulation of the public sector. The administration of President Felipe Calderón (2006–12) released a National Climate Change Strategy in 2007 which led to the development of a Special Climate Change Programme (PECC) in 2009 setting a goal of 50 per cent reductions in emissions from 2000 levels by 2050 (see Galindo 2009). In 2012, and in the context of this report, Mexico's senate approved a law that made it just the second country in the world to enshrine long-term climate targets into national legislation after the UK.

ECLAC (2010) has examined the potential economic impacts of climate change throughout Latin America and the Caribbean and its preliminary estimates indicate countries in temperate zones losing as much as 1 per cent of annual GDP up to the year 2100 under some scenarios – exceeding the entire budgets of most environment ministries. The costs are likely to be higher in Andean, Central American and Caribbean countries. In some cases, such as those in which climate change threatens biodiversity or human life, there will be irreversible consequences that cannot be quantified in economic terms (see also ECLAC 2009). A study prepared by the IDB, ECLAC and WWF estimates that Latin America and the Caribbean will suffer annual damage in the order of $100 bn by the year 2050 due to declines in agricultural yields, the disappearance of glaciers, floods, droughts and other events caused by global warming (IDB 2012). On a regional basis, the World Bank's EACC suggests that the East Asia and Pacific Region face the highest adaptation cost, and the Middle East and North Africa the lowest (see Table 6.2).

While costs increase in absolute terms over time, they should fall as a percentage of GDP, suggesting that countries become less vulnerable to climate change as their economies and investments in adaptation and mitigation grow (see World Bank 2009a). The IDB (2012), for example, notes that the adaptation costs are a small fraction of the costs of physical impacts, conservatively estimated at 0.2 per cent of GDP for the region, at current values.

The impact of climate change will be influenced by social as well as political and economic structures and the vulnerability of different social groups will vary. A community's capacity to withstand extreme events such as drought is affected by factors such as inequality, poverty, lack of representation and access to social security systems. As the poor stand to lose most, governments need adaptation strategies that take into account the most vulnerable groups and will need to take

Table 6.2 Total annual costs of adaptation for all sectors, by region, 2010–50*

Cost aggregation type	East Asia and Pacific	Europe and central Asia	Latin America and Caribbean	Middle East and North Africa	South Asia	Sub-Saharan Africa	Total
National Centre for Atmospheric Research (NCAR), wettest scenario							
Gross sum	28.7	10.5	22.5	4.1	17.1	18.9	101.8
X-sum	25.0	9.4	21.5	3.0	12.6	18.1	89.6
Net sum	25.0	9.3	21.5	3.0	12.6	18.1	89.5
Commonwealth Scientific and Industrial Research Organization (CSIRO), driest scenario							
Gross sum	21.8	6.5	18.8	3.7	19.4	18.1	88.3
X-sum	19.6	5.6	16.9	3.0	15.6	16.9	77.6
Net sum	19.5	5.2	16.8	2.9	15.5	16.9	76.8

* US$ billions at 2005 prices, no discounting.

Note: The gross aggregation method sets negative costs in any sector in a country to zero before costs are aggregated for the country and for all developing countries. The X-sums net positive and negative items within countries but not across countries and include costs for a country in the aggregate as long as the net cost across sectors is positive for the country. The net aggregate measure nets negative costs within and across countries

Source: World Bank 2009a. "The Cost to Developing Countries of Adapting to Climate Change: New Methods and Estimates", Consultation Draft 64087. Washington, DC: World Bank (http://climatechange.worldbank.org/climatechange/research).

"soft" political and institutional measures alongside hard investments in infrastructure. The EACC study examined Bolivia to analyse the impacts of climate change on different social groups taking into account such factors as levels of education, ethnicity and poverty (see World Bank 2010b). In Bolivia, the poorest groups most vulnerable to climate change tend to live in dry zones such as the central and southern Altiplano, valleys and plains, and along riverbeds in lowland areas. To meet their needs, alongside infrastructure soft investments will be required in social security coverage and education.

The creation of a global market for carbon represents one of the most innovative and important outcomes of the international effort to address climate change since the 1980s. Latin American and

Caribbean countries have so far played a limited role in this market but their involvement is increasing. There has been innovation in countries such as Costa Rica, for example, on selling carbon credits to the industrialized world. Two main mechanisms have emerged to internalize the environmental costs of GHGs and therefore to set a price on them: taxes on emissions, and emission trading.

Taxes on GHG emissions/carbon taxes. Taxation can be used to reduce emissions by putting a price on the release of CO_2 or other gases into the atmosphere, the main source of which are the emissions of fossil fuels whose carbon content is used to calculate the level of tax to be paid. A CO_2 tax may also be based on the emissions that are generated by the production of goods. Tax may be levied on both consumers and producers, creating different incentives for switching fuel and having different implications for the costs of collection and enforcement. Most countries implementing a carbon tax levy it directly on consumers through a tax on fuel consumption "at the pump". Governments often use a combination of a tax on CO_2 emissions and a tax on energy use in general, based on the energy content of power sources which can be imposed on both fossil fuels and on carbon-free sources. European countries have taken the lead in imposing carbon taxes, while many other countries have introduced general energy taxes aimed at promoting efficiency and savings. National carbon taxes have not yet been used in Latin America where governments do not consider them to be viable. Economic growth in the region has been relatively low in terms of carbon intensity – how much carbon is released per unit of energy created – meaning that if carbon taxes are introduced, what Latin American consumers end up paying would be significantly above the global average (see Medvedev and van der Mensbrugghe 2008). However, in 1997, Costa Rica imposed a 3.5 per cent carbon tax on hydrocarbon fuels in some parts of the country to generate funds for sustainable development projects.

Emission trading. Emission trading schemes (ETSs) were pioneered in the US in the 1970s and a provision for international emission trading was incorporated in the 1997 Kyoto Protocol. Since Kyoto, a limited number of mandatory schemes have been implemented at the national level and in 2005 the EU introduced the world's largest ETS (the EU-ETS). These schemes vary considerably in terms of size, environmental stringency, reporting and monitoring, or CO_2 price.

The trend in policy has been to link schemes in order to create a larger market, thereby reducing volatility in the price of allowances (WTO/UNEP 2009). Carbon trading in Latin America and the Caribbean is limited but its potential is growing. Low carbon intensity means the region stands to gain substantially from emissions trading. REDD projects also offer market mechanisms and have significant potential in Latin American countries. The Clean Development Mechanism is the main way in which the countries of Latin America and the Caribbean have so far been able to participate in the global carbon market: the region hosts about a quarter of the world's 1,555 CDM projects. Brazil is Latin America's leading developer of CDM projects and boasts the region's first carbon-trading platform hosted by Bovespa, the principal stock exchange. Membership of the main carbon trading market in the Americas, the Chicago Climate Exchange (CCX), includes several Brazilian forestry companies. Direct links that connect trading platforms are possible and indirect links have grown common, whereby emission trading schemes are linked to "offsets" based on specific projects. Carbon offsetting refers to the act of reducing or avoiding emissions in one place in order to "offset" them somewhere else, and offsets are credits generated by projects that aim to reduce emissions such as tree planting or renewable energy. Offsetting has proved an important way of enabling Latin American and Caribbean countries to participate in the carbon trading markets. The CCX has registered forest offset credits from Costa Rica, and has considered registering projects in Bolivia. Costa Rica has made headway in carbon trading as part of the country's pledge to become "carbon neutral" by 2021 by selling carbon certificates to industrialized countries. In its first carbon credit transaction in 2009, Costa Rica sold nearly 3,000 tons of carbon credits to Equator, a US company, generating about $9 m for the country's National Forestry Financing Fund to replant forests.

Political, practical and economic factors explain why carbon taxes and trading schemes have so far had limited scope in Latin America. In 2010, the region's first auction of voluntary carbon credits in Brazil ended without a single bid. There are also technical loopholes in how carbon credits are defined and regulated in areas such as forestry. Where there has been progress it has often been as the result of an international NGO or foreign fair trade initiative providing an infrastructure for some form of emissions trading. In Peru's Sierra

Piura region, for example, the ethical coffee company Cafédirect together with the local NGO Progreso has pioneered a carbon offsetting scheme whereby farmers engage in reforestation to earn carbon credits that Cafédirect then helps them sell to partners. Carbon trading has also generated divisions within the environmental lobby in Latin America. In 2010, in Costa Rica, the Foro Indígena Latinoamericano sobre el Cambio Climático (Latin American Indigenous Forum on Climate Change) attacked the use of carbon credits and any solution to global warming based on the logic of the market because many sites being proposed by governments and NGOs to participate in offset initiatives are in their territories. Indigenous groups are likely to be at the centre of disputes over who owns forest carbon that is traded commercially. In the absence of an internationally agreed price for carbon and because carbon taxes or trading schemes are not applied universally, concerns have grown about the cost of compliance for energy-intensive industries and environmental efficiency in terms of what is called "carbon leakage" – the risk of energy-intensive industries relocating to countries with weaker environmental policies. Various mechanisms have been considered to alleviate the cost of compliance for industries potentially affected, such as free allowances, exemptions or trade measures to impose a similar cost on importers (WTO/UNEP 2009). Fears about competitiveness are also behind clauses that have been written into free trade agreements that strengthen the ability of a corporation to sue a government for what it claims are damages to its business caused by environmental regulations – so called "investor-state disputes". In Peru, for example, Renco, the US mother company of a smelter shut down for financial and environmental reasons, is suing the government for $800 m in loss of earnings under the terms of the US–Peru free trade agreement of 2006. Alongside the fears for competitiveness in the developed world generated by the risk of energy-intensive industries relocating to countries with weaker environmental policies, the notion of the "carbon footprint" – which refers to the overall amount of carbon dioxide and other GHG emissions emitted during the lifecycle of a product along its supply chain and is seen as a tool for mitigating climate change in developed countries – has important implications for regions such as Latin America and the Caribbean that depend heavily on trade (see ECLAC Notes 2010).

Conclusion

Latin American and Caribbean governments have embraced the agenda of sustainable development and the region has become a laboratory of initiatives seeking ways both of assessing the environmental cost of production and financing greener forms of growth. The region's policymakers have taken a prominent role in the global effort to weigh up the costs of climate change and whether mitigation is more cost effective than adaptation. But many political and economic factors have so far limited the scope in Latin America and the Caribbean of innovative mechanisms aimed at protecting the environment such as carbon taxes and trading schemes. Its countries also remain heavily dependent on foreign capital, which it is likely will play the most important role in financing sustainable development initiatives in the future. This dependence will enable foreign investment – which heads disproportionately towards extractive sectors – to retain considerable influence over the terms of debate about the future direction of the green economy. Although it has been growing fast, the private sector remains small throughout Latin America and has only become a powerful force in the most developed economies, a factor that is likely to limit its role in providing alternative, domestic funds for green growth. The region may also remain at a disadvantage under the current norms on competitiveness that are shaping the character of the world economy, which limit what its countries can do to nurture domestic corporations strong enough to play a fuller role in funding sustainable development. Concerns about competitiveness are increasingly being used by foreign corporations, employing clauses written into free trade agreements, to challenge the restrictions posed by national environmental regulations on their activity. The issue of competitiveness therefore raises important questions about the sovereign power of Latin American and Caribbean nation states to determine how they will pursue strategies of sustainable development and develop greener economies.

Recommended reading

Arriagada, Rodrigo. 2008. "Private Provision of Public Goods: Applying Matching Methods to Evaluate Payments for Ecosystem Services in Costa Rica". Summary for Decision-makers, No. 8 September 2008,

Policy Briefs, Latin American and Caribbean Environmental Economics Program.

Ballesteros, Athena et al. 2010. "Power, Responsibility, and Accountability: Rethinking the Legitimacy of Institutions for Climate Finance." Final Report. Washington, DC: World Resources Institute.

Féres, José Gustavo. 2007. "The Role of Economic Instruments for Environmental Management: Water Charges in the Paraíba do Sul River Basin, Brazil". Summary for Decision-makers, No. 2, October 2007, Policy Briefs, Latin American and Caribbean Environmental Economics Program.

Saha, Suranjit Kumar and David Parker. 2002. *Globalisation and Sustainable Development in Latin America: Perspectives on the New Economic Order.* Cheltenham: Edward Elgar.

Useful websites

Alianza Centroamericana de Desarrollo Sostenible (ALIDES, Alliance for the Sustainable Development of Central America): www.inbio.ac.cr/estrategia/coabio/ALIDES.html

Ancient Forest International (AFI), Chile: www.ancientforests.org/

ECOFONDO, Colombia: www.ecofondo.org.co

Fondo Ambiental de El Salvador (FONAES, Environmental Fund of El Salvador): www.fonaes.gob.sv/

Fundação Nacional do Índio (FUNAI, National Indian Foundation): www.funai.gov.br/

Global Footprint Network (GFN): www.footprintnetwork.org

Millennium Ecosystem Assessment: www.millenniumassessment.org/

Programa Latinoamericano del Carbono (PLAC, Latin America Carbon Programme): www.caf.com/view/index.asp?ms=12

Rio+20: www.uncsd2012.org/

UNEP Finance Initiative: www.unepfi.org/

References

Abramson, Evan. 2009. "Soy: A Hunger for Land", in *NACLA Report on the Americas*, Vol. 42, No. 3 (May/June), pp. 34–42.

Acuña, Guillermo. 1999. *Marcos regulatorios e institucionales de América Latina y el Caribe: 1980–1990*. Santiago: Economic Commission for Latin America and the Caribbean. Available online at www.eclac.org/publicaciones/xml/0/4350/lcl1311e.pdf [accessed September 2012].

Albert, Michael. 2006. *Realizing Hope: Life beyond Capitalism*. London: Zed Books.

Alcock, Frank. 2008. "Conflicts and Coalitions within and across the ENGO Community", *Global Environmental Politics*, Vol. 8, No. 4 (November), pp. 66–91.

Alexander, Lucy. 1996. "Colombia's Pacific Plan: Indigenous and Afro-Colombia Communities Challenge the Developers", in Helen Collinson (ed.), *Green Guerrillas: Environmental Conflicts and Initiatives in Latin America and the Caribbean. A Reader*. London: Latin America Bureau.

Anderson, Robin L. 1999. *Colonization as Exploitation in the Amazon Rain Forest*. Gainesville: University Press of Florida.

Anderson, Terry L and Donald R Leal. 1991. *Free Market Environmentalism*. San Francisco, CA: Pacific Research Institute for Public Policy.

Angus, Ian (ed.). 2009. *The Global Fight for Climate Justice: Anticapitalist Responses to Global Warming and Environmental Destruction*. Winnipeg: Fernwood Publishing.

Annis, Sheldon (ed.). 1992. *Poverty, Natural Resources, and Public Policy in Central America*. New Brunswick, NJ: Transaction Publishers/Overseas Development Council.

Aravena Novielli, Claudia. 2009. "Should Chile Use Renewables, Fossil Fuel or Hydropower for Future Electricity Supply? Evidence from a Contingent Valuation Study". Summary for Decision-makers, No. 14, November 2009, Policy Briefs, Latin American and Caribbean Environmental Economics Program.

Arnell, Nigel W. 2004. "Climate Change and Global Water Resources:

SRES Scenarios Emissions and Socio-economic Scenarios", *Global Environmental Change*, Vol. 14, No. 1, pp. 31–52.

Arnold, David. 1996. *La naturaleza como problema histórico: el medio, la cultura y la expansión de Europa*. Mexico City: Fondo de Cultura Económica.

Arriaga, Laura and Leticia Gómez. 2004. *Posibles efectos del cambio climático en algunos componentes de la biodiversidad de México*. Mexico: Secretaría de Medio Ambiente y Recursos Naturales/Instituto Nacional de Ecología. Available online at www2.ine.gob.mx/publicaciones/libros/437/arriaga.html [accessed September 2012].

Arriagada, Rodrigo. 2008. "Private Provision of Public Goods: Applying Matching Methods to Evaluate Payments for Ecosystem Services in Costa Rica". Summary for Decision-makers, No. 8 September 2008, Policy Briefs, Latin American and Caribbean Environmental Economics Program.

Ascher, William. 1997. "The Politics of Rent Distribution and Latin American Natural Resource Policy", in Gordon J MacDonald, Danile L Nielson and Marc A Stern (eds), *Latin American Environmental Policy in International Perspective*. Boulder, CO: Westview Press.

Assadourian, Erik. 2010a. "The Rise and Fall of Consumer Cultures", in Linda Starke and Lisa Mastny (eds), *2010 State of the World. Transforming Cultures: From Consumerism to Sustainability*. Washington, DC: Worldwatch Institute.

——. 2010b. "Introduction, Traditions Old and New", in Linda Starke and Lisa Mastny (eds), *2010 State of the World. Transforming Cultures: From Consumerism to Sustainability*. Washington, DC: Worldwatch Institute.

Associated Press. 2011. "Greenhouse gases rise by record amount", guardian.co.uk, 4 November 2011, available online at www.guardian.co.uk/environment/2011/nov/04/greenhouse-gases-rise-record-levels [accessed August 2012].

Athanasiou, Tom and Paul Baer. 2002. *Dead Heat: Global Justice and Global Warming*. New York: Seven Stories Press.

Bacci, Massimo L. 2008. Conquest: *The Destruction of the American Indios*, translated by Carl Ipsen. Cambridge: Polity Press.

Bachram, Heidi. 2004. "Climate Fraud and Carbon Colonialism: The New Trade in Greenhouse Gases", *Capitalism Nature Socialism*, Vol. 15, No. 4 (December), pp. 1–16.

Bacon, Christopher M, V Ernesto Menendez, Stephen R Gliessman, David Goodman and Jonathan A Fox (eds). 2008. *Confronting the Coffee Crisis: Fair Trade, Sustainable Livelihoods and Ecosystems in Mexico and Central America*. Cambridge, MA: MIT Press.

Baer, Werner. 1972. "Import Substitution and Industrialization in Latin

America: Experiences and Interpretations", in *Latin American Research Review*, Vol. 7, No. 1, pp. 95–122.

Bahn, Paul G. 1993. "50,000-Year-Old Americans of Pedra Furada", *Nature*, 362 (March), pp. 114–15.

Bai, ZG, DL Dent, L Olsson and ME Schaepman. 2008. "Global Assessment of Land Degradation and Improvement. 1. Identification by Remote Sensing." Report 2008/01. Wageningen: ISRIC – World Soil Information/ UN Food and Agriculture Organization (FAO). Available online at www.isric.org/content/global-assessment-land-degradation-and-improvement-1-identification-remote-sensing [accessed January 2014].

Baitenmann, Helga. 2011. "Popular Participation in State Formation: Land Reform in Revolutionary Mexico", in *Journal of Latin American Studies*, Vol. 43, No. 1 (February), pp. 1–31.

Bakker, Karen. 2002. "From State to Market? Water Mercantilización in Spain", *Environment and Planning*, Vol. 34, No. 5, pp. 767–90.

Balée, William. 1989. "The Culture of Amazonian Forests", in Darrell A Posey and William Balee (eds), *Advances in Economic Botany*, Vol. 7. New York: The New York Botanical Garden, pp. 1–21.

——. 1999. *Footprints of the Forest: Ka'apor Ethnobotany – The Historical Ecology of Plant Utilization by an Amazonian People*. New York: Columbia University Press.

Ballesteros, Athena, et al. 2010. "Power, Responsibility, and Accountability: Rethinking the Legitimacy of Institutions for Climate Finance." Final Report. Washington, DC: World Resources Institute.

Ballvé, Teo. 2007. "Pachamama Goes Organic: Bolivia's Quinoa Farmers: Part One of a Two-part Series", *NACLA Report on the Americas*, Vol. 40, No. 4 (July/August), pp. 15–19.

Barcena, Alicia, et al. 2011. "Sustainable Development in Latin America and the Caribbean 20 Years on from the Earth Summit: Progress, Gaps and Strategic Guidelines", LC/L 3346, August 2011, 2011-457. New York: United Nations. Available online at www.eclac.org/rio20/noticias/paginas/9/43799/REV.Rio+20-Sustainable_development.pdf [accessed April 2012].

Barkdull, John and Paul G Harris. 2002. "Environmental Change and Foreign Policy: A Survey of Theory", *Global Environmental Politics*, Vol. 2, No. 2 (May), pp. 63–91.

Barkin, David. 2004. "Mexico City's Water Crisis", *NACLA Report on the Americas*, Vol. 38, No. 1 (July/August), p. 24.

Baud, Michiel, Fabio de Castro and Barbara Hogenboom. 2011. "Environmental Governance in Latin America: Towards an Integrative Research Agenda", *European Review of Latin American and Caribbean Studies*, 90 (April), pp. 79–88.

Bauer, Carl J. 1998. *Against the Current: Privatization, Water Markets, and the State in Chile*. Dordrecht: Kluwer Academic Publishers.

bbc.co.uk. 2004. "México: crece escándalo verde", bbc.co.uk, 26 February 2004. Available online at http://news.bbc.co.uk/hi/spanish/latin_america/newsid_3490000/3490452.stm [accessed December 2011].

——. 2011. "Chevron faces $10.6bn Brazil legal suit over oil spill", bbc.co.uk, 15 December 2011. Available online at www.bbc.co.uk/news/world-latin-america-16192321 [accessed January 2012].

——. 2012. "UK firm signs Cuban renewable energy deal", bbc.co.uk, 17 January 2011. Available online at www.bbc.co.uk/news/uk-scotland-scotland-business-12204109 [accessed August 2012].

Bebbington, Anthony. 1996. "Debating 'Indigenous' Agricultural Development: Indian Organizations in the Central Andes of Ecuador", in Helen Collinson (ed.), *Green Guerrillas: Environmental Conflicts and Initiatives in Latin America and the Caribbean. A Reader*. London: Latin America Bureau.

——. 2009. "The New Extraction: Rewriting the Political Ecology of the Andes?", *NACLA Report on the Americas*, Vol. 42, No. 5 (September/October), pp. 12–20.

Bebbington, Anthony and Jeffrey Bury. 2009. "Institutional Challenges to Mining and Sustainability in Peru", Proceedings of the National Academy of Sciences. Available at www.pnas.org/content/early/2009/09/23/0906057106.full.pdf+html [accessed September 2012].

Bekoff, Marc. 2003. *Nosotros los animales*. Madrid: Editorial Trotta.

Belejack, Barbara. 2002. "Bio 'Gold' Rush in Chiapas on Hold", *NACLA Report on the Americas*, Vol. 35, No. 5 (March/April), pp. 23–28.

Berger, Mark T. 2001. "Citizenship and the Struggle for Land and the Environment in Chiapas", *Latin American Perspectives*, Vol. 28, No. 4 (July), pp. 156–59.

Berke, Phillip R and Timothy Beatley. 1997. *After the Hurricane: Linking Recovery to Sustainable Development in the Caribbean*. London: Johns Hopkins University Press.

Berman Santana, Deborah. 1996. *Kicking off the Bootstraps: Environment, Development and Community Power in Puerto Rico*. Tucson: University of Arizona Press.

Bethell, Leslie (ed.). 1998. *A Cultural History of Latin America: Literature, Music and the Visual Arts in the 19th and 20th Centuries*. Cambridge: Cambridge University Press.

Biermann, Frank and Klaus Dingwerth. 2004. "Global Environmental Change and the Nation State", *Global Environmental Politics*, Vol. 4, No. 1 (February), pp. 1–22.

Birdsall, Nancy and David Wheeler. 1993. "Trade Policy and Industrial

Pollution in Latin America: Where are the Pollution Havens?", *Journal of Environment and Development*, Vol. 2, No. 1 (January), pp. 137–49.

Bishop, Joshua, et al. (eds). 2010. *The Economics of Ecosystems and Biodiversity. TEEB for Business, Executive Summary 2010*. Geneva: United Nations Environment Programme. Available online at http://www.unepfi.org/fileadmin/biodiversity/TEEBforBusiness_summary.pdf [accessed January 2014].

Bjornlund, Henning and Jeniffer McKay. 2002. "Aspects of Water Markets for Developing Countries: Experiences from Australia, Chile, and the US", *Environment and Development Economics*, Vol. 7, No. 4 (October), pp. 769–95.

Blair, David J. 2008. "Trade Liberalisation, Environmental Regulation and the Limits of Reformism: The North American Experience", *Environmental Politics*, Vol. 17, No. 5 (November), pp. 693–711.

Boelens, Rutgerd and Paul H Gelles. 2005. "Cultural Politics, Communal Resistance and Identity in Andean Irrigation Development", *Bulletin of Latin American Research*, Vol. 24, No. 3 (July), pp. 311–27.

Boyd, Stephanie and Ernesto Cabellos. 2002. *Choropampa: The Price of Gold* (documentary film). Lima: Guarango Association. Available to view online at www.youtube.com/watch?v=dW7zn0SbrV4 [accessed September 2012].

Brack, Antonio. 2003. *Perú: Diez mil años de domesticación*. Lima: Programa de las Naciones Unidas para el Desarrollo (PNUD)-Bruño.

Brading, David A. 1985. *The Origins of Mexican Nationalism*. Cambridge Latin American Miniatures. Cambridge: Centre of Latin American Studies.

Bradley, Ruth. 2006. "Chile's Environmental NGOs", Business Chile Magazine (online), 1 May 2006. Avilable online at www.businesschile.cl/en/news/reportaje-principal/chile%E2%80%99s-environmental-ngos [accessed June 2012].

Brannstrom, Christian (ed.). 2004. *Territories, Commodities and Knowledges: Latin American Environmental Histories in the Nineteenth and Twentieth Centuries*. London: Institute for the Study of the Americas.

Brannstrom, Christian and Stefania Gallini. 2004 "An Introduction to Latin American Environmental History", in Christian Brannstrom (ed.), *Territories, Commodities and Knowledges: Latin American Environmental Histories in the Nineteenth and Twentieth Centuries*. London: Institute for the Study of the Americas.

Briscoe, John, et al. 1998. *Managing Water as an Economic Resource: Reflections on the Chilean Experience*. Washington, DC: World Bank.

Broad, Robin. 1994. "The Poor and the Environment: Friends or Foes?", *World Development*, Vol. 22, No. 6, pp. 811–22.

Broad, Robin, and John Cavanagh. 1993. *Plundering Paradise: The Struggle for the Environment in the Philippines*. Berkeley and Los Angeles: University of California Press.

——. 2011. "Like Water for Gold in El Salvador", Mining Watch Canada, 15 July 2011. Available online at www.miningwatch.ca/article/water-gold-el-salvador [accessed August 2012].

Brockett, Charles D and Robert R Gottfried. 2002. "State Policies and the Preservation of Forest Cover: Lessons from Contrasting Public-Policy Regimes in Costa Rica", *Latin American Research Review*, Vol. 37, No. 1, pp. 7–40.

Brothwell, Don. 1994. "On Biological Exchanges between the Two Worlds", in Warwick Bray (ed.), *The Meeting of Two Worlds: Europe and the Americas, 1432–1650*. Oxford: Oxford University Press/British Academy.

Brown, Jonathan C. and Peter S Linder. 1998. "Oil", in Steven C Topik and Allen Wells (eds), *The Second Conquest of Latin America: Coffee, Henequen, and Oil during the Export Boom, 1850–1930*. Austin: University of Texas Press.

Brundtland, Gro Harlem, et al. 1987. "Report of the World Commission on Environment and Development: Our Common Future". Annex to General Assembly Document A/42/427, Development and International Co-operation: Environment 2 August 1987. Available online at www.un-documents.net/wced-ocf.htm [accesed September 2012].

Bruner, Aaron G, Raymond E Gullison and Andrew Balmford. 2004. "Financial Costs and Shortfalls of Managing and Expanding Protected-Area Systems in Developing Countries", *BioScience*, Vol. 54, No. 12 (December), pp. 1119–26.

Brysk, Alison. 2000. *From Tribal Village to Global Village: Indian Rights and International Relations in Latin America*. Stanford, CA: Stanford University Press.

Bueno de Mesquita, Bruce, Alastair Smith, Randolph M Siverson and James D Morrow. 2003. *The Logic of Political Survival*. Cambridge, MA: MIT Press.

Building Bridges Collective. 2010. *Space For Movement? Reflections from Bolivia on Climate Justice, Social Movements and the State*. Leeds: Building Bridges Collective. Available online at http://spaceformovement.files.wordpress.com/2010/08/space_for_movement2.pdf [accessed February 2014].

Bulkeley, Harriet and Michele M Betsill. 2003. *Cities and Climate Change: Urban Sustainability and Global Environmental Governance*. Oxford: Routledge.

Bulmer-Thomas, Victor. 1994. *The Economic History of Latin America since Independence*. Cambridge: Cambridge University Press.

Burke, Lauretta and Jonathan Maidens. 2004. *Reefs at Risk in the Caribbean*. Washington, DC: World Resources Institute.

Busch, Per-Olof, Helge Jörgens and Kerstin Tews. 2005. "The Global Diffusion of Regulatory Instruments: The Making of a New International Environmental Regime", *The Annals of the American Academy of Political and Social Science*, Vol. 598, No. 1 (March), pp. 146–67.

Call, Wendy. 2002. "Plan Puebla-Panama", *NACLA Report on the Americas*, Vol. 35, No. 5 (March/April), pp. 24–25.

Canziani, Osvaldo F and Sandra Diaz (eds). 2000. *The Regional Impacts of Climate Change*, Chapter 6, "Latin America". World Meteorological Organization/United Nations Environment Programme. www.grida.no/publications/other/ipcc_sr/?src=/climate/ipcc/regional/173.htm [accessed January 2014].

Cardoso, Eliana and Ann Helwege. 1992. *Latin America's Economy. Diversity, Trends, and Conflicts*. Cambridge, MA: MIT Press.

Carneiro da Cunha, Manuela. 1992. "Introdução a uma história indígena", in Manuela Carneiro da Cunha (ed.), *História dos Índios no Brasil*. São Paulo: Companhia das Letras.

Carruthers, David V. 2007. "Environmental Justice and the Politics of Energy on the US–Mexico Border", *Environmental Politics*, Vol. 16, No. 3 (June), pp. 394–413.

—— (ed.). 2008a. *Environmental Justice in Latin America: Problems, Promise and Practice*. London: MIT Press.

——. 2008b. "Introduction: Popular Environmentalism and Social Justice in Latin America", in David V Carruthers (ed.), *Environmental Justice in Latin America: Problems, Promise and Practice*. London: MIT Press.

Carter, Neil. 2007. *The Politics of the Environment: Ideas, Activism, Policy*. Cambridge: Cambridge University Press.

——. 2010. "The Greens in the 2009 European Parliament Election", *Environmental Politics*, Vol. 19, No. 2 (March), pp. 295–302.

Casas, Alejandro, Adriana Otero-Arnaiz, Edgar Pérez-Negrón and Alfonso Valiente-Banuet. 2007. "In situ Management and Domestication of Plants in Mesoamerica", *Annals of Botany*, Vol. 100, No. 5, pp. 1101 15.

Castro Herrera, Guillermo. 2001. "Environmental History (Made) in Latin America", H-Net Humanities and Social Sciences Online (February-April). Available online at www2.h-net.msu.edu/~environ/historiography/latinam.htm [accessed September 2012].

——. 2008. "Isthmus in the World: Elements for an Environmental History of Panama", *Global Environment. A Journal of History and Natural and Social Sciences*, Vol. 1, No. 1, pp. 10–55.

Castro, Gonzalo. 2003. "Conservation Finance: The Long Road to Sustainability". Paper presented at the Vth World Parks Congress: Sustainable

Finance Stream, Overview Session, Introduction to the Sustainable Finance Stream and the Policy Context for Protected Area Financing, Panel A, Estimating the Costs. Durban, South Africa, September 2003. Available online at www.conservationfinance.org/guide/WPC/WPC_documents/Overview_PanA_Castro_v2.pdf [accessed August 2011].

Catton, William R and Riley E Dunlap. 1978. "Environmental Sociology: A New Paradigm", *American Sociologist*, Vol. 13 (February), pp. 41–49.

CBD (Convention on Biological Diversity). 2006. *Global Biodiversity Outlook 2*. Montreal: Secretariat of the Convention on Biological Diversity. Available online at www.cbd.int/doc/gbo/gbo2/cbd-gbo2-en.pdf [accessed September 2012].

——. 2010. *Global Biodiversity Outlook 3*. Montreal: Secretariat of the Convention on Biological Diversity. Available online at www.cbd.int/doc/publications/gbo/gbo3-final-en.pdf [accessed September 2012].

Chambers, W Bradnee and Jessica F Green (eds). 2005. *Reforming International Environmental Governance: From Institutional Limits to Innovative Reforms*. Tokyo: UN University Press.

Chasteen, John Charles. 2008. *Americanos: Latin America's Struggles for Independence*. Oxford: Oxford University Press.

Chernela, Janet M. 2011. "Barriers Natural and Unnatural: Islamiento as a Central Metaphor in Kuna Ecotourism", *Bulletin of Latin American Research*, Vol. 30, No. 1 (January), pp. 35–49.

Cherneva, Iveta (ed.). 2012. *The Business Case for Sustainable Finance*. Oxford: Routledge.

Chestney, Nina. 2012. "Emissions set to surge 50 pct by 2050: OECD", Reuters, 15 March 2012. Available online at www.reuters.com/article/2012/03/15/us-oecd-environment-idUSBRE82E0FF20120315 [accessed August 2012].

Clapp, Jennifer. 1998. "The Privatization of Global Environmental Governance: ISO 14000 and the Developing World", *Global Governance*, Vol. 4, No. 3 (July–September), pp. 295–316.

Clay, Jason W. 1988. *Indigenous Peoples and Tropical Forests: Models of Land Use and Management in Latin America*. Cambridge: Cultural Survival.

Cleary, David. 2001. "Towards an Environmental History of the Amazon: From Prehistory to the NineteenthCentury", *Latin American Research Review*, Vol. 36, No. 2, pp. 64–96.

Clemons, Karlie Shea. 2009. "Hydroelectric Dams: Transboundary Environmental Effects and International Law", *Florida State University Law Review*, Vol. 36, pp. 487–536.

Coates, Kenneth. 2004. *A Global History of Indigenous Peoples: Struggle and Survival*. Basingstoke: Palgrave Macmillan.

Collier, Paul and Anke Hoeffler. 2004. "Greed and Grievance in Civil War", *Oxford Economic Papers*, Vol. 56, No. 4, pp. 563–95.

Colloredo-Mansfeld, Rudi. 1999. *The Native Leisure Class: Consumption and Cultural Creativity in the Andes*. London: University of Chicago Press.

Conca, Ken. 2001. "Consumption and Environment in a Global Economy", *Global Environmental Politics*, Vol. 1, No. 3 (summer), pp. 53–71.

——. 2004. "Ecology in an Age of Empire: A Reply to (and Extension of) Dalby's Imperial Thesis", *Global Environmental Politics*, Vol. 4, No. 2 (May), pp. 12–19.

Conca, Ken, Thomas Princen and Michael F Maniates. 2001. "Confronting Consumption", *Global Environmental Politics*, Vol. 1, No. 3 (August), pp. 1–10.

Congleton, Roger D. 1992. "Political Institutions and Pollution Control", *Review of Economics and Statistics*, Vol. 74, No. 3 (August), pp. 412–21.

Cook, Noble David and Alexandra Parma Cook. 2007. *People of the Volcano: Andean Counterpoint in the Colca Valley of Peru*. Durham, NC: Duke University Press.

Cooper, Alix. 2007. *Inventing the Indigenous: Local Knowledge and Natural History in Early Modern Europe*. Cambridge: Cambridge University Press.

Cope, R Douglas. 2010. "Indigenous Agency in Colonial Spanish America", *Latin American Research Review*, Vol. 45, No. 1, pp. 203–14.

Cronon, William. 1996. "The Trouble with Wilderness: Or, Getting Back to the Wrong Nature", in William Cronon (ed.), *Uncommon Ground: Rethinking the Human Place in Nature*. New York: W.W. Norton.

Crosby, Alfred W. 1972. *The Columbian Exchange: Biological and Cultural Consequences of 1492*. Westport, CT: Greenwood Press.

——. 1986. *Ecological Imperialism: The Biological Expansion of Europe 900–1900*. Cambridge: Cambridge University Press.

——. 1991. "The Biological Consequences of 1492", in *The Conquest of Nature 1492–1992*, special edn., *NACLA Report on the America*, Vol. 25, No. 2 (September), pp. 6–13.

Da Cunha, Euclides. 2006. *The Amazon: Land Without History* (translated by R. Sousa). Oxford: Oxford University Press.

Dalby, Simon. 2004. "Ecological Politics, Violence, and the Theme of Empire", *Global Environmental Politics*, Vol. 4, No. 2 (May), pp. 1–11.

Dalton, Russell J, Steve Recchia and Robert Rohrschneider. 2003. "The Environmental Movement and the Modes of Political Action", *Comparative Political Studies*, Vol. 36, No. 7 (September), pp. 743–71.

Dangl, Benjamin. 2010. *Dancing with Dynamite: Social Movements and States in Latin America*. Oakland, CA: AK Press.

Davis, Mike. 2001. *Late Victorian Holocausts: El Niño Famines and the Making of the Third World*. London: Verso.

De Acosta, José. 2002. *The Natural and Moral History of the Indies* (translated by Frances López-Morillas). Durham, NC: Duke University Press.

De la Torre, Augusto, Pablo Fajnzylber and John Nash. 2009. *Low Carbon, High Growth: Latin American Responses to Climate Change*. Washington, DC: World Bank.

De Vos, Paula Susan. 2006. "The Science of Spices: Empiricism and Economic Botany in the Early Spanish Empire", *Journal of World History*, Vol. 17, No. 4 (December), pp. 399–427.

Dean, Warren. 1995. *With Broadax and Firebrand: The Destruction of the Brazilian Atlantic Forest*. London: University of California Press.

Deere, Carolyn L and Daniel C Esty (eds). 2002. *Greening the Americas: NAFTA's Lesson for Hemispheric Trade*. Cambridge, MA: MIT Press.

Denevan, William M. 1992. "The Pristine Myth: The Landscape of the Americas in 1492", *Annals of the American Association of Geographers*, Vol. 82, No. 3 (September), pp. 369–85.

——. 2001 *Cultivated Landscapes of Native Amazonia and the Andes*. Oxford: Oxford University Press.

Denevan, William M and Kent Mathewson (eds). 2009. *Carl Sauer on Culture and Landscape: Readings and Commentaries*. Baton Rouge: Louisiana State University Press.

Descola, Philippe. 1994. *In the Society of Nature: A Native Ecology in Amazonia*. Cambridge: Cambridge University Press.

Di John, Jonathan. 2009. *From Windfall to Curse? Oil and Industrialization in Venezuela, 1920 to the Present*. University Park: Pennsylvania State University Press.

Diamond, Jared. 2005. *Collapse: How Societies Choose to Fail or Succeed*. New York: Viking.

Díaz-Briquets, Sergio and Jorge Pérez-López. 2000. *Conquering Nature: The Environmental Legacy of Socialism in Cuba*. Pittsburgh: University of Pittsburgh Press.

DiBio (Dirección de Biodiversidad)/SERNA (Secretaria de Recursos Naturales y Ambiente). 2007. *Draft/Proposal for a National Biosafety Framework, Honduras, November 2007*. Tegucigalpa: Secretaria de Recursos Naturales y Ambiente /Dirección General de Biodiversidad. Available online at http://hqweb.unep.org/chinese/biosafety/Documents/Honduras%20NBF.pdf [accessed January 2014].

Díez, Jordi and OP Dwivedi (eds). 2008. *Global Environmental Challenges: Perspectives from the South*. Peterborough, ON: Broadview Press.

Díez, Jordi and Susan Francheschet (eds). 2012. *Comparative Public Policy in Latin America*. London: University of Toronto Press.

Dobson, Andrew and Derek Bell (eds). 2006. *Environmental Citizenship*. Cambridge, MA: MIT Press.

Dore, Elizabeth. 1991. "Open Wounds", in *The Conquest of Nature 1492–1992*, special edn., *NACLA Report on the Americas*, Vol. 25, No. 2 (September), pp. 6–13.

——. 1996a. "Capitalism and Ecological Crisis: Legacy of the 1980s", in Helen Collinson (ed.), *Green Guerrillas: Environmental Conflicts and Initiatives in Latin America and the Caribbean. A Reader*. London: Latin America Bureau.

——. 1996b. "How Sustainable were Pre-Columbian Civilizations?", in Helen Collinson (ed.), *Green Guerrillas: Environmental Conflicts and Initiatives in Latin America and the Caribbean. A Reader*. London: Latin America Bureau.

Dorsey, Michael K. 2006. "Future Markets in Biology: Life After Bioprospecting", *NACLA Report on the Americas*, Vol. 39, No. 5 (March/April), pp. 31–34.

Dourojeanni, Axel and Andrei Jouravlev. 1999. *El Código de Aguas en Chile: entre la ideología y la realidad*. Santiago: Economic Commission for Latin America and the Caribbean.

Durham, William. 1979. *Scarcity and Survival in Central America*. Stanford, CA: Stanford University Press.

——. 1994. "Political Ecology and Environmental Destruction in Latin America", in Michael Painter and William H Durham (eds), *The Social Causes of Environmental Destruction in Latin America*. Ann Arbor: University of Michigan Press.

Durning, Alan. 1992. *Guardians of the Land: Indigenous Peoples and the Health of the Earth*. Worldwatch Paper No. 112. Washington, DC: Worldwatch Institute.

ECLAC (Economic Commission for Latin America and the Caribbean). 2002. *Financing for Sustainable Development in Latin America and the Caribbean: From Monterrey to Johannesburg*. World Summit on Sustainable Development, Johannesburg, 2002. Johannesburg: Economic Commission for Latin America and the Caribbean.

——. 2004. *Social Panorama of Latin America 2004*. Santiago: Economic Commission for Latin America and the Caribbean.

——. 2007a. *Estadísticas de recursos naturales y del medio ambiente, Anuario estadístico de América Latina y el Caribe 2006*. Santiago: Economic Commission for Latin America and the Caribbean. Available online at www.eclac.cl/publicaciones/xml/3/28063/LCG2332B_3.pdf [accessed September 2012].

——. 2007b. *Panorama de la Inserción Internacional de América Latina y el Caribe. Tendencias 2008*. Santiago: Economic Commission for Latin America and the Caribbean.

——. 2009. *Economics of Climate Change in Latin America and the Caribbean. Summary*. Santiago: Economic Commission for Latin America and the Caribbean. Available online at www.cepal.org/publicaciones/xml/3/38133/02_Economics_of_Climate_Change_-_Summary_2009.pdf [accessed August 2012].

——. 2010. *Economics of Climate Change in Latin America and the Caribbean, Summary 2010*. Santiago: Economic Commission for Latin America and the Caribbean. Available online at www.eclac.cl/dmaah/publicaciones/xml/9/41909/2010-914-Climate_change-COMPLETO_WEB.pdf [accessed January 2012].

——. 2011a. *Financing for Development and Middle Income Countries: New Challenges*. Santiago: Economic Commission for Latin America and the Caribbean.

——. 2011b. *Foreign Direct Investment in Latin America and the Caribbean*. Briefing Paper. Santiago: Economic Commission for Latin America and the Caribbean. Available online at www.eclac.cl/publicaciones/xml/2/46572/2012-182-LIEI-WEB.pdf [accessed September 2012].

——. 2011c. *Statistical Yearbook for Latin American and the Caribbean 2011*. Santiago: Economic Commission for Latin America and the Caribbean.

——. 2012a. *Foreign Direct Investment in Latin America and the Caribbean, 2011*. Briefing Paper. Santiago: Economic Commission for Latin America and the Caribbean. Available online at www.eclac.cl/publicaciones/xml/2/46572/2012-182-LIEI-WEB.pdf [accessed July 2012].

——. 2012b. *Social Panorama of Latin America 2011*. Santiago: Economic Commission for Latin America and the Caribbean. Available online at www.eclac.cl/publicaciones/xml/5/45175/PSE2011-Social-panorama-of-Latin-America.pdf [accessed September 2012].

ECLAC Notes. 2010. "Carbon Footprint May Deepen Latin America Trade Vulnerability", Notes No. 66 (November). Available online at www.eclac.cl/notes/66/Titulares1.html [accessed June 2012].

The Economist. 2010. *Latin American Green City Index: Assessing the Environmental Performance of Latin America's Major Cities*. Munich: The Economist/Siemens. Available online at www.siemens.com/entry/cc/features/greencityindex_international/all/en/pdf/report_latam_en.pdf [accessed January 2012].

Ellis, Reuben. 2001. *Vertical Margins: Mountaineering and the Landscapes of Neoimperialism*. Madison: University of Wisconsin Press.

Espach, Ralph. 2006. "When is Sustainable Forestry Sustainable? The Forest Stewardship Council in Argentina and Brazil", *Global Environmental Politics*, Vol. 6, No. 2 (May), pp. 55–84.

Esty, Daniel C. 1994. *Greening the GATT: Trade, Environment, and the Future*. Washington, DC: Institute for International Economics.

Eurostat. 2002. *SERIEE Environmental Protection Expenditure Accounts – Compilation Guide*, Theme 2, Economy and Finance. Luxembourg: EUROSTAT/European Commission. Available online at http://epp.eurostat.ec.europa.eu/cache/ITY_OFFPUB/KS-BE-02-001/EN/KS-BE-02-001-EN.PDF [accessed September 2012].

Evans, Sterling. 1999. *The Green Republic: A Conservation History of Costa Rica*. Austin: University of Texas Press.

Faber, Daniel. 1991. "A Sea of Posion", *The Conquest of Nature 1492–1992*, special edn., *NACLA Report on the Americas*, Vol. 25, No. 2 (September), pp. 31–36.

——. 1993. *Environment Under Fire: Imperialism and the Ecological Crisis in Central America*. New York: Monthly Review.

——. 2002. "A Revolution in Environmental Justice and Sustainable Development: The Political Ecology of Nicaragua", in John Byrne, Leigh Glover and Cecilia Martinez (eds), *Environmental Justice: International Discourses in Political Economy, Energy and Environmental Policy*. London: Transaction.

Fair, James. 1996. "Can Ecotourism Save Ecuador's Threatened Cloud Forests?", in Helen Collinson (ed.), *Green Guerrillas: Environmental Conflicts and Initiatives in Latin America and the Caribbean. A Reader*. London: Latin America Bureau.

FAO (Food and Agriculture Organization). 2005. *Global Forest Resources Assessment 2005*. Rome: United Nations Food and Agriculture Organization.

——. 2007a. *State of the World's Forests, 2007*. Rome: UN Food and Agriculture Organization. Available online at www.fao.org/docrep/009/a0773e/a0773e00.htm [accessed September 2012].

——. 2007b. *Tierra y agua. Día internacional del agua*. UN Food and Agriculture Organization, Oficina regional para América Latina y el Caribe. Available online at http://web.archive.org/web/20110705155323/http://www.rlc.fao.org/es/tierra/agua07.htm [accessed January 2014].

——. 2008. FAOSTAT Statistics Division database. Rome: UN Food and Agriculture Organization. Available online at http://faostat.fao.org/#.

——. 2009. *State of the World´s Forests 2009*. Rome: UN Food and Agriculture Organization.

Féres, José Gustavo. 2007. "The Role of Economic Instruments for Environmental Management: Water Charges in the Paraíba do Sul River Basin, Brazil". Summary for Decision-makers, No. 2, October 2007, Policy Briefs, Latin American and Caribbean Environmental Economics Program.

FIDA (Foro Interamericano de Derecho Ambiental). 2008. Draft Background Note, National Focal Points' Meeting, Inter-American Forum on Environmental Law (FIDA), Supreme Court of Justice Brasilia, 7, 8 and 9 May 2008.

Finley-Brook, Mary. 2007. "Green Neoliberal Space: The Mesoamerican Biological Corridor", *Journal of Latin American Geography*, Vol. 6, No. 1, pp. 101–24.

Firor, John and Judith Jacobsen. 2002. *The Crowded Greenhouse: Population, Climate Change, and Creating a Sustainable World*. New Haven, CT: Yale University Press.

Forero, Oscar A and Michael R Redclift. 2006. "The Role of the Mexican State in the Development of Chicle Extraction in Yucatán, and the Continuing Importance of Coyotaje", *Journal of Latin American Studies*, Vol. 38, No. 1 (February), pp. 65–93.

Fougner, Tore. 2006. "The State, International Competitiveness and Neoliberal Globalisation: Is There a Future Beyond 'The Competition State'?", *Review of International Studies*, Vol. 32, No. 1, pp. 165–85.

Foweraker, Joe. 2001. "Grassroots Movements and Political Activism in Latin America: A Critical Comparison of Chile and Brazil", *Journal of Latin American Studies*, Vol. 33, No. 4 (November), pp. 839–65.

Foweraker, Joe, Todd Landman and Neil Harvey. 2003. *Governing Latin America*. Cambridge: Polity Press.

Frankenhoff, Charles A. 1962. "The Prebisch Thesis: A Theory of Industrialism for Latin America", *Journal of Inter-American Studies*, Vol. 4, No. 2 (April), pp. 185–206.

Franko, Patrice. 1999. *The Puzzle of Latin American Economic Development*. Lanham, MD: Rowman & Littlefield.

Frenkel, Stephen. 1996. "Jungle Stories: North American Representations of Tropical Panama", *Geographical Review*, Vol. 86, No. 3 (July), pp. 317–33.

Funes Monzote, Reinaldo. 2008. *From Rainforest to Cane Field in Cuba: An Environmental History since 1492*. Chapel Hill: University of North Carolina Press.

Furley, Peter A. (ed.). 1994. *The Forest Frontier: Settlement and Change in Brazilian Roraima*. London: Routledge.

Gade, Daniel W. 1999. *Nature and Culture in the Andes*. Madison: University of Wisconsin Press.

Galaz, Victor. 2004. "Stealing from the Poor? Game Theory and the Politics of Water Markets in Chile", *Environmental Politics*, Vol. 13, No. 2, pp. 414–37.

Galindo, Luis Miguel (ed.). 2009. *La Economía del Cambio Climático en México. Síntesis*. Mexico City: Secretarías de Hacienda y Crédito

Público and Secretaría del Medio Ambiente y Recursos Naturales. Available online at http://era-mx.org/biblio/SintesisEconCambioClimatico2090617.pdf [accessed August 2012].

Gallagher, Kevin P. 2004. *Free Trade and the Environment: Mexico, NAFTA and Beyond.* Stanford, CA: Stanford University Press.

——. 2008 "China Matters: China's Economic Impact in Latin America", *Latin American Research Review*, Vol. 43, No. 1, pp. 185–202.

Gallagher, Kevin P and Jacob Werksman (eds). 2002. *The Earthscan Reader on International Trade and Sustainable Development.* London: Earthscan.

Gallagher, Kevin P and Lyuba Zarsky. 2007. *The Enclave Economy: Foreign Investment and Sustainable Development in Mexico's Silicon Valley.* Cambridge, MA: MIT Press.

Gallagher, Kevin P, et al. (eds). 2008. *Foreign Investment and Sustainable Development Lessons from the Americas.* Working Group on Development and the Environment in the Americas. Washington, DC: Heinrich Böll Foundation North America.

Gallini, Stefania. 2004. "A Maya-Mam Agro-ecosystem in Guatemala's Coffee Revolution: Costa Cuca, 1830s–1880s", in Christian Brannstrom (ed.), *Territories, Commodities and Knowledges: Latin American Environmental Histories in the Nineteenth and Twentieth Centuries.* London: Institute for the Study of the Americas.

Gan, Lin. 2002. "Research Note. Promoting Green Electricity Development from Industrial to Developing Countries: What Needs to be Done?", *Environmental Politics*, Vol. 11, No. 1 (spring), pp. 163–83.

Garcia Canclini, Néstor. 1989. *Culturas Híbridas: Estrategias para Entrar y Salir de la Modernidad.* Mexico: Grijalbo.

Gardner, Toby A, Isabelle M Côté, Jennifer A Gill, Alastair Grant and Andrew R Watkinson. 2003. "Long-Term Region-Wide Declines in Caribbean Corals", *Science*, Vol. 301, No. 5635, pp. 958–60.

Garfield, Seth. 2001. "A Nationalist Environment: Indians, Nature, and the Construction of the Xingu National Park in Brazil", *Luso-Brazilian Review*, Vol. 41, No. 1, pp. 139–67.

GEF (Global Environment Facility). 2010. *Indigenous Communities and Biodiversity.* Washington, DC: Global Environment Facility.

——. 2012. *Behind the Numbers: A Closer Look at GEF Achievements.* Washington, DC: Global Environment Facility. Available online at www.thegef.org/gef/sites/thegef.org/files/publication/GEF_Behind_the_Numbers_CRA.pdf [accessed July 2012].

Gelles, Paul H. 1995. "Equilibrium and Extraction: Dual Organization in the Andes", *American Ethnologist*, Vol. 22, No. 4 (November), pp. 710–42.

——. 2000. *Water and Power in Highland Peru: The Cultural Politics of*

Irrigation and Development. New Brunswick, NJ: Rutgers University Press.

GFN (Global Footprint Network). 2010. *Global Footprint Network 2010 Annual Report*. Oakland: Global Footprint Network.

Glennie, Jonathan. 2011. "Colombia's new index to measure poverty merits a cautious welcome", guardian.co.uk, 30 August 2011. Available online at www.guardian.co.uk/global-development/poverty-matters/2011/aug/30/colombia-new-poverty-measurement-index [accessed June 2012].

Godoy, Emilio. 2012. "The waste mountain engulfing Mexico City", guardian.co.uk, 9 January 2012. Available online at www.guardian.co.uk/environment/2012/jan/09/waste-mountain-mexico-city [accessed June 2012].

Gómez-Galvarriato, Aurora and Jeffrey G Williamson. 2009. "Was it Prices, Productivity or Policy? Latin American Industrialisation after 1870", *Journal of Latin American Studies*, Vol. 41, No. 4 (November), pp. 663–94.

Goodman, David and Michael Redclift (eds). 1991. *Environment and Development in Latin America: The Politics of Sustainability*. Manchester: Manchester University Press.

Gose, Peter. 1993. "Segmentary State Formation and the Ritual Control of Water under the Incas", *Comparative Studies in Society and History*, Vol. 35, No. 3 (July), pp. 480–514.

Grove, Richard. 1997. *Ecology, Climate and Empire: Colonialism and Global Environmental History, 1400–1940*. Cambridge: White Horse.

Gwynne, Robert N and Cristóbal Kay. 2004. "Latin America Transformed: Globalization and Neoliberalism", in Robert N. Gwynne and Cristóbal Kay (eds.), *Latin America Transformed: Globalization and Modernity*, 2nd edn. London: Arnold.

Haines, Andrew, Paul R Epstein and Anthony McMichael, 1993: "Global health watch: monitoring impacts of environment change", *Lancet*, Vol. 342, No. 8885 (December), pp. 1464–69.

Hall, Gillette and Harry Anthony Patrinos. 2005. *Indigenous Peoples, Poverty and Human Development in Latin America: 1994–2004*. Washington, DC: World Bank. Available online at http://siteresources.worldbank.org/INTLAC/Resources/FinalExecutiveSummary_Eng_May05.pdf [accessed June 2012].

Hall, Thomas D and James V Fenelon. 2009. *Indigenous Peoples and Globalization: Resistance and Revitalization*. Boulder, CO: Paradigm Publishers.

Hames, Robert and William Vickers (eds). 1983. *Adaptive Responses of Native Amazonians*. New York: Academic Press.

Hamilton, Sarah and Edward F Fischer. 2003. "Non-Traditional

Agricultural Exports in Highland Guatemala: Understandings of Risk and Perceptions of Change", *Latin American Research Review*, Vol. 38, No. 3, pp. 82–110.

Hanley, Nick, Jason F Shogren and Ben White. 2001. *Introduction to Environmental Economics*. Oxford: Oxford University Press.

Haraway, Donna J. 1997. *Modest_Witness@Second_Millennium. FemaleMan_Meets_Onco Mouse: Feminism and Technoscience*. New York: Routledge.

Harris, Richard. 2002. "Resistance and Alternatives to Globalization in Latin America and the Caribbean", *Latin American Perspectives*, Vol. 29, No. 6 (November), pp. 136–51.

Harvey, Fiona. 2011. "World headed for irreversible climate change in five years, IEA warns", guardian.co.uk, 9 November 2011. Available online at www.guardian.co.uk/environment/2011/nov/09/fossil-fuel-infrastructure-climate-change [accessed August 2012].

Haufler, Virginia. 2001. *A Public Role for the Private Sector: Industry Self-Regulation in the Global Economy*. New York: Carnegie Endowment for International Peace.

Haughton, Graham. 2002. "Market Making: Internationalisation and Global Water Markets", *Environment and Planning*, Vol. 34, No. 5, pp. 791–807.

Hayden, Cori. 2003. *When Nature Goes Public: The Making and Unmaking of Bioprospecting in Mexico*. Princeton, NJ: Princeton University Press.

——. 2006. "Bioprospecting: The 'Promise' and Threat of the Market", *NACLA Report on the Americas*, Vol. 39, No. 5 (March/April), pp. 26–31.

Hecht, Susanna B and Alexander Cockburn. 1990. *The Fate of the Forest: Developers, Destroyers, and Defenders of the Amazon*. New York: HarperCollins.

Hecht, Susanna B and Darrell A Posey. 1989. "Preliminary Findings on Soil Management of the Kayapó Indians", in Darrell A Posey and William L Balée (eds), *Resource Management in Amazônia: Indigenous and Folk Strategies*. New York: New York Botanical Garden.

Henley, Paul. 1996. "Review Essay. Recent Themes in the Anthropology of Amazonia: History, Exchange, Alterity", *Bulletin of Latin American Research*, Vol. 15, No. 2 (May), pp. 231–45.

Highfield, Roger. 2011. "Bolivia's stunning salt flats", *New Scientist* online, 9 June 2011. Available online at www.newscientist.com/blogs/shortsharpscience/2011/06/bolivias-stunning-salt-flats.html [accessed August 2012].

Hillstrom, Kevin and Laurie Collier-Hillstrom. 2004. *Latin America and the Caribbean: A Continental Overview of Environmental Issues*. Santa Barbara, CA: ABC-CLIO.

Hines, Colin. 2000. *Localization: A Global Manifesto*. London: Earthscan.

Hoad, Darren. 2002. "Profile – GATS, Sustainable Tourism and the International Year of Ecotourism (IYE 2002)", *Environmental Politics*, Vol. 11, No. 2 (summer), pp. 159–64.

Hochstetler, Kathryn and Margaret E Keck. 2007. *Greening Brazil: Environmental Activism in State and Society*. Durham, NC: Duke University Press.

Honey, Martha. 2003. "Giving a Grade to Costa Rica's Green Tourism", *NACLA Report on the Americas*, Vol. 36, No. 6 (May/June), p. 39.

Honty, Gerardo. 2011. *Cambio Climático: Negociaciones y Consecuencias para America Latina*. Montevideo: Centro Latino Americano de Ecología Social. Available online at www.intercambioclimatico.com/wp-content/uploads/2011/02/HontyCambioClimatico2011.pdf [accessed August 2012].

Horton, Lynn R. 2006. "Contesting State Multiculturalisms: Indigenous Land Struggles in Eastern Panama", *Journal of Latin American Studies*, Vol. 38, No. 4 (November), pp. 829–58.

Houck, Oliver A. 2000. "Environmental Law in Cuba", *Journal of Land Use and Environmental Law*, Vol. 16, No. 1, pp. 1–81.

IAI (Inter-American Institute for Global Change Research). 2011. "Science Snapshots 6: Heat, Dust, and People", IAI Communiqués. Brazil: Inter-American Institute for Global Change Research. Available online at www.iai.int/index.php?option=com_content&view=article&id=109&Itemid=108 [accessed July 2011].

IDB (Inter-American Development Bank). 2012. *The Climate and Development Challenge for Latin America and the Caribbean: Options for Climate-Resilient, Low-Carbon Development*. Washington, DC: Inter-American Development Bank/Economic Commission of Latin America and the Caribbean/World Wildlife Fund. Available online at www.iadb.org/intal/cartamensual/cartas/Articulo.aspx?Id=61634927-831e-41b0-8b5e-ec63a46c43ae&lang=en [accessed August 2012].

IEA (International Energy Agency). 2008. *World Energy Outlook 2008*. Paris: International Energy Agency. Available online at www.worldenergyoutlook.org/media/weowebsite/2008-1994/WEO2008.pdf [accessed September 2011].

——. 2009. *World Energy Outlook 2009*. Paris: International Energy Agency. Available online at www.worldenergyoutlook.org/media/weowebsite/2009/WEO2009.pdf [accessed September 2011].

IFAD (International Fund for Agricultural Development). 2003. *The Adoption of Organic Agriculture among Small Farmers in Latin America and the Caribbean: Thematic Evaluation*. Rome: International Fund for Agricultural Development.

Igelsias Utset, Marial. 2011. *A Cultural History of Cuba During the US Occupation 1898–1902* (translated by Russ Davidson). Chapel Hill: University of North Carolina Press.

ILO (International Labour Organization). 2009. *Global Employment Trends, January 2009*. Geneva: International Labour Organization.

INPE (Instituto Nacional de Pesquisas Espaciais). 2009. "Projeto PRODES: Monitoramento da floresta amazônica brasileira por satélite". São José dos Campos: Instituto Nacional de Pesquisas Espaciais. Available online at www.obt.inpe.br/prodes/index.php [accessed September 2012].

IOM (International Organization for Migration). 2009. *Climate Change, Environmental Degradation and Migration: Addressing Vulnerabilities and Harnessing Opportunities*. Geneva: International Organization for Migration.

IPCC (Intergovernmental Panel on Climate Change). 1996. *IPCC Second Assessment Report: Climate Change 1995*. Impacts, Adaptations and Mitigation of Climate Change: Scientific-Technical Analyses. Contribution of Working Group II to the Second Assessment Report of the Intergovernmental Panel on Climate Change. Cambridge: Intergovernmental Panel on Climate Change/Cambridge University Press. Available online at www.ipcc.ch/publications_and_data/publications_and_data_reports.shtml#1 [accessed September 2012].

——. 2007. *Climate Change 2007 Synthesis Report* (Contribution of Working Groups I, II and III to the Fourth Assessment Report of the Intergovernmental Panel on Climate Change, AR4). Geneva: Intergovernmental Panel on Climate Change. Available online at www.ipcc.ch/publications_and_data/ar4/syr/en/contents.html [accessed September 2012].

IPCC Working Group II. 1997. "The Regional Impacts of Climate Change: An Assessment of Vulnerability". Summary for Policymakers. IPCC Special Report: Intergovernmental Panel on Climate Change/United Nations Environment Programme/World Maritime Organization.

Irvine, Dominique. 1989. "Succession Management and Resource Distribution in an Amazonian Rainforest", in Darrell A Posey and William Balee (eds), *Advances in Economic Botany*, Vol. 7. New York: The New York Botanical Garden.

Irwin, Alan. 2001. *Sociology and the Environment: A Critical Introduction to Society, Nature and Knowledge*. Polity Press: Cambridge.

IUCN (International Union for Conservation of Nature). 2008a. *An Analysis of Amphibians on the 2008 IUCN Red List of Threatened Species*. Gland: International Union for Conservation of Nature. Available online at www.iucnredlist.org/amphibians [accessed September 2012].

——. 2008b. *An Analysis of Mammals on the 2008 IUCN Red List*. Gland: International Union for Conservation of Nature. Available online at www.iucnredlist.org/mammals [accessed September 2012].

——. 2008c. *Red List Summary Statistics*. Gland: International Union for Conservation of Nature. Available online at www.iucnredlist.org/about/summary-statistics [accessed September 2012].

IUCN/UNEP-WCMC (United Nations Environment Programme-World Conservation Monitoring Centre). 2011. *The World Database on Protected Areas (WDPA): January 2011*. Cambridge: International Union for Conservation of Nature, United Nations Environment Programme, World Conservation Monitoring Centre.

Jackson, Tim. 2011. *Prosperity without Growth: Economics for a Finite Planet*. London: Routledge.

Jaffee, Daniel. 2007. *Brewing Justice: Fair Trade Coffee, Sustainability, and Survival*. Berkeley: University of California Press.

James, Clive. 2006. "Global Status of Commercialized Biotech/GM Crops", ISAAA Briefs No. 35. Ithaca, NY: International Service for the Acquisition of Agri-Biotech Applications.

Jenkins, Rhys. 2003. "Has Trade Liberalization Created Pollution Havens in Latin America?", *CEPAL Review*, 80 (August), pp. 81–95.

Jiménez, Carolina, Pilar Huante and Emmanuel Rincón. 2006. *Restauración de minas superficiales en México*. Mexico: Secretaría de Medio Ambiente y Recursos Naturales.

Johnson, Sherry. 2011. *Climate and Catastrophe in Cuba and the Atlantic World in the Age of Revolution*. Chapel Hill: University of North Carolina Press.

Johnston, Barbara Rose (ed.). 2011. *Life and Death Matters: Human Rights, Environment, and Social Justice*. Walnut Creek, CA: Left Coast Press.

Jones, Eric L. 1991. "The History of Natural Resource Exploitation in the Western World", *Research in Economic History*, Supplement 6, pp. 235–52.

Joseph, Gilbert, Catherine LeGrand and Ricardo Salvatore (eds). 1998. *Close Encounters of Empire: Writing the Cultural History of US-Latin American Relations*. Durham, NC: Duke University Press.

Kaimowitz, David. 1996. "Social Pressure for Environmental Reform in Latin America", in Helen Collinson (ed.), *Green Guerrillas: Environmental Conflicts and Initiatives in Latin America and the Caribbean. A Reader*. London: Latin America Bureau.

Kalkstein, LS. 1993. "Direct Impacts in Cities", *Lancet*, Vol. 342, No. 8884, pp. 1397–99.

Karl, Terry Lynn. 1997. *The Paradox of Plenty: Oil Booms and Petro-States*. Berkeley: University of California Press.

Kawell, JoAnn. 2002. "Who Owns Knowledge?", *NACLA Report on the Americas,* Vol. 35, No. 5 (March/April), pp. 14–17.

Kay, Cristóbal. 2004. "Rural Livelihoods and Peasant Futures", in Robert N Gwynne and Cristóbal Kay (eds), *Latin America Transformed: Globalization and Modernity*, 2nd edn. London: Arnold.

Killeen, Timothy J. 2007. *A Perfect Storm in the Amazon Wilderness: Development and Conservation in the Context of the Initiative for the Integration of the Regional Infrastructure of South America (IIRSA).* Advances in Applied Biodiversity Science, No. 7. Arlington, VA: Center for Applied Biodiversity Science/Conservation International. Available online at www.conservation.org/publications/Documents/AABS.7_Perfect_Storm_English.low.res.pdf [accessed February 2012].

Kimerling, Judith. 1996. "Oil, Lawlessness and Indigenous Struggles in Ecuador's Oriente", in Helen Collinson (ed.), *Green Guerrillas: Environmental Conflicts and Initiatives in Latin America and the Caribbean. A Reader.* London: Latin America Bureau.

Kingstone, Peter. 2010. *The Political Economy of Latin America: Reflections on Neoliberalism and Development*. New York: Routledge.

Kirdar, Uner (ed.). 1992. *Change: Threat or Opportunity for Human Progress? Ecological Change*. New York: United Nations.

Klooster, Dan. 2003a. "Campesinos and Mexican Forest Policy during the Twentieth Century", *Latin American Research Review,* Vol. 38, No. 2 (June 2003).

——. 2003b. "Forest Transitions in Mexico: Institutions and Forests in a Globalized Countryside", *Professional Geographer,* Vol. 55, No. 2 (May), pp. 227–37.

Kozloff, Nikolas. 2004. "From Lakeshore Village to Oil Boom Town: Lagunillas under Venezuelan Dictator Juane Vicente Gómez, 1908–1935", in Christian Brannstrom (ed.), *Territories, Commodities and Knowledges: Latin American Environmental Histories in the Nineteenth and Twentieth Centuries*. London: Institute for the Study of the Americas.

——. 2006. "Asserting State Authority through Environmental Monitoring: Venezuela in the Post-Gómez Era, 1935–1945", *Bulletin of Latin American Research*, Vol. 25, No. 2 (April), pp. 282–300.

——. 2010. *No Rain in the Amazon: How South America's Climate Change Affects the Entire Planet*. Basingstoke: Palgrave Macmillan.

Kütting, Gabriela. 2004. "Book Review Essay: Environmental Justice", *Global Environmental Politics*, Vol. 4, No. 1 (February), pp. 115–21.

Lacoste, Pablo. 2007. "Complejidad de la industria vitivinícola colonial: Crianza biológica de vino (reino de Chile siglo XVIII)", *Latin American Research Review*, Vol. 42, No. 2, pp. 154–68.

Laird, Sarah A, Walter V Reid and Carrie A Meyer. 1993. *Biodiversity Prospecting: Using Genetic Resources for Sustainable Development*. Washington, DC: World Resources Institute.

Lall, Sanjaya, John Weiss and Hiroshi Oikawa. 2005. "People's Republic of China's Competitive Threat to Latin America: An Analysis for 1990–2002", *Oxford Development Studies*, Vol. 33, No. 2, pp. 163–94.

Lambin, Eric F, Helmut J Geist and Erika Lepers. 2003. "Dynamics of Land-Use and Land-Cover Change in Tropical Regions", *Annual Review of Environment and Resources*, Vol. 28, No. 1, pp. 205–41.

Larrain, Jorge. 2000. *Identity and Modernity in Latin America*. Cambridge: Polity.

Latin Business Chronicle. 2008. "Latin America More Globalized", fourth annual Latin Globalization Index, Latin Business Chronicle online, 10 December 2008.

Latinobarómetro. 2011. *Informe 2011*. Santiago: Corporación Latinobarómetro. Available online at www.latinobarometro.org/latino/latinobarometro.jsp [accessed July 2012].

Latour, Bruno. 1993. *We Have Never Been Modern* (translated by Catherine Porter). Cambridge, MA: Harvard University Press.

Lederman, Daniel and William F Maloney (eds). 2007. *Natural Resources: Neither Curse nor Destiny*. Washington, DC: World Bank /Stanford University Press.

Lederman, Daniel, Marcelo Olarreaga and Guillermo Perry. 2006. *Latin America and the Caribbean's Response to the Growth of China and India: Overview of Research Findings and Policy Implications*. Washington, DC: World Bank, Latin America and the Caribbean Region.

Leighton, Michelle and Aaron Frank. 1997. *Environmental Degradation and Migration: The US–Mexico Case Study*. The Natural Heritage Institute, ECSP Report 4: Special Report. Washington, DC: Wilson Center, Environmental Change and Security Program.

Lele, Sharachchandra M. 1991. "Sustainable Development: A Critical Review", *World Development*, Vol. 19, No. 6, pp. 607–21.

Lemos, Maria Carmen and Arun Agrawal. 2006. "Environmental Governance", *Annual Review of Environment and Resources*, Vol. 31, No. 3 (November), pp. 297–325.

Levy, David and Daniel Egan. 1998. "Capital Contests: National and Transnational Channels of Corporate Influence on Climate Change Negotiations", *Politics and Society*, Vol. 26, No. 3 (September), pp. 337–61.

Liverman, Diana and Silvina Vilas. 2006. "Neoliberalism and the Environment in Latin America', *Annual Review of Environment and Resources*, No. 31 (November), pp. 327–63.

Lloyd-Sherlock, Peter. 1997. “The Recent Appearance of Favelas in Sao Paulo City: An Old Problem in a New Setting”, *Bulletin of Latin American Research*, Vol. 16, No. 3 (September), pp. 289–305.

Lohmann, Larry. 2006. “Carbon Trading: A Critical Conversation on Climate Change, Privatization and Power”, Development Dialogue No. 48. Uppsala: The Dag Hammarskjöld Centre.

Loker, William. 2004. *Changing Places: Environment, Development and Social Change in Rural Honduras*. Durham, NC: Carolina Academic Press.

Lora, Eduardo, Andrew Powell, Bernard MS van Praag and Pablo Sanguinetti (eds). 2010. *The Quality of Life in Latin American Cities: Markets and Perception*. Washington, DC: Inter-American Development Bank.

Lövbrand, Teresia Rindefjäll and Joakim Nordqvist. 2009. “Closing the Legitimacy Gap in Global Environmental Governance? Lessons from the Emerging CDM Market”, *Global Environmental Politics*, Vol. 9, No. 2 (May), pp. 74–100.

Ludlam, Steve. 2009. “Cuban Socialism: Recovery and Change”, in Geraldine Lievesley and Steve Ludlam (eds), *Reclaiming Latin America: Experiments in Radical Social Democracy*. London: Zed Books.

Luke, Timothy W. 1998. “The (Un)Wise (Ab)Use of Nature: Environmentalism as Globalized Consumerism”, *Alternatives: Global, Local, Political*, Vol. 23, No. 2 (April), pp. 175–212.

Lyons, Colleen Scanlan. 2009. “Battle in Bahia: A New Port Faces Growing Resistance”, *NACLA Report on the Americas*, Vol. 42, No. 5 (September/October), pp. 30–34.

MacDonald, Gordon J and Marc Stern. 1997. “Environmental Politics and Policy in Latin America”, in Gordon J MacDonald, Daniel L Nielson and Marc A Stern (eds), *Latin American Environmental Policy in International Perspective*. Boulder, CO: Westview Press.

MacDonald, Gordon J and Daniel L Nielson 1997. “Conclusion: Latin American Foreign Policy and International Environmental Regimes”, in Gordon J MacDonald, Daniel L. Nielson and Marc A Stern (eds), *Latin American Environmental Policy in International Perspective*. Boulder, CO: Westview Press.

Macdonald, Ken. 2012. “Strathclyde University scientists end marabu weed nightmare”, bbc.co.uk, 17 January 2012. Available online at www.bbc.co.uk/news/uk-scotland-glasgow-west-16597459 [accessed August 2012].

MacDonald, Laura. 1997. *Supporting Civil Society: The Political Role of Non-Governmental Organisations in Central America*. Basingstoke: Macmillan.

Macnaghten, Phil and John Urry. 1998. *Contested Natures*. London: Sage.

MacNeish, Richard S. 1992. *The Origins of Agricultura and Settled Life*. London: University of Oklahoma Press.

Maffi, Luisa. 2002. "Endangered Languages, Endangered Knowledge", *International Social Science Journal*, Vol. 54, No. 173 (September), pp. 385–93.

Magrin, Graciela, Carlos Gay García, et al. 2007. "Latin America", in ML Parry et al. (eds), *Climate Change 2007: Impacts, Adaptation and Vulnerability. Contribution of Working Group II to the Fourth Assessment Report of the Intergovernmental Panel on Climate Change*. Cambridge: Cambridge University Press. Available online at www.ipcc.ch/pdf/assessment-report/ar4/wg2/ar4-wg2-chapter13.pdf [accessed September 2012].

Malhi, Yadvinder, et al. 2008. "Climate Change, Deforestation, and the Fate of the Amazon", *Science*, Vol. 319, No. 5860 (November), pp. 169–72.

Mander, Jerry and Victoria Tauli-Corpuz (eds). 2006. *Paradigm Wars: Indigenous Peoples' Resistance to Globalization*. San Francisco, CA: Sierra Club Books.

Markandya, Anil and Kirsten Halsnaes (eds). 2002. *Climate Change and Sustainable Development: Prospects for Developing Countries*. London: Earthscan.

Marquardt, Steve. 2002. "Pesticides, Parakeets, and Unions in the Costa Rican Banana Industry, 1938–1962", *Latin American Research Review*, Vol. 37, No. 2, pp. 3–36.

Martin, Edward J. 2003. "Liberation Theology, Sustainable Development, and Postmodern Public Administration", *Latin American Perspectives*, Vol. 30, No. 4, *Struggle and Neoliberal Threats* (July), pp. 69–91.

Mas, Jean-François, et al. 2004. "Assessing Land Use/Cover Changes: A Nationwide Multidate Spatial Database for Mexico", *International Journal of Applied Earth Observation and Geoinformation*, Vol. 5, No. 4 (October), pp. 249–61.

McCarthy, John D and Mayer N Zald. 1977. "Resource Mobilization and Social Movements", *American Journal of Sociology*, Vol. 82, No. 6 (May), pp. 1212–41. Available online at http://uni-leipzig.de/~sozio/mitarbeiter/m29/content/dokumente/595/mccarthyzald77.pdf [accessed September 2012].

McCarthy, Stephen and Tacconi, Luca. 2011. "The Political Economy of Tropical Deforestation: Assessing Models and Motives", *Environmental Politics*, Vol. 20, No. 1 (February), pp. 115–32.

McCook, Stuart. 2002a. "'Giving Plants a Civil Status': Scientific Representations of Nature and Nation in Costa Rica and Venezuela, 1885–1935", *The Americas*, Vol. 58, No. 4 (April), pp. 513–36.

——. 2002b. *States of Nature: Science, Agriculture, and Environment in the Spanish Caribbean, 1760–1940*. Austin: University of Texas Press.

McD[onald] Beckles, H. 1996. *Inside Slavery*. Kingston, Jamaica: Canoe Press

MDSP Bolivia (Ministerio de Desarrollo Sostenible y Planificación). 2000. *Informe del Gobierno de Bolivia, Implementación de la Convención de las Naciones Unidas de Lucha Contra la Desertificación*. La Paz: Ministerio de Desarrollo Sostenible y Planificación.

Meadows, Donella H, et al. (eds). 1972. *The Limits to Growth: A Report for Club of Rome's Project*. New York: Universe Books.

Medvedev, Denis and Dominique van der Mensbrugghe. 2008. "Climate Change in Latin America: Impacts and Mitigation Policy Options", 19 November 2008. Paper presented at the 12th Annual Conference on Global Economic Analysis, Santiago, Chile, 2009.

Meggers, Betty. 1971. *Amazonia: Man and Culture in a Counterfeit Paradise*. Washington, DC: Smithsonian Institution Press.

Melville, Elinor. 1997. *A Plague of Sheep: Environmental Consequences of the Conquest of Mexico*. New York: Cambridge University Press.

Millennium Ecosystem Assessment. 2005. *Millennium Ecosystem Assessment, General Synthesis Report*. Washington, DC: Island Press.

Miller, Shawn William. 2000. *Fruitless Trees: Portuguese Conservation and Brazil's Colonial Timber*. Stanford, CA: Stanford University Press.

——. 2007. *An Environmental History of Latin America*. Cambridge: Cambridge University Press.

Mintz, Sidney W. 1991. "A Bittersweet Tale", *The Conquest of Nature 1492–1992*, special edn., *NACLA Report on the Americas*, Vol. 25, No. 2 (September), pp. 22–25.

Mittermeier, Russell A, et al. 1997. *Megadiversidad: Los países biológicamente más ricos del mundo*. Mexico City: Cemex.

MMA Brasil (Ministerio de Medio Ambiente). 2000. *Informe Nacional sobre la Implementación de la Convención de las Naciones Unidas de Lucha Contra la Desertificación*. Brazilia: Ministerio de Medio Ambiente.

Mol, Arthur P. 2010. "Environmental Authorities and Biofuel Controversies", *Environmental Politics*, Vol. 19, No. 1 (February), pp. 61–79.

Monseff Perissinotto, Renato. 2003. "State and Coffee Capital in São Paulo's Export Economy (Brazil 1889–1930)", *Journal of Latin American Studies*, Vol. 35, No. 1 (February), pp. 1–23.

Moody, Roger (ed.). 1988. *The Indigenous Voice: Visions and Realities*, Vols. 1–2. London: Zed Books.

Moore, Donald S. 1996. "Marxism, Culture, and Political Ecology: Environmental Struggles in Zimbabwe's Eastern Highland", in Richard Peet and Michael Watts (eds), *Liberation Ecologies: Environment, Development, and Social Movements*. London: Routledge.

Moret, Erica. 2008. "Afro-Cuban Religion, Ethnobotany and Healthcare in the Context of Global Political and Economic Change", *Bulletin of Latin American Research*, Vol. 27, No. 3 (July), pp. 333–50.

Morgan, Faith. 2006. *The Power of Community: How Cuba Survived Peak Oil* (documentary film). AlchemyHouse Productions/Arthur Morgan Institute for Community Solutions, available to watch online at www.youtube.com/watch?v=L2TzvnRo6_c [accessed September 2012].

Mumme, Stephen P and Edward Korzetz. 1997. "Democratization, Politics, and Environmental Reform in Latin America", in Gordon J MacDonald et al. (eds), *Latin American Environmental Policy in International Perspective*. Boulder, CO: Westview Press.

Muñoz, Heraldo. 1997. "Free Trade and Environmental Policies: Chile, Mexico, and Venezuela", in Gordon J MacDonald, Daniel L Nielson and Marc A Stern (eds), *Latin American Environmental Policy in International Perspective*. Boulder, CO: Westview Press.

Muñoz-Piña, Carlos, Alejandro Guevara, Juan Manuel Torres and Josefina Braña. 2008. "Paying for the Hydrological Services of Mexico's Forests: Analysis, Negotiations and Results", *Ecological Economics*, Vol. 65, No. 4 (May), pp. 725–36.

Murray, Warwick E. 2002. "The Neoliberal Inheritance: Agrarian Policy and Rural Differentiation in Democratic Chile", *Bulletin of Latin American Research*, Vol. 21, No. 3 (July), pp. 425–41.

Nabhan, Gary Paul. 2002. *Enduring Seeds: Native American Agriculture and Wild Plant Conservation*. Tucson: University of Arizona Press.

Newell, Peter. 2009. "Bio-Hegemony: The Political Economy of Agricultural Biotechnology in Argentina", *Journal of Latin American Studies*, Vol. 41, No. 1 (February), pp. 27–57.

Nielson, Daniel L and Marc A Stern. 1997. "Endowing the Environment: Multilateral Development Banks and Environmental Lending in Latin America", in Gordon J MacDonald, Daniel L Nielson and Marc A Stern (eds), *Latin American Environmental Policy in International Perspective*. Boulder, CO: Westview Press.

Niezen, Ronald. 2003. *The Origins of Indigenism: Human Rights and the Politics of Identity*. Berkeley: University of California Press.

North, Peter. 2006. *Alternative Currencies as a Challenge to Globalisation? A Case Study of Manchester's Local Currency Networks*. Farnham: Ashgate.

Nugent, Stephen. 1993. *Amazonian Caboclo Society: An Essay on Invisibility and Peasant Economy*. Providence: Berg.

O'Brien, Karen L. 1998. *Sacrificing the Forest: Environmental and Social Struggles in Chiapas*. Boulder, CO: Westview Press.

O'Donnell, Guillermo. 1973. *Modernization and Bureaucratic Authoritarianism: Studies in South American Politics*. Berkeley: Institute of International Studies, University of California.

Ocampo, José Antonio. 2009. "Foreword", in Kevin P Gallagher and Daniel Chudnovsky (eds), *Rethinking Foreign Investment for Sustainable Development: Lessons from Latin America*. London: Anthem Press.

OECD (Organization for Economic Cooperation and Development). 2007. *OECD Environmental Data. Compendium, 2006/2007. Environmental Expenditure and Taxes*. Paris: Organization for Economic Cooperation and Development.

——. 2008. *OECD Environmental Data Compendium, 2006–2008*, updates from the 2008 OECD/Eurostat Questionnaire on the State of the Environment. Paris: Organization for Economic Cooperation and Development.

——. 2010. *OECD Factbook 2010: Economic, Environmental and Social Statistics*. Paris: Organization for Economic Cooperation and Development. Available online at http://dx.doi.org/10.1787/826022128246 [accessed June 2012].

Offen, Karl H. 2004. "The Geographical Imagination, Resource Economies and Nicaraguan Incorporation of the Mosquitia, 1838–1909", in Christian Brannstrom (ed.), *Territories, Commodities and Knowledges: Latin American Environmental Histories in the Nineteenth and Twentieth Centuries*. London: Institute for the Study of the Americas.

Olivares Gallardo, Alberto. 2010. "El Nuevo Marco Institucional Ambiental En Chile", *Revista Catalana De Dret Ambiental*, Vol. 1, No. 1, pp. 1–23.

Omar Farouk, I. 2007. *Annual Report 2007*. Vienna: Organization of the Petroleum Exporting Countries.

Onursal, Bekir and Surhid P Gautam. 1997. *Vehicular Air Pollution: Experiences from Seven Latin American Urban Centers*, World Bank Technical Paper No. 373. Washington, DC: World Bank.

Orihuela R, Carlos Enrique. 2008. "Estimating Genuine Investment for the Peruvian Mining Sector during 1992–2005". Summary for Decisionmakers, No. 6, April 2008, Policy Briefs, Latin American and Caribbean Environmental Economics Program (LACEEP).

Orlove, Ben. 2002. *Lines in the Water: Nature and Culture at Lake Titicaca*. Berkeley: University of California Press.

Ortiz Monasterio, Fernando, Isabel Fernández, Alicia Castillo, José Ortiz Monasterio and Alfonso Bulle Goyri. 1987. *Tierra Profanada: Historia Ambiental de México*. Mexico City: Instituto Nacional de Antropología e Historia, Secretaría de Desarrollo Urbano y Ecología.

Otero, Gerardo (ed.). 2008. *Food for the Few: Neoliberal Globalism and Biotechnology in Latin America*. Austin: University of Texas Press.

——. 2009. "Is Biotechnology the Answer? The Evidence From NAFTA", *NACLA Report on the Americas*, Vol. 42, No. 3 (May/June), pp. 27–31.

Padgham, J. 2009. "Agricultural Development Under a Changing Climate:

Opportunities and Challenges for Adaptation." Environment and Agriculture and Rural Development Department Joint Discussion Paper. Washington, DC: World Bank.

Pádua, José Augusto. 1987. "O movimento ecológico no Brasil (1974–1986)", in José Augusto Pádua et al., *Ecologia e política no Brasil*, Rio de Janeiro : Editora Espaço e Tempo/Instituto Universitário de Pesquisas do Rio de Janeiro.

——. 2012. *Um Sopro de Destruição*. Rio de Janeiro: Jorge Zahar Editor (Kindle).

Paehlke, Robert C. 2003. *Democracy's Dilemma: Environment, Social Equity, and the Global Economy*. Cambridge, MA: MIT Press.

Pagiola, Stefano, Agustin Arcenas and Gunars Platais. 2005. "Can Payments for Environmental Services Help Reduce Poverty? An Exploration of the Issues and the Evidence to Date from Latin America", *World Development*, Vol. 33, No. 2 (February), pp. 237–53.

PAHO (Pan American Health Organization). 2005. "An Assessment of Health Effects of Exposures to Ambient Air Pollutants in Latin America and the Caribbean", *Epidemiology*, Vol. 16, No. 5 (September), p. S111.

Painter, Michael and William Durham (eds). 1995. *The Social Causes of Environmental Destruction in Latin America*. Ann Arbor: University of Michigan Press.

Panizza, Francisco. 2009. *Contemporary Latin America: Development and Democracy Beyond the Washington Consensus*. London: Zed Books.

Parsons, Talcott. 1954. *Essays in Sociological Theory*. New York: The Free Press.

Partido Verde Brazil. 2011. "Programa", Partido Verde, Convenção Nacional, Brasília/DF, 2005. Available online at http://pv.org.br/ [accessed December 2011].

Passananti, Thomas P. 2007. "'Nada De Papeluchos!' Managing Globalization in Early Porfirian Mexico", *Latin American Research Review*, Vol. 42, No. 3, pp. 101–28.

Paterson, Matthew. 2000. *Understanding Global Environmental Politics*. London: Macmillan.

Pattberg, Philipp. 2007. "Conquest, Domination and Control: Europe's Mastery of Nature in Historic Perspective", *Journal of Political Ecology*, Vol. 14, pp. 1–9. Available online at http://jpe.library.arizona.edu/volume_14/pattberg.pdf [accessed September 2012].

Pattullo, Polly. 1996. "Green Crime, Green Redemption: The Environment and Ecotourism in the Caribbean", in Helen Collinson (ed.), *Green Guerrillas: Environmental Conflicts and Initiatives in Latin America and the Caribbean. A Reader*. London: Latin America Bureau.

Payne, Rodger. 1995. "Freedom and the Environment", *Journal of Democracy*, Vol. 6, No. 3 (July), pp. 41–55.

Peard, Julyan G. 1999. *Race, Place, and Medicine: The Idea of the Tropics in Nineteenth-Century Brazilian Medicine*. Durham, NC: Duke University Press.

Peet, Richard and Michael Watts (eds). 1996. *Liberation Ecologies: Environment, Development, Social Movements*. London: Routledge.

Pepper, David. 1993. *Eco-Socialism: From Deep Ecology to Social Justice*. London: Routledge.

Pérez, Louis A. 2001. *Winds of Change: Hurricanes and the Transformation of Nineteenth-Century Cuba*. Chapel Hill: University of North Carolina Press.

Pérez, Mamerto, Sergio Schlesinger and Timothy A Wise. 2008. *The Promise and the Perils of Agricultural Trade Liberalization: Lessons from Latin America*. Washington, DC and Medford, OR: Working Group on Development and Environment in the Americas/Global Development and Environment Institute, Tufts University.

Peterson, Jeanette Favrot. 1993. *The Paradise Garden Murals of Malinalco: Utopia and Empire in Sixteenth-century Mexico*. Austin: University of Texas Press.

Petras, James. 2002 "Una historia de los foros", *Rebelión*, 18 February 2002. Available online at www.rebelion.org/hemeroteca/petras/petrasportoalegre180202.htm [accessed August 2012].

Phillips, Oliver L, et al. 2002. "Increasing Dominance of Large Lianas in Amazonian Forests", *Nature*, 418 (August), pp. 770–74.

Pollard, Duncan (ed.). 2010. *Living Planet Report 2010: Biodiversity, Biocapacity and Development*. Gland, London and Oakland, CA: WWF International/Zoological Society of London/Global Footprint Network. Available online at www.footprintnetwork.org/en/index.php/GFN/page/publications/ [accessed July 2011].

Ponzio, Carlos Alejandro. 2005. "Globalisation and Economic Growth in the Third World: Some Evidence from Eighteenth-Century Mexico", *Journal of Latin American Studies*, Vol. 37, No. 3 (August), pp. 437–67.

Poole, Deborah. 2010a. "El buen vivir: Peruvian Indigenous Leader Mario Palacios", *NACLA Report on the Americas*, Vol. 43, No. 5 (September/October), pp. 30–33.

——. 2010b. "Extractivism Spills Death and Injustice in Peru", *NACLA Report on the Americas*, Vol. 43, No. 5 (September/October), pp. 32–34.

Porritt, Jonathon. 1984. *Seeing Green: The Politics of Ecology Explained*. London: Blackwell.

Posey, Darrell A. 1985. "Indigenous Management of Tropical Forest Ecosystems: The Case of the Kayapó", *Agroforestry Systems*, Vol. 3, No. 2 (June), pp. 139–58.

——. (ed.). 1999. *Cultural and Spiritual Values of Biodiversity*. London: United Nations Environmental Programme/Intermediate Technology Publications.

Price, Marie. 1994. "Ecopolitics and Environmental Nongovernmental Organizations in Latin America", *Geographical Review*, Vol. 84, No. 1 (January), pp. 42–58.

Pugliano, Valentina. 2009. "Essay Review: Non-Colonial Botany or, the Late Rise of Local Knowledge?", *Studies in History and Philosophy of Biological and Biomedical Sciences*, Vol. 40, No. 4 (December), pp. 321–28.

Rabelo, Carla. 1998. "The Brazilian Green Party: A historical Summary", *Synthesis/Regeneration*, 15 (winter). Available online at www.greens.org/s-r/15/15-03.html [accessed October 2011].

Raffles, Hugh. 1999. "Exploring the Anthropogenic Amazon: Estuarine Landscape Transformations in Amapa, Brazil", in Christine Padoch et al. (eds), *Várzea: Diversity, Development and Conservation of Amazonia's Whitewater Floodplains*. New York: The New York Botanical Garden Press.

——. 2002. *In Amazonia: A Natural History*. Princeton, NJ: Princeton University Press.

Raffles, Hugh and Antoinette Winkler Prins. 2003. "Further Reflections on Amazonian Environmental History: Transformations of Rivers and Streams", *Latin American Research Review*, Vol. 38, No. 3, pp. 165–87.

Rathbone, John Paul. 2011. "Pristine Forest is Finite Resource", *Sustainable Business: Amazonia, Special Report, Financial Times*, 29 November 2011, p. 1.

Raynolds, Laura T. 2008. "The Organic Agro-Export Boom in the Dominican Republic: Maintaining Tradition or Fostering Transformation?", *Latin American Research Review*, Vol. 43, No. 1, pp. 161–85.

Redford, Kent H. 1991. "The Ecologically Noble Savage", *Cultural Survival Quarterly*, Vol. 15, No. 1 (spring), pp. 46–48.

Reitz, Karl. 2001. "Indigenous Peoples in Resistance: History with an Anthropological Perspective", *Latin American Perspectives*, Vol. 28, No. 6 (November), pp. 85–87.

Richards, Patricia. 2010. "Of Indians and Terrorists: How the State and Local Elites Construct the Mapuche in Neoliberal Multicultural Chile", *Journal of Latin American Studies*, Vol. 42, No. 1 (February), pp. 59–90.

Rival, Laura. 1998. "Domestication as a Historical and Symbolic Process: Wild Gardens and Cultivated Forest in the Ecuadorian Amazon", in William Balee (ed.), *Advances in Historical Ecology*. New York: Columbia University Press.

Roberts, J Timmons and Nikki Demetria Thanos. 2003. *Trouble in Paradise: Globalization and Environmental Crises in Latin America*. London: Routledge.

Robins, Nicholas A. 2011. *Mercury, Mining, and Empire: The Human and Ecological Cost of Colonial Silver Mining in the Andes*. Bloomington: Indiana University Press.

Robinson, William I. 2007. "Beyond the Theory of Imperialism: Global Capitalism and the Transnational State", *Societies without Borders*, Vol. 2, pp. 5–26.

——. 2008. *Latin America and Global Capitalism: A Critical Globalization Perspective*. Baltimore, MD: Johns Hopkins University Press.

Roosevelt, Anna C. 1981. *Parmana: Prehistoric Maize and Manioc Subsistence along the Amazon and Orinoco*. New York: Academic Press.

——. 1991. *Moundbuilders of the Amazon: Geophysical Archaeology on Marajo Island, Brazil*. San Diego, CA: Academic Press.

——. (ed.). 1994. *Amazonian Indians from Prehistory to the Present: Anthropological Perspectives*. Tucson: University of Arizona Press.

——. 1999. "Twelve Thousand Years of Human–Environment Interaction in the Amazon Floodplain", in Christine Padoch et al. (eds), *Várzea: Diversity, Development and Conservation of Amazonia's Whitewater Floodplains*. New York: The New York Botanical Garden Press.

Roseberry, William. 1991. "To the Last Drop", *The Conquest of Nature 1492–1992*, special edn., *NACLA Report on the Americas*, Vol. 25, No. 2 (September), pp. 26–30.

Rostow, Walt W. 1962. *The Stages of Economic Growth: A Non-Communist Manifesto*. Cambridge: Cambridge University Press.

Rothstein, Frances Abrahamer. 2007. *Globalization in Rural Mexico: Three Decades of Change*. Austin: University Press of Texas.

Rowbotham, Michael. 2000. *Goodbye America: Globalisation, Debt and the Dollar Empire*. Charlbury: Jon Carpenter Books.

Ruiz-Marrero, Carmelo. 2011. "Latin American Progressive Governments Still Bet on 'Extractivismo'", *Synthesis/Regeneration*, 55 (spring). Available online at www.greens.org/s-r/55/55-01.html [accessed June 2012] (article originally published in *Energy and Environment Monitor*: http://energyandenvironmentmonitor.blogspot.com/2010/10/issue-4.html.

Runge, C Ford, et al. 1994. *Freer Trade, Protected Environment: Balancing Trade Liberalization and Environmental Interests*. New York: Council on Foreign Relations Press.

Ryan, John C. 1991. "The Shrinking Forest", *The Conquest of Nature 1492–1992*, special edn., *NACLA Report on the Americas*, Vol. 25, No. 2 (September), pp. 18–19.

Sá, Lúcia. 2007. *Life in the Megalopolis – Mexico City and São Paulo*. Oxford: Routledge.

Sabatier, Paul A and Hank C Jenkins-Smith (eds). 1993. *Policy Change and Learning: An Advocacy Coalition Approach*. Boulder, CO: Westview Press.

Sabin, Paul. 1998. "Searching for Middle Ground: Native Communities and Oil Extraction in the Northern and Central Ecuadorian Amazon, 1967–1993", *Environmental History*, Vol. 3, No. 2 (April), pp. 144–68.

Saha, Suranjit Kumar and David Parker. 2002. *Globalisation and Sustainable Development in Latin America: Perspectives on the New Economic Order*. Cheltenham: Edward Elgar.

Sáiz, Angel Valencia. 2005. "Globalisation, Cosmopolitanism and Ecological Citizenship", *Environmental Politics*, Vol. 14, No. 2 (April), pp. 163–78.

Saldarriaga, Carlos A and Carlos A Vergara. 2008. "Evaluation of the Fuel Conversion Program in Vehicles in the Aburrá Valley (Colombia)". Summary for Decisionmakers, No. 5, April 2008, Policy Briefs, Latin American and Caribbean Environmental Economics Program.

Sale, Kirkpatrick. 1990. *The Conquest of Paradise: Christopher Columbus and the Columbian Legacy*. New York: Knopf.

——. 2000. *Dwellers in the Land: The Bioregional Vision*. Athens: University of Georgia Press.

Sánchez-Azofeifa, GA, et al. 2009. "Land Cover and Conservation in the Area of Influence of the Chamela–Cuixmala Biosphere Reserve, Mexico", *Forest Ecology and Management*, Vol. 258, No. 6, pp. 907–12.

Saney, Isaac. 2004. *Cuba: A Revolution in Motion*. London: Zed Books.

Santiago, Myrna I. 1998. "Rejecting Progress in Paradise: Huastecs, the Environment, and the Oil Industry in Veracruz, Mexico, 1900–1935", *Environmental History*, Vol. 3, No. 2 (April), pp. 169–88.

——. 2006. *The Ecology of Oil: Environment, Labor, and the Mexican Revolution, 1900–1938*. Cambridge: Cambridge University Press.

Sauer, Carl O. 1952. *Agricultural Origins and Dispersals*. New York: American Geographical Society.

Sawers, Larry. 2000. "Income Distribution and Environmental Degradation in the Argentine Interior", *Latin American Research Review*, Vol. 35, No. 2, pp. 3–33.

——. 2005a. "Nontraditional or New Traditional Exports: Ecuador's Flower Boom", *Latin American Research Review*, Vol. 40, No. 3, pp. 40–67.

——. 2005b. *Sustainable Floriculture in Ecuador*, Working Paper, No. 2005-03 (March 2005), Department of Economics, American University, Washington, DC.

Sawyer, Suzana. 2004. *Crude Chronicles: Indigenous Politics, Multinational Oil, and Neoliberalism in Ecuador*. Durham, NC: Duke University Press.

Scartascini, Carlos, Pablo Spiller, Ernesto Stein and Mariano Tommasi (eds). 2011. *El juego político en América Latina: ¿Cómo se deciden las políticas públicas?* Colombia: Inter-American Development Bank.

Schalatek, Liane (ed.). 2004. *Globalization and the Environment: Lessons from the Americas.* Working Group on Development and Environment in the Americas. Washington, DC: The Heinrich Böll Foundation North America. Available online at http://ase.tufts.edu/gdae/workinggroup.htm [accessed November 2011].

Schatan, Claudia. 1999. *Contaminación industrial en los países latinoamericanos pre y post reformas económicas. Serie medio ambiente y desarrollo 22.* Santiago: Economic Commission for Latin America and the Caribbean. Available online at www.eclac.org/publicaciones/xml/2/4352/lcl1331e.pdf [accessed July 2012].

Scheper-Hughes, Nancy. 2006. "Biopiracy and the Global Quest for Human Organs", *NACLA Report on the Americas*, Vol. 39, No. 5 (March/April), pp. 14–21.

Schlosberg, David. 2004. "Reconceiving Environmental Justice: Global Movements and Political Theories", *Environmental Politics*, Vol. 13, No. 3 (autumn), pp. 517–40.

Scholte, Jan Aart. 2005. *Globalization: A Critical Introduction.* Basingstoke: Palgrave Macmillan.

Scrieciu, Serban S. 2007. "Can Economic Causes of Tropical Deforestation be Identified at a Global Level?", *Ecological Economics*, Vol. 62, Nos. 3–4 (May), pp. 603–12.

SEMARNAT (Secretaría del Medio Ambiente y Recursos Naturales). 2006. *Informe de la Situación del Medio Ambiente en México 2005.* Tlalpan, Mexico: Secretaría del Medio Ambiente y Recursos Naturales.

SEMARNAT/INE (Instituto Nacional de Ecología). 2006. *México Tercera Comunicación Nacional ante la Convención Marco de las Naciones Unidas sobre Cambio Climático.* Mexico City. Tlalpan, Mexico: Secretaría del Medio Ambiente y Recursos Naturales/Instituto Nacional de Ecología.

Shaw, Justine M. 2003. "Climate Change and Deforestation: Implications for the Maya Collapse", *Ancient Mesoamerica*, Vol. 14, No. 1 (January), pp. 157–67.

Sherbondy, J. 1998. "Andean Irrigation in History", in Rutgerd Boelens and Gloria Dávila (eds), *Searching for Equity: Conceptions of Justice and Equity in Peasant Irrigation.* Assen: Van Gorcum.

Shiva, Vandana and Gitanjali Bedi (eds). 2002. *Sustainable Agriculture and Food Security: The Impact of Globalization.* London: Sage.

Sick, Deborah. 2008. "Coffee, Farming Families, and Fair Trade in Costa Rica: New Markets, Same Old Problems?" *Latin American Research Review*, Vol. 43, No. 3, pp. 193–208.

Sieder, Rachel (ed.). 2002. *Multiculturalism in Latin America: Indigenous Rights, Diversity and Democracy*. Basingstoke: Palgrave Macmillan.

Silva, Eduardo. 1995. "Environmental Policy in Chile: The Politics of the Comprehensive Law", in Frank Fischer and Michael Black (eds), *Greening Environmental Policy – The Politics of a Sustainable Future*. London: Chapman.

——. 1996. "Democracy, Market Economics, and Environmental Policy in Chile", *Journal of Interamerican Studies and World Affairs*, Vol. 38, No. 4 (winter), pp. 1–33.

——. 1997. "Conservation, Sustainable Development, and the Politics of Native Forest Policy in Chile", in Gordon J MacDonald et al. (eds), *Latin American Environmental Policy in International Perspective*. Boulder, CO: Westview Press.

Silvius, Kirsten M, Richard E Bodmer and José MV Fragoso. 2005. *People in Nature: Wildlife Conservation in South and Central America*. New York: Columbia University Press.

Simms, Andrew and Hannah Reid. 2006. *Up in Smoke? Latin America and the Caribbean: The Threat from Climate Change to the Environment and Human Development. The third report from the Working Group on Climate Change and Development*. London: New Economics Foundation/International Institute for Environment and Development/Progressio. Available online at www.foe.co.uk/resource/reports/upinsmokelatamerica.pdf [accessed September 2012].

Slater, Candace. 1996. "Amazonia as Edenic Narrative", in William Cronon (ed.), *Uncommon Ground: Rethinking the Human Place in Nature*. New York: W.W. Norton.

Slater, David (ed.). 1985. *New Social Movements and the State in Latin America*. Amsterdam: CEDLA.

Smith, Fred L. 1995. "Markets and the Environment: A Critical Reappraisal", *Contemporary Economic Policy*, Vol. 13, No. 1 (January), pp. 62–73.

Smith, Mick. 2001. "Review Article – Bioregional Visions", *Environmental Politics*, Vol. 10, No. 2 (summer), pp. 140–44.

——. 2007. "Wild-life: Anarchy, Ecology, and Ethics", *Environmental Politics*, Vol. 16, No. 3 (June), pp. 470–87.

Sobrevila, Claudia. 2008. *The Role of Indigenous Peoples in Biodiversity Conservation: The Natural but Often Forgotten Partners*. Washington, DC: World Bank.

Soluri, John. 2000. "People, Plants, and Pathogens: The Eco-social Dynamics of Export Banana Production in Honduras, 1875–1950", in *Hispanic American Historical Review*, Vol. 80, No. 3 (August), pp. 463–501.

——. 2004. "Bananas, Biodiversity and the Paradox of Commodification", in Christian Brannstrom (ed.), *Territories, Commodities and Knowledges: Latin American Environmental Histories in the Nineteenth and Twentieth Centuries*. London: Institute for the Study of the Americas.

——. 2006. *Banana Cultures: Agriculture, Consumption and Environmental Change in Honduras and the United States*. Austin: University of Texas Press.

Sponsel, Leslie (ed.). 1995. *Indigenous Peoples and the Future of Amazonia: An Ecological Anthropology of an Endangered World*. Tucson: University of Arizona Press.

——. 2011. "The Master Thief: Gold Mining and Mercury Contamination in the Amazon", in Barbara Rose Johnston (ed.), *Life and Death Matters: Human Rights, Environment, and Social Justice*. Walnut Creek, CA: Left Coast Press.

Spray, Sharon L and Karen L McGlothlin (eds). 2002. *Global Climate Change*. Lanham, MD: Rowman and Littlefield.

Stallings, Barbara and Wilson Peres. 2000. *Growth, Employment, and Equity: The Impact of the Economic Reforms in Latin America and the Caribbean*. Washington, DC/Santiago: Brookings Institution/CEPAL.

Stein, Ernesto, Mariano Tommasi, Koldo Echebarría, Eduardo Lora and Mark Payne (eds). 2005. *The Politics of Policies. Economic and Social Progress in Latin America, 2006 Report*. New York: Inter-American Development Bank/David Rockefeller Center for Latin American Studies. Available online at www.iadb.org/en/research-and-data/publication-details,3169.html?pub_id=b-2006 [accessed September 2012].

Stern, Nicholas. 2007. *The Economics of Climate Change: The Stern Review*. Cambridge: Cambridge University Press.

Stern, Steve. 1998. "The Decentered Center and the Expansionist Periphery: The Paradoxes of Foreign-Local Encounter", in Gilbert Joseph et al. (eds), *Close Encounters of Empire: Writing the Cultural History of US–Latin American Relations*. Durham, NC: Duke University Press.

Stewart, Sarah. 1996. "The Price of a Perfect Flower: Environmental Destruction and Health Hazards in the Colombian Flower Industry", in Helen Collinson (ed.), *Green Guerrillas: Environmental Conflicts and Initiatives in Latin America and the Caribbean. A Reader*. London: Latin America Bureau.

Stockholm Environment Institute. 2005. *Linking Water Scarcity to Population Movements: From Global Models to Local Experiences*. Stockholm: Stockholm Environment Institute. Available online at www.sei-international.org/mediamanager/documents/Publications/

Risk-livelihoods/SEI_Dow_Water_Migration_2005.pdf [accessed September 2012].

Stoddart, Hannah (ed.). 2011. *A Pocket Guide to Sustainable Development Governance*, 1st edn. London: Stakeholder Forum/Commonwealth Secretariat.

Stott, Philip and Sian Sullivan (eds). 2000. *Political Ecology: Science, Myth and Power.* London: Arnold.

Strathern, Marilyn. 1981. "No Nature, No Culture: The Hagen Case", in Carol MacCormack and Marilyn Strathern (eds), *Nature, Culture, and Gender.* Cambridge: Cambridge University Press.

Striffler, Steve and Mark Moberg (eds). 2003. *Banana Wars: Power, Production and History in the Americas.* Durham, NC: Duke University Press.

Strzepek, Kenneth M and Alyssa L McCluskey. 2010. *Economics of Adaptation to Climate Change: Modeling the Impact of Climate Change on Global Hydrology and Water Availability.* Washington, DC: World Bank, Discussion Paper No. 8, September 2010 (56801).

Sundberg, Juanita. 2008. "Tracing Race: Mapping Environmental Formations in Environmetal Justice Research in Latin America", in David V Carruthers (ed.), *Environmental Justice in Latin America: Problems, Promise, and Practice.* London: MIT Press.

Sunderlain, William DE, Jeffrey Hatcher and Megan Liddle. 2008. *From Exclusion to Ownership? Challenges and Opportunities in Advancing Tenure Reform.* Washington, DC: Rights and Resources Initiative.

Sunkel, Osvaldo. 1969. "National Development Policy and External Dependence in Latin America", *Journal of Development Studies*, Vol. 6, No. 1 (October), pp. 23–48.

Sunkel, Osvaldo and Nicolo Gligo (eds). 1980. *Estilos de Desarrollo y Medio Ambiente en América Latina.* Mexico City: Fondo de Cultura Económica.

Tarrow, Sidney. 1994. *Power in Movement: Social Movements, Collective Action, and Politics.* Cambridge: Cambridge University Press.

Tate, C Neal, and Torbjörn Vallinder (eds). 1995. *The Global Expansion of Judicial Power.* New York: NY University Press.

Tauli-Corpuz, Victoria. 2010. "The Importance of Indigenous Peoples in Biodiversity Conservation", *Environment Matters: Banking on Biodiversity.* Washington, DC: World Bank.

Tecklin, David, Carl Bauer and Manuel Prieto. 2011. "Making Environmental Law for the Market: The Emergence, Character, and Implications of Chile's Environmental Regime", *Environmental Politics*, Vol. 20, No. 6 (November), pp. 879–98.

TEEB (The Economics of Ecosystems and Biodiversity). 2010. *The Economics of Ecosystems and Biodiversity: Mainstreaming the Economics of Nature. A*

Synthesis of the Approach, Conclusions and Recommendations of TEEB. Geneva: United Nations Environment Programme. Available online at www.teebweb.org/InformationMaterial/TEEBReports/tabid/1278/Default.aspx [accessed June 2012].

Thrupp, Lori Ann. 1996. "New Harvests, Old Problems: The Challenges Facing Latin America's Agro-Export Boom", in Helen Collinson (ed.), *Green Guerrillas: Environmental Conflicts and Initiatives in Latin America and the Caribbean. A Reader*. London: Latin America Bureau.

Timberlake, Lloyd. 1986. *Africa in Crisis: The Causes, the Cures of Environmental Bankruptcy*. London and Washington, DC: Earthscan/International Institute for Environment and Development.

Topik, Steven C. 1998. "Coffee", in Steven C Topik and Allen Wells (eds), *The Second Conquest of Latin America: Coffee, Henequen, and Oil during the Export Boom, 1850–1930*. Austin: University of Texas Press.

Topik, Steven C and Allen Wells (eds). 1998. *The Second Conquest of Latin America: Coffee, Henequen, and Oil during the Export Boom, 1850–1930*. Austin: University of Texas Press.

Topik, Steven C, Carlos Marichal and Zephyr Frank (eds) 2006. *From Silver to Cocaine: Latin American Commodity Chains and the Building of the World Economy, 1500–2000*. Durham, NC: Duke University Press.

Torras, Mariano and James K Boyce. 1998. "Income, Inequality and Pollution: A Reassessment of the Environmental Kuznets Curve", *Ecological Economics*, Vol. 25, No. 2 (May), pp. 147–60.

Torres, Blanca. 1997. "Transnational Environmental NGOs: Linkages and Impact on Policy", in Gordon J MacDonald, Daniel L Nielson and Marc A Stern (eds), *Latin American Environmental Policy in International Perspective*. Boulder, CO: Westview Press.

Tortolero, Alejandro. 2004. "Transforming the Central Mexican Waterscape: Lake Drainage and its Consequences during the Porfiriato (1877–1911)", in Christian Brannstrom (ed.), *Territories, Commodities and Knowledges: Latin American Environmental Histories in the Nineteenth and Twentieth Centuries*. London: Institute for the Study of the Americas.

Tosun, Jale. 2009. *Environmental Policy in Chile and Mexico: Explaining the Effect of Economic Integration on Regulatory Standards*. Saarbrücken: VDM Verlag Dr. Mueller.

Townsend, Janet. 1996 "Pioneer Women and the Destruction of the Rainforests", in Helen Collinson (ed.), *Green Guerrillas: Environmental Conflicts and Initiatives in Latin America and the Caribbean. A Reader*. London: Latin America Bureau.

Trujillo Cabrera, María del Pilar. 2010. "Flujos de madera en la frontera amazónica de Colombia, Brasil y Perú: Comprendiendo la magnitud, las causas y los efectos de la extracción no controlada en la economía local". Summary for Decisionmakers, No. 16, February 2010, Policy Briefs, Latin American and Caribbean Environmental Economics Program. Available online at www.laceep.org/publications/policy-briefs [accessed November 2011].

Tucker, Richard P. 2000. *Insatiable Appetite: The United States and the Ecological Degradation of the Tropical World*. Berkeley: University of California Press.

Turner, Will R, et al. 2012. "Global Biodiversity Conservation and the Alleviation of Poverty", *BioScience*, Vol. 62, No. 1 (January), pp. 85–92.

UN (United Nations). 1990. *The Human Development Report 1990*. New York: Oxford University Press.

——. 2010a. *Millennium Development Goals, Advances in Environmentally Sustainable Development in Latin America and the Caribbean*. United Nations Publication LC/G 2428-P, Santiago de Chile.

——. 2010b. *The Millennium Development Goals Report 2010*. New York: United Nations.

UN HABITAT, 2008. *The State of World Cities, 2008/2009: Harmonious Cities*. Nairobi, Kenya.

UNDP (United Nations Development Programme). 2003. *World Resources, 2002–2004*. UN Development Programme. Washington, DC: World Resources Institute/UNEP.

UNEP (United Nations Environment Programme). 2007. *Global Environment Outlook. GEO-4: Environment and Development*. Nairobi: United Nations Environment Programme.

——. 2008. "'Global Green New Deal' – Environmentally Focused Investment Historic Opportunity for twenty-first Century Prosperity and Job Generation", news release, 22 October 2008. London/Nairobi: United Nations Environment Programme.

——. 2009. *Global Green New Deal – A Policy Brief*. Geneva: United Nations Environment Programme. Available online at www.unep.org/pdf/A_Global_Green_New_Deal_Policy_Brief.pdf [accessed March 2012].

——. 2010. *Latin America and the Caribbean: Environment Outlook GEO LAC 3*. Panama City: United Nations Environment Programme. Available online at www.unep.org/publications/contents/pub_details_search.asp?ID=4149 [accessed July 2011].

——. 2012. *GEO5 Global Environment Outlook: Environment for the Future We Want*. Nairobi: United Nations Environment Programme. Available online at www.unep.org/geo/pdfs/geo5/GEO5_report_full_en.pdf [accessed August 2012].

UNEP FI (United Nations Environment Programme Finance Initiative). 2010. *UNEP FI 2010 Overview*. Geneva: United Nations Environment Programme Finance Initiative. Available online at www.unepfi.org/

fileadmin/documents/unepfi_overview_2010_01.pdf [accessed August 2012].

UNEP FI/PRI (Principles for Responsible Investment). 2010. *Universal Ownership: Why Environmental Externalities Matter to Institutional Investors*. Geneva: UNEP Finance Initiative/Principles for Responsible Investment Association.

UNEP/IISD (International Institute for Sustainable Development). 2005. *Environment and Trade: A Handbook*, 2nd edn. Geneva/Winnipeg: United Nations Environment Programme/International Institute for Sustainable Development.

UNESCO-WWAP (United Nations Educational, Scientific and Cultural Organization, World Water Assessment Programme). 2006. "Water: A Shared Responsibility", United Nations World Water Development Report 2. Paris: United Nations Educational, Scientific and Cultural Organization, World Water Assessment Programme. Available online at http://unesdoc.unesco.org/images/0014/001454/145405E.pdf [accessed September 2012].

UNFPA (United Nations Population Fund). 2008. *State of World Population 2008. Reaching Common Ground: Culture, Gender and Human Rights*. New York: United Nations Population Fund.

——. 2011. *State of World Population 2011: People and Possibilities in a World of Seven Billion*. New York: United Nations Population Fund.

UN-HABITAT. 2007. *Enhancing Urban Safety and Security: Global Report On Human Settlements 2007*. London: UN Human Settlements Programme/ Earthscan.

——. 2011a. *Global Report on Human Settlements 2011. Cities and Climate Change: Policy Directions*. Nairobi: UN Human Settlements Programme.

——. 2011b. *State of the World's Cities: Trends in Latin America & the Caribbean, Urbanization & Metropolitanization*. Features/Backgrounder, UN-HABITAT Features/Media centre. Nairobi: UN Human Settlements Programme.

University of Manchester. 2009. "Trade Sustainability Impact Assessment (SIA) of the Association Agreement under Negotiation between the European Community and Mercosur, Final Report", revised March 2009. Manchester: University of Manchester, Impact Assessment Research Centre/Institute for Development Policy and Management.

UNWTO (United Nations World Tourism Organization). 2012. "International Tourism Receipts Surpass US$ 1 trillion in 2011", press release, PR12027, 7 May 2012. Madrid: UN World Tourism Organization. Available online at http://media.unwto.org/en/press-release/2012-05-07/international-tourism-receipts-surpass-us-1-trillion-2011 [accessed June 2012].

Vaccaro, Ismael, Laura C Zanotti and Jennifer Sepez. 2009. "Commons and Market: Opportunities for Development of Local Sustainability", *Environmental Politics*, Vol. 18, No. 4 (July), pp. 522–38.

Valbo-Jorgensen, John, Doris Soto and Angel Gumy. 2008. *La pesca continental en América Latina: su contribución económica y social e instrumentos normativos asociados*. COPESCAL Documento Ocasional, No. 11. Rome: UN Food and Agriculture Organization.

Valiela, Ivan, Jennifer L Bowen and Joanna K York. 2001, "Mangrove Forests – One of the World's Threatened Major Tropical Environments", *BioScience*, Vol. 51, No. 10 (October), pp. 807–15.

Van Cott, Donna Lee. 2005. *From Movements to Parties in Latin America: The Evolution of Ethnic Politics*. Cambridge: Cambridge University Press.

Van den Hombergh, Heleen. 2004. *No Stone Unturned: Building Blocks of Environmentalist Power versus Transnational Industrial Forestry in Costa Rica*. Amsterdam: Dutch University Press.

Van Dijck, Pitou. 2013. *The Impact of the IIRSA Road Infrastructure Programme on Amazonia*. Oxford: Routledge.

Van Dooren, Robine and German A Zarate-Hoyos. 2003. "The Insertion of Rural Areas into Global Markets: A Comparison of Garment Production in Yucatán and La Laguna, Mexico", *Journal of Latin American Studies*, Vol. 35, No. 3 (August), pp. 571–92.

Van Leeuwen, Mathijs. 2010. "To Conform or to Confront? CSOs and Agrarian Conflict in Post-Conflict Guatemala", *Journal of Latin American Studies*, Vol. 42, No. 1 (February), pp. 91–119.

Van Roozendaal, Gerda. 2009. "The Inclusion of Environmental Concerns in US Trade Agreements", *Environmental Politics*, Vol. 18, No. 3 (May), pp. 431–38.

Vasconcelos, Alvaro de (ed.). 2012. *Global Trends 2030 – Citizens in an Interconnected and Polycentric World*. European Strategy and Policy Analysis System. Paris: European Union Institute for Security Studies.

Véliz, Claudio. 1980. *The Centralist Tradition of Latin America*. Princeton, NJ: Princeton University Press.

Vergara, Walter and Sebastian M Scholz (eds). 2011. *Assessment of the Risk of Amazon Dieback*. Washington, DC: World Bank.

Vié, Jean-Christophe, Craig Hilton-Taylor and Simon N Stuart (eds). 2009. *Wildlife in a Changing World – An Analysis of the 2008 IUCN Red List of Threatened Species*. Gland, Switzerland: International Union for Conservation of Nature. Available online at http://data.iucn.org/dbtw-wpd/edocs/RL-2009-001.pdf [accessed February 2014].

Viola, Eduardo J. 1997. "The Environmental Movement in Brazil: Institutionalization, Sustainable Development, and Crisis of Governance since 1987", in Gordon J MacDonald et al. (eds), *Latin American*

Environmental Policy in International Perspective. Boulder, CO: Westview Press.

Vitale, Luis, 1983. *Hacia una Historia del Ambiente en América Latina: De las culturas aborígenes a la crisis ecológica actual*. Mexico City: Nueva Sociedad/Editorial Nueva Imagen.

Vogel, David. 2006. "International Trade and Environmental Regulation", in Norman Vig and Michael Kraft (eds), *Environmental Policy: New Directions for the Twenty-First Century*, 6th edn. Washington, DC: CQ Press.

Walker, Rob. 2012. "Peru's gold rush pits illegal miners against government", bbc.co.uk, 11 July 2012, available online at www.bbc.co.uk/news/world-latin-america-18524330 [accessed July 2012].

Wallerstein, Immanuel. 1974. *The Modern World-System*, Vol. 1, *Capitalist Agriculture and the Origins of the European World-Economy in the Sixteenth Century*. London: Academic Press.

Ward, Hugh. 2008. "Liberal Democracy and Sustainability", *Environmental Politics*, Vol. 17, No. 3 (June), pp. 386–409.

Weber, Martin. 2001. "Competing Political Visions: WTO Governance and Green Politics", *Global Environmental Politics*, Vol. 1, No. 3 (August), pp. 92–113.

Weber, Max. 1947/1997. *The Theory of Social and Economic Organization* (translated by AM Henderson and Talcott Parsons). New York: The Free Press.

Wells, Allen. 1998. "Henequen", in Steven C Topik and Allen Wells (eds), *The Second Conquest of Latin America: Coffee, Henequen, and Oil during the Export Boom, 1850–1930*. Austin: University of Texas Press.

Wessendorf, Kathrin (ed.). 2011. *The Indigenous World 2011*. Copenhagen: International Work Group for Indigenous Affairs. Available online at www.iwgia.org/iwgia_files_publications_files/0454_THE_INDIGENOUS_ORLD-2011_eb.pdf [accessed November 2011].

White, Lynn Jr. 1967. "The Historical Roots of Our Ecological Crisis", *Science*, Vol. 155, No. 3767 (March), pp. 1203–07.

Wilkins, Mira. 1998. "An Alternative Approach", in Steven C Topik and Allen Wells (eds), *The Second Conquest of Latin America: Coffee, Henequen, and Oil during the Export Boom, 1850–1930*. Austin: University of Texas Press.

Williams, Heather L. 2001. *Social Movements and Economic Transition: Markets and Distributive Conflict in Mexico*. Cambridge: Cambridge University Press.

Williams, Marc. 2001. "Trade and Environment in the World Trading System: A Decade of Stalemate?", in *Global Environmental Politics*, Vol. 1, No. 4 (November), pp. 1–9.

Williams, Raymond. 1980. "Ideas of Nature", in Raymond Williams (ed.), *Problems in Materialism and Culture: Selected Essays*. London: Verso.

Williams, Robert G. 1986. *Export Agriculture and the Crisis in Central America*. Chapel Hill: University of North Carolina Press.

Williamson, Edwin. 1992. *The Penguin History of Latin America*. Harmondsworth: Penguin Books.

Winpenny, James. 1994. *Managing Water as an Economic Resource*. London: Routledge.

World Bank. 2001. *Making Sustainable Commitments*. Washington, DC: World Bank.

——. 2005. *Indigenous Peoples, Poverty and Human Development in Latin America: 1994–2004*. Washington, DC: World Bank.

——. 2007. "WDR/Latin America and the Caribbean: Developed Country Subsidies, an Obstacle for Agricultural Development", press release 2008/080/DEC, 19 October 2007. Washington, DC: World Bank.

——. 2008. "Development and Climate Change: A Strategic Framework for the World Bank Group", Consultation Draft, 21 August 2008. Available at http://siteresources.worldbank.org/EXTCC/Resources/407863-1219339233881/DevelopmentandClimateChange.pdf.

——. 2009a. "The Cost to Developing Countries of Adapting to Climate Change: New Methods and Estimates", Consultation Draft 64087. Washington, DC: World Bank. Available online at http://climatechange.worldbank.org/climatechange/research [accessed October 2011].

——. 2009b. *World Development Indicators 2009*. Washington, DC: World Bank.

——. 2010a. *Economic Evaluation of Climate Change Adaptation Projects. Approaches for the Agricultural Sector and Beyond (Development and Climate Change)*. Washington, DC: World Bank.

——. 2010b. *Economics of Adaptation to Climate Change: Social Synthesis Report*. Washington, DC: World Bank. Available online at http://climatechange.worldbank.org/sites/default/files/documents/EACCSocialSynthesisFinal.pdf [accessed September 2012].

——. 2010d. *Environment Matters: Banking on Biodiversity*. Washington, DC: World Bank. Available online at www.worldbank.org/reference/ [accessed July 2011].

——. 2012a. *Global Development Finance 2012: External Debt of Developing Countries*. Available online at http://data.worldbank.org/sites/default/files/gdf_2012.pdf [accessed April 2011].

——. 2012b. *Justice for Forests: Improving Criminal Justice Efforts to Combat Illegal Logging*. Washington, DC: World Bank. Available online at http://siteresources.worldbank.org/EXTFINANCIALSECTOR/Resources/Illegal_Logging.pdf [accessed March 2012].

World Water Assessment Programme. 2009. *The United Nations World Water Development Report 3: Water in a Changing World*. Paris and London: United Nations Educational, Scientific and Cultural Organization/ Earthscan.

Worster, Donald. 1990. "Transformations of the Earth: Toward an Agroecological Perspective in History", *Journal of American History*, Vol. 76, No. 4 (March), pp. 1087–106.

Wright, Ronald. 2005. *A Short History of Progress*. Edinburgh: Canongate Books.

Wright, SJ and Osvaldo Calderón. 2005. "Seasonal, El Niño and Longer Term Changes in Flower and Seed Production in a Moist Tropical Forest", *Ecology Letters*, Vol. 9, No. 1 (January 2006), pp. 35–44.

WSP (Water and Sanitation Programme). 2007. *Saneamiento para el desarrollo. ¿Cómo estamos en 21 países de América Latina y el Caribe?* Latinosan 2007 conferencia Latinoamericana de saneamiento. Water and Sanitation Programme, Peru. Available online at www.wsp.org/wsp/sites/wsp.org/files/11142007111614_Latinosan_Final.pdf [accessed September 2012].

WTO (World Trade Organization). 2001. *Ministerial Declaration*. Ministerial Conference – Fourth Session, Doha, 9–14 November 2001, WTO/MIN(01)/DEC/1. Geneva: World Trade Organization (WTO).

WTO/UNEP (United Nations Environment Programme). 2009. *Trade and Climate Change: A Report by the United Nations Environment Programme and the World Trade Organization*. Geneva: World Trade Organization/ United Nations Environment Programme.

WWF (World Wildlife Fund). 2012. *Living Planet Report 2012*. Gland: World Wide Fund For Nature. Available online at http://wwf.panda.org/about_our_earth/all_publications/living_planet_report/ [accessed June 2012].

Young, Kenneth R. 2005. "Nature's Role in Latin American Governance and History", *Latin American Research Review*, Vol. 40, No. 3 (October), pp. 457–68.

Zarembo, Alan. 2001. "The canal from hell", www.newsweek.com, 20 May 2001. Available online at www.newsweek.com/2001/05/20/the-canal-from-hell.html [accessed August 2012].

Zedillo, Ernesto (ed.). 2008. *Global Warming: Looking Beyond Kyoto*. Washington, DC: Brookings Institution Press.

Zeltsman, Corinna. 2007. "Choropampa: The Price Of Gold/Tambogrande: Mangos, Murder, Mining", *NACLA Report on the Americas*, Vol. 40, No. 4 (July/August), pp. 52–54.

Index